WHAT WE BELIEVE

This book, written by Dr. E. Harold Henderson, is based on the Doctrinal Statement of the Baptist Missionary Association of America.

All true doctrines come from the Bible. They have their origin in the Word of God. Neither individuals, churches, nor denominations have the right to formulate doctrine. Doctrine is what the Bible teaches; so doctrine originates with God. We must diligently search the Bible in order to understand the teachings of the heavenly Father.

Disciple**Guide**

BMA
BAPTIST MISSIONARY ASSOCIATION ◢AMERICA

CONTENTS

CONTENTS

CONTENTS

THE ONE TRUE GOD

The belief in the existence of God is practically universal. Every culture, however primitive, has some concept of God. That truth is written in the conscience of the whole human race. Ideas of the nature of God vary, but the existence of God is accepted. The person who denies the existence of God rejects the evidence because of an evil heart which is set against the truth (Romans 1:20).

Knowledge of the one living and true God is the highest knowledge a person can ever attain. Coming to know God in truth changes a person; he can never be the same again. We Christians rejoice that we have a complete revelation of God through nature, the inspired Scriptures, and through Jesus Christ, the Son of God.

This study is designed to help you better understand Him who is beyond understanding and to know Him whom to know aright is to have life eternal. Tread softly here; this is holy ground.

GOD

We believe there is one living and true God who is revealed in the unity of the Godhead as God the Father, God the Son, and God the Holy Spirit. That statement of doctrine contains five great truths about the nature of our God.

God is one. The pagans have their many gods, but the Christian has but one. We agree with the Shema of ancient Israel, which reads, "Hear, O Israel: The LORD our God is one LORD" (Deuteronomy 6:4). "To us there is but one God, the Father, of whom are all things, and we in him; and one Lord Jesus Christ, by whom are all things, and we by him" (I Corinthians 8:6). Our belief in the trinity of God does not make Him three Gods. He is one.

God is living. The idols and images before which people bow in worship are lifeless items of stone, wood, or metal. But our God is "the most High . . . that liveth for ever . . . from generation to generation" (Daniel 4:34). We speak of that as the eternity of God. When He would make a vow, He swears by himself (since there is none greater than He), saying, "As I live, saith the Lord

GOD" (Ezekiel 14:16, 18, 20). As the living God, He swears by His life. Pause now and talk with Him who lives forever, your Lord and your God.

God is true. He is "a God of truth and without iniquity, just and right is he" (Deuteronomy 32:4). Because He is true He always speaks truth, does right, and receives those who seek Him in truth. Because He is true you can believe His promises and rely upon Him with safety.

God is Creator. The first announcement of the Bible is, "In the beginning God created the heavens and the earth" (Genesis 1:1). We worship Him with these words, "Thou, even thou, art LORD alone; thou hast made heaven, the heaven of heavens, with all their host, the earth, and all things that are therein, the seas, and all that is therein, and thou preservest them all" (Nehemiah 9:6). Unbelievers may deny that statement, claiming it to be unscientific. But "through faith we understand that the worlds were framed by the word of God" (Hebrews 11:3).

God is tri-unity. Here is one of the greatest mysteries of the doctrine of God. How can He be three persons and yet one God? We believe it, whether we can explain it or not. The doctrine was intimated in the Old Testament with the plural name for deity (Elohim) and the use of plural pronouns in reference to God ("us," "our"). The doctrine is stated in the New Testament in the baptismal formula: "in the name (singular) of the Father, and of the Son, and of the Holy Ghost" (Matthew 28:19). It is stated in the apostolic benediction (II Corinthians 13:14); and even Jesus indicated it by saying the Father would send the Spirit in response to the request of the Son (John 14:16). God the Father, Son, and Spirit are equally deity.

GOD THE FATHER— ETERNAL DEITY

What is the scope of His fatherhood? It is not a "fatherhood of God and brotherhood of man" which bypasses the doctrine of salvation. His fatherhood is manifest in three areas.

(1) He is the Father of all people by creation, according to Malachi 2:10 and Deuteronomy 32:6.

2) He is the Father of the Son by eternal generation. Jesus was the Son of God in eternity before His birth to a human mother.

(3) He is the Father of believers in Jesus by regeneration, according to John 1:11-12; 3:5-7; Galatians 3:26. How do you claim His fatherhood over you?

What were the intimations of His fatherhood in the Old Testament? He is called "a father of the fatherless, and a judge of the widows" (Psalm 68:5). He is said to pity us as a father pities his own dear children (Psalm 103:13). God is pictured as the Father of national Israel (Jeremiah 31:9). But those were just dim glimpses of the New Testament revelation.

What is the revelation of His fatherhood in the New Testament? The Bible states quite clearly that God is the Father of Jesus, the son of Mary (Matthew 3:17; John 14—17). Jesus is called His "beloved Son" and Jesus calls Him "Father."

God is the Father of those who receive Jesus by faith. As a Father, He is concerned about our welfare (Matthew 6:25-34), hears our prayers (Matthew 6:5-15), disciplines us (Hebrews 12:5-11), comforts us (II Thessalonians 2:16), gives good things to us (Matthew 7:11; II Peter 1:3), and makes us His heirs (Romans 8:15-17; I Corinthians 2:9).

Do not think in physical terms when you speak of God as Father. God is spirit. We understand our fatherhood among people because it is a reflection of God's fatherhood over us. Pause at this point and thank God for being your Father in Christ.

GOD THE SON—DEITY INCARNATE

Jesus Christ was human in every sense of the word. He was born by natural development and birth to a normal human mother. Only her conception was miraculous.

Jesus grew up in a normal human body, the same as every other person who lives on the earth. He grew, was tired, had to eat to sustain His life, was tempted, and was otherwise fully human. Jesus, the son of man, is fully human.

At the same time, Jesus Christ is eternal Deity. He lived before He was born! He had a relationship with the Father "before the world was" (John 17:5). That is one reason why His birth had to be by a miraculous conception instead of natural human generation. In personal testimony Jesus spoke of His being with the Father in eternity, coming down from the Father, doing the work of the Father while on earth, and returning to the Father in heaven. He draws all of that into focus by the words, "I and my Father are one" (John 10:30). "He that hath seen me hath seen the Father" (John 14:9). But the crowning proof of the eternal deity of Jesus was His resurrection from death (Romans 1:14). He laid down His life, and He took it up again by His own power. Only God could do that.

Jesus Christ did the work of God during His earthly ministry. He revealed God as no other person ever had or could. "We beheld his glory, the glory as of the only begotten of the Father, full of grace and truth" (John 1:14).

He atoned for sin by His own death (Romans 3:21-26). He freely gave His life as the payment for human sin. He died and was buried. Then He arose from death on the third day. By His death He paid the penalty for sin, and by His resurrection He broke the power of sin. We are reconciled to God because He died, and we are saved by God because He lives (Romans 5:10).

He ascended back to the Father in heaven where He sat down at the right hand of God. He continues His blessed ministry of intercession in that high place (Romans 8:34). One day He will return in glory to receive us to himself (Acts 1:11; I Thessalonians 4:16-18).

Pause now and worship the Son of God, Incarnate Deity.

GOD THE SPIRIT— DEITY PRESENT

Jesus promised that when He returned to heaven He would request the Father to send the Holy Spirit. (Note the three persons of Holy Trinity in John 14:16.) That is just what happened according to the record of Acts 1 and 2. Jesus called the Holy Spirit "another" companion. That word another means "another of the same kind." Thus the Holy Spirit has the same nature of deity as does Jesus Christ.

The Holy Spirit is not some vague, misty, ghostly apparition. He is a real person, a divine person. Personal pronouns ("he") are ascribed to Him. Personal actions (convict, lead, teach, speak) are ascribed to Him. Personal emotions (grief) are ascribed to Him. And those actions are things only God can do. The Holy Spirit is called "God" in Acts 5:4.

The Holy Spirit was active in creation. He convicts of sin. He confers spiritual gifts. He performs the new birth in one who repents and trusts Jesus. He inspires Holy Scripture and illuminates the mind to understand it. He anoints and empowers for service. He sanctifies, comforts, fills, and produces spiritual fruit. He does the work only God can do.

The Holy Spirit is Deity. Your relation and reaction to Him is your relation and reaction to God. Do not ignore Him or resist His leadings. He is God— God living in you now.

How can the human mind express adequately the person and nature of Him whom we call God? This writer feels the discussion above is far too weak to speak of our Father, His eternal Son, and the blessed Holy Spirit. God is far more majestic than I have been able to express.

It is of utmost importance that we recognize the majesty of God. A loss of awe in His presence causes us to lose our spirit of worship and the ability to fellowship with Him in our meditation. A thousand evils enter our lives when we are no longer sensing the holy ground of His presence.

No people ever rises above its religion, and no religion is ever higher than its concept of God. More important than the buildings, programs, goals, and accomplishments of a church is her concept of God.

What comes to your mind when you think about God? The answer to that question indicates what sort of person you are and the direction your life is taking. More than correct theology is involved here. Practical Christian living flows from our concept of God.

When a person sees himself in the presence of the sovereign God, he recognizes his faults and need for forgiveness. When a believer enters a personal relationship with God, all of life takes on a new dimension; he is a new creature. May God use this study to purify and elevate your concept of God. And may that concept influence your life so that you pass it on to your children. God is not like us. But He has made it possible for us to become like Him through Jesus Christ our Lord.

Pause here and worship Him who is so worthy of worship.

1. In what way is the belief in God universal?
2. How is knowledge of God the highest knowledge possible?
3. What do we mean by saying that God is one?
4. What is the importance of the fact that He is a living God?
5. Why is the doctrine of the Trinity so important?
6. How is God pictured as a Father in the Old Testament?
7. How is God pictured as a Father in the New Testament?
8. Why do we call Jesus "Deity Incarnate"?
9. How do you know that the Holy Spirit is God?
10. Why is a correct doctrine of God so essential to your life?

GOD'S INERRANT REVELATION

Do we really believe that the Bible is God's words in human language, without error in its content, but true word by word? We answer with a positive "YES!" Such a belief requires us to be "people of the Book." Since the Bible is the book of God and we are the people of God, the Bible is the most important book in the world to us.

There are many people today, some even in the Christian community, who question or deny that the Bible is an absolutely true revelation from God. But their denials do not change our conviction. We have met God in the Word. We have His testimony concerning the Word. We say, "Let God be true, but every man a liar" (Romans 3:4). God has said that the Bible is His revelation and that it has no error. We accept that as true.

THE BIBLE IS REVELATION

It is the record of God's disclosure, not of man's discovery. To reveal means to unveil, to make plain, to draw back the curtain. God drew back the curtain and made plain to human writers divine truth which they wrote as Sacred Scripture. First Corinthians 2:9-16 teaches four things about that disclosure.

1. The unseen things of God cannot be understood by natural man. Man in his natural state can never see, hear with understanding, or conceive in his human mind the things of God. No one can know the mind of the Lord or search out the judgments based on God's wisdom and knowledge, because His ways are past our finding out (Romans 11:33).

2. The unseen things of God have been revealed to chosen men. To read "God hath revealed them to us by his Spirit" is to witness a miracle of grace (I Corinthians 2:10). He chose what to reveal, when to reveal it, and to whom to reveal it. Thus our Bible came over a period of about fifteen hundred years, written by scores of different persons. Yet the message is always consistent because the one God spoke through each writer.

3. The unseen things of God have been given through Spirit-taught words: "not in

the words which man's wisdom teacheth" (I Corinthians 2:13). That means the very words of the Bible are God's words. Finite humans wrote the words, but only as "they were moved by the Holy Ghost" (II Peter 1:21). The Bible is God's words expressed in human language.

4. The Spirit-taught words are understood only by spiritually minded believers in Jesus (I Corinthians 2:14-16). That explains why there are so many opinions about the Bible and so many interpretations of its text. The Holy Spirit joins spiritual truth to spiritual minds, but to no other. Ask yourself, "How well do I understand the Bible?" That will tell you something about the quality of your spiritual mind.

It is God's disclosure of what was formerly unknown. The New Testament, particularly Paul's epistles, makes reference to a "mystery." It does not refer to something which is so difficult to comprehend that very few people know of it. It refers instead to something formerly unknown but now revealed in Jesus Christ (Colossians 1:26, 27; Ephesians 3:3, 4, 9). In a sense we could say that all of the Bible truth was formerly unknown by carnal people but is now made known in the Holy Bible.

It is God's disclosure by a special revelation. God has revealed himself in nature (Psalm 19:1), in visions (Genesis 15:1), in providence (Isaiah 46:4), and especially in Jesus Christ (Hebrews 1:1, 2; John 1:14, 18). All of those revelations are recorded in the Bible. At this point we are concerned with the truth revealed. In a section below we will consider how that revealed truth was recorded without error.

It is God's disclosure which is preserved for all generations. What happened centuries before was written in the Bible for our instruction (I Corinthians 10:11). Since the Word of God stands forever (Isaiah 40:8), all generations of mankind will have a witness to the truth from God himself.

The Bible is the divinely revealed Word of God.

THE BIBLE IS INERRANT

We believe the Bible is without error. It has no mistakes in any subject to which it makes reference. It is historically accurate in every statement. It is the standard of truth by which all other opinions are to be measured.

We use two theological terms to describe that doctrine. First, we say the Bible is inerrant. That means it is without error, making no mistake. Second, we say the Bible is infallible. That means it is incapable of error and never wrong.

How can such a statement be made about books written by finite humans in such differing situations over so many centuries? It can be said because God directed the writers of Holy Scripture so that they wrote without error what God revealed to them. Each used his own vocabulary and reflected his own personality, but what was written was the Word of God, not the words of men. That is the miracle of the Bible.

There is no error in the Bible. Its references to history, science, psychology, astrology, geology, sociology, religion, or any other subject continue to be true today. It is the inerrant Word of God. What a book!

The Bible declares itself to be the inspired and inerrant Word of God. It declares that "his work is perfect" (Deuteronomy 32:4). He "keepeth truth for ever" (Psalm 146:6). "Every word of God is pure . . . . Add thou not unto his words, lest he reprove thee, and thou be found a liar" (Proverbs 30:5, 6). It will not change or pass away, for it is eternal truth (Matthew 5:18). Psalm 19:7-9 describes it as "perfect," "sure," "right," "pure," "clean," "true and righteous altogether."

Study the Bible. There is no other book like it in all the world.

THE BIBLE IS COMPLETE

It is God's final revelation until Jesus returns in person. Nothing was left out; hence, nothing needs to be added. Not one unnecessary word was included, so nothing needs to be taken out. The Word of God is so complete that God pronounces a most severe judgment upon one who would add to or take from the book (Revelation 22:18, 19).

God's revelation is recorded in the sixty-six books of the Holy Bible. It is understood today by illumination, in which the Holy Spirit opens one's mind to the meaning and application of the truth revealed and recorded in the Bible. We need no "new" revelation to know the truth of God. God is not giving new revelation today. The Holy Spirit, who is the real author of the Bible, is present with each believer in Jesus to interpret the Bible to him.

We have a responsibility to know the Word and to obey the Word. But we have no authority to try to correct it or improve upon it. Here is God's word to us: "What thing soever I command you, observe to do it: thou shalt not add thereto, nor diminish from it" (Deuteronomy 12:32).

There have been some who claim to have received later revelations which add to God's revelations in the Bible. (I refer to books like The Book of Mormon and Science and Health With a Key to the Scriptures, held sacred by Mormons and Christian Scientists.) But all such revelations fall far short of God's word in the Bible and are to be rejected (Isaiah 8:20). The Bible is complete in its sixty-six books.

THE BIBLE IS INSPIRED

A revelation has to do with God giving the truth to human minds; inspiration has to do with the recording of that truth in human language. Inspiration is the supernatural influence of the Holy Spirit upon chosen people, with the result that their writing is the Word of God rather than their own ideas or opinions.

Second Timothy 3:16 declares inspiration for the whole Bible: "All scripture is given by inspiration of God" (II Timothy 3:16). Sections of law, history, poetry, prophecy, biography, and epistles are equally and totally inspired. You can read at any place in the Bible and be assured that it is the Word of God.

The theories of inspiration are many.

(1) Natural inspiration holds that the writers were simply great men of literary genius.

(2) Dictation inspiration sees the writers as passive instruments through which God wrote.

(3) Partial inspiration sees some parts of the Bible inspired and other parts uninspired.

(4) Plenary/verbal inspiration views the very words of the Bible as God's words so there is unerring accuracy in every statement, even in every word. The writers used the exact words which God approved for them to use (Exodus 4:12; I Corinthians 2:13).

THE BIBLE IS THE STANDARD

It is the standard for doctrine. We follow the principle of Isaiah 8:20 in estimating all religious teaching: "To the law and to the testimony: if they speak not according to this word, it is because there is no light in them." All other books of religion and all religious doctrine are to be judged by the teaching of the Bible. What agrees with the Bible is true, and what disagrees is untrue. The Bible is the standard for doctrine.

It is the standard for conduct. It is by hiding God's Word in the heart (memorizing the Bible) that you can be kept from sin (Psalm 119:11). This book will instruct, reprove, correct, and keep you in the way of righteousness (II Timothy 3:16, 17).

It is the standard for ajudication, the principle by which God will judge. Jesus said the words He spoke would judge people at the last day (John 12:47, 48). We must learn to live by it now, for we shall be judged by its standards then.

It is the standard for fellowship, "the true basis for Christian fellowship." We can have free fellowship with any who live by this book. But we must not extend Christian fellowship to those who rebel against it (Romans 16:17; I Timothy 6:3-5; II Timothy 3:2-5). Do you test your friends by the Word of God?

This book contains the mind of God, the state of man, the way of salvation, the doom of sinners, and the happiness of believers. Its doctrines are holy, its precepts are binding, its histories are true, and its decisions are immutable. Read it to be wise, believe it to be saved, and practice it to be holy. It will reward the greatest labor and condemn all who trifle with its sacred contents. It is the book of books—God's Book—the revelation of God to man.

1. In what way is the Bible God's words in man's language?

2. How is the Bible a record of God's revelation?

3. In what way is the Bible written in Spirit-taught words?

4. What do we mean by saying that the Bible is inerrant?

5. What passages declare the Bible to be without error?

6. Why is it important to say that the Bible is complete in sixty-six books?

7. Why do we need illumination rather than revelation today?

8. What does it mean to say that the Bible is inspired?

9. Why should we accept the Bible as our standard for life?

10. How can you give the Bible a larger place in your time?

THE PERSONALITY OF SATAN

What do you believe about the devil? What a person believes about Satan will influence his lifestyle, just as what he believes about God will do so. The doctrine of the devil and his demons (called "devils" in the King James Version of the Bible) is a very biblical doctrine. It is important that we understand that teaching.

An understanding of the doctrine of Satan is not just for an intellectual exercise or to satisfy curiosity. We must not become enamored with the doctrine, but we must be informed about it. Unless we know our spiritual enemy, we will not be strong in the spiritual warfare. That is why this study is scheduled in a review of Bible doctrine. It has a very practical application to daily life.

THE EVIL PERSON

Is the devil really a person? A definite answer is possible only from the Bible. Satan deceives people concerning his very existence, and apart from the Bible each is left to his personal opinion. What does the Bible say about Satan?

The devil is referred to in seven different books of the Old Testament and in every book of the New Testament. That would be inexplainable if he were not a person with whom we had to be concerned.

Jesus spoke of the devil as a person. He said that Satan is a liar and a murderer. He said Satan binds people with physical infirmity. He said Satan sows tares (weeds) where good wheat has been sown to confuse the harvest. He said Satan has a kingdom. That sounds like Jesus thought of Satan as a person.

Jesus spoke to the devil. In His temptation experience in the wilderness (Matthew 4:1-11), Jesus spoke to Satan three times, quoting a passage from the Bible each time. Jesus was not deceived, neither was He play-acting. He knew that the devil is a real person, and He treated him that way.

The saints of God have experiences which indicate that the devil is a real person as they face him in temptation and spiritual warfare. Unbelievers might not recognize Satan's work, but he puts a lie in their hearts and leads them in sin. Yes, Satan is real. Those who deny his reality are deceived.

What is Satan like? That Satan has personality is proven by his possessing a mind which plans his devices (II Corinthians 11:3), emotions by which he can have a great wrath (Revelation 12:17), and a will by which he plans and performs (II Timothy 2:26). He is morally responsible for his actions (Matthew 24:51).

Satan is a creature, meaning he has not eternally existed. The Bible does not tell of his origin except perhaps in Ezekiel 28:14, 15 where the description goes far beyond any earthly king. Everything is created but God; He is the Creator: "By him were all things created, that are in heaven, and that are in earth, visible and invisible, whether they be thrones, or dominions, or principalities, or powers: all things were created by him, and for him" (Colossians 1:16). That includes the devil himself.

Satan is a spirit being, belonging to an order of angels. The fact that Michael, the archangel, did not dare to rebuke Satan when disputing over the body of Moses indicates that Satan may have been the highest of the angels before his fall (Jude 8, 9). He still is ruler over the dominion of fallen angels and demon spirits.

Satan is the enemy of God and His people. He is called slanderer, adversary, accuser of the brethren, enemy, tempter, wicked one, destroyer, sower of discord, and other degrading names which indicate his evil spirit toward all that is good. He is your personal enemy, even if you are not aware of it.

Satan is the wicked one. He can be no other. A person who yields to Satan's influence will be wicked also. Beware!

What is Satan's position and power today? He is called the prince of this world (John 12:31), the prince of the power of the air (Ephesians 2:2), and the god of this age (II Corinthians 4:4). He is strong enough to resist and delay the archangel of God in his mission (Daniel 10:5-13), and is the ruler of the unsaved (Acts 26:18; I John 5:19). It is serious to stand against the devil. We must have the help of our Lord.

HIS EVIL WORK

The consuming desire of Satan is to thwart the plan of God in every area and by every means. Note the Bible record of how he has attempted that evil work.

He tempted Christ to sin (Matthew 4:1-11). I can understand his tempting us, but what audacity he showed in tempting the very Son of God! He offered to Jesus a demonic version of the benefits of the atonement without the suffering of the cross. Jesus turned aside from it. That temptation was repeated in various ways several times after the wilderness temptation (Matthew 16:23; John 8:44; 13:27).

He tempts the nations of mankind. His great purpose is to deceive the nations into believing that they can prosper well without God or in opposition to God. He has been quite successful in that attempt, as our present culture indicates. Even after one thousand years of great peace and prosperity, the nations will listen to his lies and align themselves against God (Revelation 20:8). How tragic it is that people will believe the devil's lies!

He blinds the minds of unbelievers. He does not want them to understand and respond to the gospel. When one hears the message of salvation, Satan comes immediately to take it away as the birds eat grain which falls upon the pathway.

He tempts believers to sin, accuses and slanders them, employs demons to try to defeat them, and incites persecution against them. He opposes them because he opposes God, and they belong to God by faith in Jesus Christ.

However, Satan can be faced and defeated. If believers in Jesus are sober and watchful, give no place to the devil, resist him after putting on the whole armor of God, are informed of his devices, walk in the Spirit, and use the Word of God, they can overcome him by the blood of the Lamb and the Word of their testimony. No Christian can truly say, "The devil made me do it." He can overcome the devil because "greater is he that is in you, than he that is in the world" (I John 4:4).

HIS EVIL END

Satan will not be victorious in his war against God's people. Four great defenses of the Christian assure that he will not be defeated.

First, no one can condemn the believer for whom Christ is making continual intercession before the Father (Roman 8:34; Hebrews 7:25). Rejoice, O Christian!

Second, no demonic power can overcome one who is strong in the Lord and in the power of His might from having put on the whole armor of God. He can stand against all the wiles of the devil (Ephesians 6:11-16).

Third, Satan was defeated through the death and resurrection of Jesus. The cross was his Waterloo (John 12:31).

Fourth, the Christian has the strength of the Lord to resist the devil so that Satan flees from him (I Peter 5:9; James 4:7). When the battle is over, the Christian is still standing (Ephesians 6:11-13). Christian, claim your victory!

Satan is under the perpetual judgment of God. He was judged when he was barred from his original position in heaven (Ezekiel 28:16). He was judged in the Garden of Eden when he deceived the woman (Genesis 3:14, 15). He was judged at the cross of Jesus, whose death effected redemption for those who were enslaved to the devil (John 12:31). He was judged when he was cast out of heaven and barred from access (Revelation 12:13). He will be judged when he is cast into the abyss to be confined for one thousand years (Revelation 20:2). He will be judged when he is cast into the lake of fire and kept there in eternal punishment (Revelation 20:10).

The devil may appear to have a temporary victory in our world. But take the longer view and see him as your defeated foe.

Do not take the devil too lightly, for he is a fierce and determined foe. Do not take him too seriously, for he is a defeated foe through Jesus Christ. He is powerful and active now as ruler over an innumerable host of demon spirits, but his doom is certain and sealed.

"Ye are of God, little children, and have overcome them: because greater is he that is in you, than he that is in the world" (I John 4:4). Glory!

1. Why do we need to understand the Bible doctrine of Satan?

2. What is the significance of Satan being a person?

3. How do you know Satan is a person?

4. What is Satan like?

THE DEPRAVITY OF MANKIND

Baptists hold to a biblical doctrine of the total depravity of the human race. That doctrine magnifies the grace of God in the salvation of sinners.

Our salvation is based solely on the redemptive work of Jesus Christ and is available by God's free grace without any merit whatsoever on our part. We only receive by faith what God freely gives by grace. There is no merit in the sinner which would recommend him to God.

THE MEANING OF DEPRAVITY

Many people reject the doctrine of depravity because they misunderstand what it means. It does not mean that everyone is as wicked as he can be, will indulge in every sin, cannot value good or do good things, or has no conscience or sense of moral values.

The doctrine means that the entire (total) nature of every person is weakened and warped toward sin and that, left to themselves, there is no desire in a person to come to God and no merit to claim when he responds to God's call.

The Bible is very clear in teaching these doctrines which underlie the doctrine of depravity.

(1) All people are sinners before God in their natural state (Rom. 3:23, Ps 51:5).

2) That universal sinful condition is related to Adam's rebellion which brought the fall of the human race (Rom. 5:13-14, 18-19).

(3) The whole human race is condemned apart from saving grace (Rom. 2:6, John 3:16).

(4) Unregenerate persons are children of the devil, not children of God (Eph. 2:1).

(5) The whole human race is in helpless captivity to the enslaving power of sin. No one is righteous apart from Jesus Christ (John 8:34, Rom. 3:10).

THE CONDITION OF DEPRAVITY

The human condition of separation from and enmity toward God did not exist from the beginning of the human race. Both man and woman were created by the direct work of God (Genesis 1:26, 27). They were made in the "image and likeness" of God. They were created free from sin. There is no biblical information about how long Adam and Eve lived in the beautiful Garden of Eden before sin entered human experience. They could have lived forever if they had refrained from sin.

What is the "image and likeness" of God which our first ancestors bore? It was not a physical likeness. (Nowhere does the Bible say God is six feet tall with brown hair!) God is spirit, and has no single physical form. Neither was "the image and likeness of God" the power of rule over the created earth. Additionally, being created in the "image and likeness of God" does not mean that Adam and Eve were gods. Instead, the idea of being created in "the image and likeness of God" implies that humans are created to represent and reflect God's glory (Isa. 43:7).

Think about some of the ways scripture describes the difference between God Himself and those created in "the image and likeness of God:"

- God is unchanging. Man is not.
- God is unmovable. Man is not.
- God cannot be tempted. Man is subject to temptation.

Humankind was free from depravity until the first couple chose to sin. That sin brought the "fall" of the human race into total depravity. Although still created in the image of God, the image is now marred by sin when humans enter the world.

THE FALL INTO DEPRAVITY

We are all born into sin (Ps. 51:5, Rom 3:23) as a result of Adam's sin (Rom 5:19). The first human sin is recorded in Gensis 3. Satan entered the garden as a serpent and tempted Eve to partake of the fruit which God had forbidden.

Up to that time the man and woman had been unclothed in the presence of each other without embarrassment. But when they sinned, they felt shame at being unclothed and sought to fashion garments from leaves to cover their nakedness. What had changed? They had.

Sin had depraved every part of them. This is the meaning of "total depravity." It does not mean humans do every bad thing they could potentially do. It simply means that sin affects every part of man totally. There is nothing-not one small part left within us- that is pleasing to God.

God knew it would be merciless to let the man and woman live forever in that condition. So, in Genesis 3:15, He announced the coming of a Savior to rescue them from spiritual death which came because of their sin. This is the first proclamation of the gospel.

However, consequences still exist for our sin. Adam and Eve died a physical death, just as God had said (Gen. 2:17). Likewise, barring the Lord's return, every human will also experience physical death (Rom 3:23) but, the gift of God is eternal life.

What happened to the first humans passed on to all of their descendants, much as human genes pass on physical characteristics. Since the parents were fallen and depraved, so all of their descendants are fallen also.

THE CONDITION OF DEPRAVITY

The natural man (as he is by nature apart from God) is void of spiritual life. He is dead in sin—separated from God because of his sin. When he is saved, he is raised out of spiritual death into spiritual life in Christ (Ephesians 2:1).

The natural man is enslaved to Satan. The whole world of mankind, which includes every living person, is under the power of the wicked one (I John 5:19). He is a bondslave to sin (Romans 6:16). That is why the Bible speaks of salvation as redemption from bondage.

The natural man is powerless to save himself. Dead in sin and enslaved by sin, how can he deliver himself from sin? All he is, does, or desires is defiled. Even his best deeds are as filthy rags before God (Isaiah 64:6). He must have a Savior who has the power to save him.

The natural man is corrupted in every part. His spirit is darkened, his soul is debased, his body is death-ridden, his will is weakened, and his conscience is dulled. He has a mind of the "flesh" and a heart that is deceitful. He is spiritually dead, under wrath and judgment, utterly lost, a guilty sinner before God, and a child of the devil (Eph. 2:1-3). He is to be pitied and directed to the Savior.

Only the righteousness of Christ is acceptable to God. Like the animal skins that God used to cover Adam and Eve's nakedness and shame, Christ clothes us with His righteousness. When the Father sees a redeemed human, He sees the righteousness of Christ rather than filthy rags.

THE EXTENT OF DEPRAVITY

Depravity is universal in the created universe. (1) It is universal in the human race. Every person is born with a depraved nature. And every part of the human nature (mind, emotion, will, spirit, and body) is depraved. That is true of you, me, and every other person. Even the best person suffers the same spiritual malady. (2) It is universal in the created earth. The inanimate creation is subject to the curse of human sin and is waiting to be delivered from it by Jesus (Romans 8:19-21). That deliverance will come when the present earth passes away and the new heavens and earth are made (II Peter 3). Everything and every person suffers the curse of depravity because of sin.

THE REMEDY FOR DEPRAVITY

There is one exception to the depravity of the human race—Jesus of Nazareth, whom we know as the Christ of God and our personal Savior. He "did no sin, neither was guile found in his mouth" (I Peter 2:22). He is "holy, harmless, undefiled, separate from sinners" (Hebrews 7:26). Because He is sinless He has offered the perfect sacrifice for sin. "Wherefore he is able also to save them to the uttermost that come unto God by him" (Hebrews 7:25).

Paul's treatment of depravity in Romans 5:12-21 can be summarized in one statement: "As the one act of Adam brought sin and death upon all, so the act of Jesus brought forgiveness and life to all." "The wages of sin is death; but the gift of God is eternal life through Jesus Christ our Lord" (Romans 6:23).

"There is therefore now no condemnation to them which are in Christ Jesus" (Romas 8:1). Christ's total salvation is the only answer to mankind's total depravity.

SAVED BY GOD'S GRACE

What do we mean when we speak of being "saved"? To be saved means "to be rescued or preserved from harm or danger; to make or keep safe." We might say the firemen "saved an infant from a burning house" and mean that they rescued the child from harm or danger. We might say the seatbelt in a car "saved the passenger from critical injury" and mean that it kept the passenger from serious injury.

In the religious realm, to be saved means "to be rescued or preserved from harm or danger; to make or keep safe," just as it means in the secular realm. However, it has the added meaning that the harm or danger from which one is rescued or preserved is the penalty of death and eternal judgment which comes upon impenitent sinners.

"Saved" is a great Bible word. It is used in the King James Version of the Bible more than 180 times, with the meaning "to rescue or preserve." That does not include the usage with the meaning "except," as in "who is a rock save our God?" (Psalm 18:31). More than three dozen times God is called our "Saviour." The theme of salvation binds all the Bible together, both the Old and the New Testaments.

There are two concepts of the way of salvation. (1) Some hold that we are saved by our deeds of merit plus an addition of the grace of God. (2) Others say we are saved by God's free grace, totally apart from human merit. Let us review Bible teaching to see which is the truth.

THE MEANING OF SALVATION

The Bible stresses six truths which explain what salvation is. Let's review them.

(1) Salvation is the work of God. Jonah learned that in the belly of the great fish and cried out, "Salvation is of the LORD" (Jonah 2:9). Isaiah testified,"God is my salvation" because he hath clothed me with the garments of salvation, he hath covered me with the robe of righteousness" (Isaiah 12:2; 61:10). Notice that it is God who did the clothing and the covering, not man who clothed himself. The righteousness which is received in Christ is His own perfect righteousness, not our own. Salvation is a personal

transaction with God. It is His gift of grace.

(2) Salvation is the deliverance of sinners from sin and its penalty. The announcement of Jesus' birth included the prophecy of His ministry: "He shall save his people from their sins" (Matthew 1:21). If we say salvation is the rescue or protection from harm or danger, we must ask what harm or danger threatens us. It is the danger of eternal death and eternal hell. Our sins so blind us that we can never find our way to God. He came in the person of Jesus to seek out we who were lost (Luke 19:10). "Christ Jesus came into the world to save sinners" (I Timothy 1:15). Aren't you glad He did?

(3) Salvation is declaring and making righteous the person who believes in Jesus. To be righteous means to have a right standing before God, to be accepted by Him in peace. Romans 3:20-22 teaches that man can never attain that right standing before God by his own works. By faith in Jesus Christ, the believer receives the righteousness of God Himself. Think about that! On a scale of 1 to 10, with 10 being the highest, how righteous are you? You are a 10, because you have the perfect righteousness of God himself imputed to you. Glory! God makes you right with Himself and announces it to your heart.

(4) Salvation is freeing the sinner from condemnation. He who does not trust Jesus is already condemned (John 3:18). He who does trust Jesus is delivered from condemnation and stands free before God (Romans 8:1). God's forgiveness removes the guilt of sin; and when guilt is gone, the penalty is removed also.

(5) Salvation is establishing peace with God. Justified by faith, each believer has peace with God through the Lord Jesus Christ (Romans 5:1; Ephesians 2:14). Through the blood of His cross, Jesus gave us peace with God and with those who trust Him as do we (Colossians 1:20). God becomes our loving Father, and we are His dear children. No wonder we have peace.

(6) Salvation is assurance of future glory. The chain of God's saving purpose has five links: foreknowledge, predestination, calling, justification, and glorification (Romans 8:28-30). Note that the divine purpose reaches from eternity before time (foreknowledge) to eternity beyond time (glorification). Our presence with Him in glory is as certain as our present certainty of forgiveness of sin. When God saves, He saves eternally.

There are many other blessings which accompany salvation. But those six principles are sufficient for our understanding and our joy in being saved by grace.

THE WAY OF SALVATION

Salvation is received by faith. Even a casual reading of Jesus' words to Nicodemus (John 3:14, 15, 18, 36) leaves no doubt that "by grace are ye saved through faith" (Ephesians 2:8). It is by believing that we have eternal life (John 20:31).

Salvation is totally apart from any works of merit. It is "not of works, lest any man should boast" (Ephesians 2:9). Settle it once for all in your mind that salvation is "not by works of righteousness which we have done, but according to his mercy he saved us" (Titus 3:5). That is why salvation is said to be a free gift of grace; it is not merited by our works.

Salvation is by repentance of sin. To repent means to turn from sin to God. God promised, "If the wicked will turn from all his sins . . . , he shall surely live, he shall not die" (Ezekiel 18:21). When the wicked forsakes his way and the unrighteous man his thoughts, God will have mercy upon him (Isaiah 55:7). There can be no turning to God if there is no turning from sin. Hence, repentance is necessary to salvation.

Salvation is by faith in Jesus. The Bible speaks of our "being justified by faith" (Romans 5:1). That was the way Abraham was saved (Galatians 3:6). That was the way Paul told the Philippian jailer to be saved (Acts 16:30-32). And that is the way you must be saved.

But what is faith? Faith is more than accepting doctrines. It is personal confidence (to the point of trust) in a person. Faith might be defined by using its spelling as an acrostic to read, "Forsaking All I Trust Him." That is saving faith—transferring all confidence from every other person or thing and setting it upon Jesus alone.

THE PROVISION OF SALVATION

Salvation is by the death of Jesus. He is "the Lamb of God, which taketh away the sin of the world" (John 1:29). God established the law that sin brings death, so the forgiveness of sin must rest upon the death of an innocent sacrifice. Jesus' sacrifice was like that of "a lamb without blemish and without spot" (I Peter 1:19). He died for our sins, "and not for our's only, but also for the sins of the whole world" (I John 2:2). Salvation is free to us today because He paid the debt for our sins by His own death. He died for us (in our place and for our good). We believe in a vicarious, substitutionary atonement.

Salvation is without respect of persons. When we say Jesus died for "the whole world," or that He "gave himself a ransom for all," or that He tasted death "for every person" by the grace of God, we speak in literal and specific terms. He died for all so that the invitation "whosoever will" could be given to the whole human race. You will never share the gospel with a person for whom Jesus did not die. "We see Jesus, who was made a little lower than the angels for the suffering of death . . . ; that he by the grace of God should taste death for every man" (Hebrews 2:9). That includes you. Rejoice!

THE PROBLEM OF SALVATION

In the salvation of sinners, God's sovereignty and man's freedom to choose seem to collide. How can God decree the salvation of sinners and still leave them free to choose whether or not to be saved? Both principles are taught in the Bible.

Salvation is provided by divine sovereignty. God decreed in eternity before time that He would save sinners by the sacrifice of His only begotten Son and chose us in Him before the world was created or a human being ever existed (Ephesians 1:3-6). His purpose and grace were given to us in Christ Jesus before the world began (II Timothy 1:9). It was not the carpricious choice of blind fate, but in the light of His perfect knowledge of all things past, present, and future He chose us (I Peter 1:2). The five links in God's sovereign work of salvation are foreknowledge, predestination, calling, justification, and glorification (Romans 8:29, 30). That means salvation is of the Lord from beginning to end and all the way between those two. The sovereign God saves sovereignly.

Salvation is received by a free act of the will. That "whosoever will" invitation is sincere. Anyone who will can come to Christ and be saved. He is not blocked from salvation by any decree of God or man. God's invitation is that all the people in all parts of the earth should look to Him and be saved (Isaiah 45:22). He tells how He invited sinners, and they refused His invitation by the act of their own will (Isaiah 30:15; Romans 10:21). Jesus said to sinners of His day, "Ye will not come to me, that ye might have life" (John 5:40). The problem was not that they could not come, but that they would not come. God is a loving Father "who will have all men to be saved, and to come unto the knowledge of the truth" (I Timothy 2:4). God wants you to be saved. He receives anyone who will come to Him.

God promises, "Whosoever shall call upon the name of the Lord shall be saved" (Romans 10:13). But to whom does that promise apply? "The promise is unto you, and to your children, and to all that are afar off, even as many as the Lord our God shall call" (Acts 2:39). Believe it. Call upon Him. Receive salvation. And rejoice!

SET APART FOR GOD

Sanctification! What a blessed Bible doctrine. But how tragically it has been neglected by many Baptists. The truth is that each believer in Jesus Christ has been sanctified (set apart to God), and that is what makes each one a saint. What doctrine of the Christian life is more wonderful than that?

Sanctification means "to separate for a holy use." The term is applied to both persons and things in biblical usage. All the firstborn of man and beast, for instance, were set apart for God after the death of the firstborn in Egypt (Exodus 13:2; Numbers 8:17).

We are concerned with sanctification as it applies to the people of God. An excellent summary statement may be found in Leviticus 20:26: "Ye shall be holy unto me: for I the LORD am holy, and have severed you from other people, that ye should be mine." To be severed from other people makes one sanctified to the Lord.

There are two elements in sanctification: position and practice. Positional sanctification occurs when God saves one and sets him apart for Himself as His own dear child. Practical sanctification continues in the Christian as he grows in Christ's likeness and lives for His glory.

The Bible speaks of both positional sanctification and practical sanctification.

POSITIONAL SANCTIFICATION: WHAT YOU ARE IN CHRIST

What is positional sanctification? It is the place, the position, you have because God has set you apart for His own. One who has been sanctified has been "perfected forever" (Hebrews 10:14) because God has placed him "in Christ." He is separated from things unclean before God. His body has become the sanctuary of the Holy Spirit (I Corinthians 6:19). He does not belong to himself but to God. His very body is a limb of Christ (I Corinthians 6:15). In his position, he is sanctified. His challenge is to make his life-style match his placing.

To whom are believers in Christ set apart? They are set apart to God. The Spirit of God sanctifies their bodies and the bodies are to so express their redeemed spirits that they glorify God in both body and spirit (I Corinthians 6:19, 20). The members of the body (hands, eyes, ears, etc.) are never to be used in the service of sin but always to be used in the work of righteousness. They are uniquely, personally, and eternally His.

When are believers in Christ set apart to God? They are sanctified the moment of their conversion. That is when they are born again (John 3), raised from death to life (Ephesians 2:1), translated from darkness to light (Colossians 1:13), transferred from death to life (John 5:24), made new creations in Christ (II Corinthians 5:17), and justified, sanctified, and washed (I Corinthians 6:11).

The Bible speaks of the "seal" of the Holy Spirit (Ephesians 1:13; 4:30). That seal is a brand, as the rancher brands his cattle. The "brand" which the Christian wears, and which identifies him as belonging to Christ, is the indwelling presence of the Holy Spirit. He indwells only believers, and He indwells every believer. That sanctifies each believer for God.

PRACTICAL SALVATION: HOW YOU BEHAVE IN CHRIST

Practical sanctification is the application to daily conduct the fact that you have been set apart for God. It continues through all of your life. You come to behave more and more like what you have become in Christ. You grow up in the grace, Word, righteousness, and holiness of God. You become more and more like Jesus, being conformed into His image by the ministry of God within you (II Corinthians 3:18). This is called "practical" sanctification because it relates principle to practice in Christian living.

Grow in grace. When II Peter 3:18 calls upon us to "grow in grace," it is making an appeal to practical sanctification. You can grow in grace in two ways. (1) You grow in grace as you understand and appreciate more fully the grace God has shown to you. (2) You grow in grace as you manifest grace (undeserved and unmerited favor) toward people about you.

"Giving all diligence, add to your faith virtue, . . . knowledge, . . . temperance, . . . patience, . . . godliness, . . . brotherly kindness, and . . . charity" (II Peter 1:5-7). As you move toward maturity by developing those graces in your life, you will experience increasing practical sanctification. You will be behaving more and more like Jesus, in whom all those virtues existed in perfection. Grace will enable you to manifest those virtues.

Grow in the Word. "As newborn babes, desire the sincere milk of the word, that ye may grow thereby" (I Peter 2:2). There are two ways you can grow in the Word of God. (1) You grow in the Word by increasing your understanding of the Word. Therefore, study your Bible regularly and diligently. It will feed your spirit, and you will grow in Christlikeness.

(2) You grow in the Word by applying the principles of God's Word to your daily life. Jesus said God's truth will sanctify you. Jesus cleanses His church "with the washing of water by the word" (Ephesians 5:26). The fruit of righteousness is produced in the person who lives by the Word of God.

Grow in righteousness. You are already perfect in the imputed righteousness of Jesus Christ. All the fullness of Deity dwells permanently in Him, and you have received His fullness because you are in Him (Colossians 1:9, 10). You have already been made the righteousness of God in Christ (II Corinthians 5:21). That can never be improved or increased. But you can grow in your manifesting His imputed righteousness in your spirit by conduct which agrees with your confession.

In fact, the goal of every Christian is to purify himself just as Christ is pure. The will of God is that we live sanctified lives in which the body is made subject to the Spirit. So we present our bodies to the Lord as a living sacrifice and resolve to be separated from the evil world system in which we live. We flee from the lusts of the flesh and refuse to satisfy them in ways which God would not approve. We hear God's command, "Ye were sometimes darkness, but now ye are light in the Lord: walk as children of light" (Ephesians 5:8). Each of us has both the responsibility and the opportunity to be "a vessel unto honour, sanctified, and meet for the master's use" (II Timothy 2:21).

Grow in holiness. Holiness is the withdrawal from what is unclean plus consecration to what is divine, sacred, and pure. Both withdrawal and consecration are involved. In New Testament usage, holiness also includes the carrying forward and completing of the spiritual-ethical requirements involved in being set apart (sanctified) for God.

Holiness is demanded of all of God's saints. They live under the imperative, "Let us cleanse ourselves from all filthiness of flesh and spirit, perfecting holiness in the fear of God" (II Corinthians 7:1). They recognize that without holiness no one will see the Lord (Hebrews 12:14). God calls to each of them, "Be ye holy; for I am holy" (I Peter 1:16). To fail to live a holy lifestyle is to sin against God.

Holiness is possible in each believer in Christ. But it does not come easily. God knew we needed help to grow in that lifestyle, so He designed the church to assist us. In the church He placed apostles, prophets, evangelists, pastors, and teachers in order to equip the saints that they might serve one another, with the result of the maturing of the body of Christ (Ephesians 4:11-16). Had you thought that your pastor's great ministry is to help you develop a holy lifestyle in the Lord? It is. Seek to increase in holiness daily.

The Christian life begins with birth. It continues with growth. It is the privilege of each Christian to develop the likeness of Jesus in his life and be a "Christ-ian" in truth. Remember this truth: It is not enough to give God the best you are; you must give Him the best you can become!

1. How would you define sanctification?

2. How does Leviticus 20:26 explain sanctification?

3. How is sanctification related to your being a saint?

4. What is your position as a believer in Christ?

5. How were you sanctified unto the Lord?

6. How can you grow in grace?

7. How can you grow in the Word?

8. How can you grow in righteousness?

9. How can you grow in holiness?

10. Why must you give God the best you can become?

ETERNALLY SECURE

God wants us to have no question about whether or not we are saved (I John 5:13). Neither would He have us question whether or not we are secure in Christ. All three persons of the Holy Trinity are committed to our security in salvation.

The doctrine of eternal security of the believer in Jesus Christ is a blessed truth. But it is greatly misunderstood. Many think it means that one can trust Jesus, live any reprobate lifestyle, and still go to heaven. Some fear it is an encouragement for careless living by a Christian. Only a misunderstanding of the doctrine would produce such thoughts. The doctrine praises the grace of God and challenges the believer to live in holiness because God has saved him with an eternal salvation.

The believer can feel secure in his salvation. His security is based on three things: the power of God the Father, the ministry of God the Son, and the agency of God the Spirit.

THE POWER OF GOD THE FATHER

The Father "borns" us into His family. John 1:11-13 distinguishes between natural birth and spiritual birth. We Christians are not merely born of the flesh (thereby making us the people of God), but we are born of God, who gives us His Holy Spirit. Anyone who believes in Jesus is born of God (I John 5:1). The Word of God leads us to the truth of sin and salvation; so the Bible says we are "born again, not of corruptible seed, but of incorruptible, by the word of God, which liveth and abideth forever" (I Peter 1:23).

The Father places us "in Christ" where we become new persons, just as if we were created anew. That means His providential care watches over us continually that the good work which He has begun in us will be performed until the day of Jesus Christ (Philippians 1:6). He works continually in us to create the desire and perform the fullness of His design for us. Therefore, "all things work together for good to them that love God, to them that are the called according to his purpose" (Romans 8:28).

The Father keeps us by His power until we receive our inheritance—incorruptible, undefiled, unfading—which is reserved in heaven for each of His dear children (I Peter 1:3-

5). We are in the hand of the Father and the Son. There is no power which is able to take us out of His hand (John 10:28-30). We do not fear because we know He is able to keep us from falling and to present us faultless before His presence with exceeding joy (Jude 24).

The Father redeems us eternally. His chain of sovereign grace reaches from before time (foreknowledge and predestination), through time (called and justified), and even beyond time (glorification) as Romans 8:29, 30 so clearly states. Because He purposes for us in view of eternity, He never quits loving us in time. His love does not change in view of difficulties we face from the world: tribulation, distress, persecution, famine, nakedness, peril, or sword. Neither does His love change in the face of enemies of the spiritual realm: death, life, angels, principalities, powers, things present, things to come, height, depth, or anything else in creation. Read Romans 8:35-59 and rejoice in the unchanging love the Father has for you.

THE MINISTRY OF GOD THE SON

What God the Father purposed in eternity before time, God the Son performed in time. The theme of Jesus' ministry was, "I came down from heaven, not to do mine own will, but the will of him that sent me" (John 6:38). What the Father predicted in the Old Testament, the Son fulfilled in the New Testament. Again and again Matthew says of events in the life of Jesus, "This was done that it might be fulfilled which was spoken by the prophet, saying . . . ."

The ministry of the Son may be gathered up under two great categories: (1) what He did for us in His incarnate ministry on earth and (2) what He is doing for us in His infinite ministry in heaven. On earth He redeemed us by His death and resurrection. In heaven He intercedes for us before the Father.

He redeemed us by His death and resurrection. God's law that "without shedding of blood is no remission" (Hebrews 9:22) explains the necessity of the death of our Savior. We had sinned; universally and inexcusably the whole human race had sinned (Romans 3:9-19). The only way for us to be rescued from our sins was by the death of an innocent and perfect sacrifice in our place. Jesus came and died "for us" (in our place and on our behalf) so we could come to God through Him. God has made it possible for us to "have redemption through his blood, the forgiveness of sins, according to the riches of his grace" (Ephesians 1:7). Think about it! "When we were enemies we were reconciled to God by the death of his Son" (Romans 5:10).

That means our sins are forgiven, removed as far from us as the east is from the west (Psalm 103:12), remembered no more (Jeremiah 31:34), buried in the sea (Micah 7:19), washed away (Revelation 1:5), and removed so that the guilt of forgiven sin will never face us again.

That is the "eternal redemption" mentioned in Holy Scripture (Hebrews 9:12). It is so complete that nothing needs to be added to it. You may accept His offer just as it is and be saved totally and eternally, today. Knowing the truth of it, enter into the good of it by repentance and faith.

He intercedes for us before the Father. Jesus' work on our behalf did not cease upon His return to the Father in heaven. At His corornation He received the name that is above every name (Philippians 2:9) and sat down at the right hand of the Majesty on high (Hebrews 1:3; 8:1). But even there He represents our interests by making intercession to God for us. Oh, how much He must love us!

His intercession assures us of our security. "He is able also to save them to the uttermost that come unto God by him, seeing he ever liveth to make intercession for them" (Hebrews 7:25). His intercession explains how we are "preserved in Jesus Christ" (Jude 1).

His intercession is personal and compassionate. He has experienced every trial we face and understands perfectly our needs. He knows the will of God and intercedes for us according to the divine purpose. He who is both God and man represents man before God. No power or person can by accusation overcome Him who preserves us by intercession (Romans 8:34). Rejoice!

He is our advocate (I John 2:1). As an attorney represents our interests in a court of law, so Jesus represents our interests before the Judge of all. Where else could you find anyone who could represent you before God?

Note that Jesus' intercession never ceases. It is a present intercession. It is a continuing intercession. Hebrews 7:25 teaches that He always lives in the ministry of making intercession for us. His grace has brought us safe thus far, and His grace will take us on to the end of the way.

Pause at this point and thank God for the intercessory ministry of Jesus. Even as you thank Him, He is interceding for you before the Father. When you forget to thank Him, He is interceding for you before the Father. His intercession continues when you rebel and when you obey. Thank you, Lord Jesus.

THE AGENCY OF THE HOLY SPIRIT

What the Father purposed and what the Son performed, the Holy Spirit applies to the life of one who believes in Jesus.

The first ministry of the Spirit is to enlighten the mind of the sinner so he can comprehend spiritual truth and receive the Gospel (Acts 16:14). Then He convinces us of the seriousness of sin, of our lack of righteousness, and of the certainty of coming judgment (John 16:8-11). When there is the response of repentance from sin and faith in Jesus Christ, the Spirit "borns" the believer into the family of God (John 3:1-8). That is when a person is saved and sealed eternally.

The Holy Spirit then moves into the believer and takes up a personal residence within. His blessed presence is the proof or "seal" (mark, brand, identification) that one is truly a child of God (Ephesians 1:13, 14; 4:30). The Holy Spirit remains with and within the believer from that conversion experience until he stands before God in eternity. He lives the life of God in a human body. He lives the life of eternity right here in time. Think about what it means to be sealed by the Holy Spirit of promise until the day of redemption. Think of it and rejoice!

The Holy Spirit becomes a witness to us that we are truly the sons of God (Romans 8:14-16). Assurance of salvation is not based on our fluctuating emotions but on the consistent witness of the Spirit of God. There is a basis for our assurance. God himself says we are saved.

The Holy Spirit becomes all we need to live the Christian life in a non-Christian world. He is our Companion (called a "Comforter" in John 14:16). Jesus' promise never to leave us or forsake us is fulfilled in the personal presence of the Holy Spirit with us and within us. Rejoice, dear Christian. He is there totally apart from our feelings, whether we feel His presence or not. Rejoice!

The Holy Spirit is active in us. He teaches us, leads us, convicts us of wrongs, assures us, empowers us, and takes the things of God to make them real to us. Every contact we have with God, whether in our prayers to Him or His ministry to us, is through the agency of the Holy Spirit. No wonder the Bible counsels us, "Grieve not the Holy Spirit of God" (Ephesians 4:30).

We have reviewed the ministry of God the Father, God the Son, and God the Spirit. Why? Because our security of the believer in Jesus is the work of God, not the accomplishment of man. It is the power of the Father, the redemption of the Son, and the ministry of the Spirit that makes you secure.

Because God is at work in your life, you can be sure you have eternal life and shall never perish (John 3:16). You are kept by the power of God until you enter your inheritance which is reserved in heaven just for you (I Peter 1:3-5).

THE TRUE CHURCH

What do you mean when you speak of the "church"? The word is used in so many different ways in our English language that we almost need to ask for a definition when we hear it.

Church is used geographically, as "the church of England." It is used denominationally, as "the Baptist church" or "the Methodist church." It is used institutionally, as when we say, "Jesus instituted the church." It is used locally to refer to the assembly of Christians in a particular place, as defined in the following comments.

Our confusion is not due to God's failure to reveal the truth about the church. In the New Testament the term church refers to a local congregation of Christians in every instance in which it is used. The Greek term ekklesia, which is commonly translated "church" in its religious usage, refers to an assembly of people who are called together to consider a matter. Some things are said of the local congregation of Christians which are true of the whole family of God, but the thrust of the New Testament is on the church as a local assembly. That is the meaning to be applied as the term is used in this study.

THE NATURE OF THE CHURCH

The church is a local congregation. That is evident from the consideration of the usage of the term ekklesia used in the Greek New Testament and commonly translated as "church." The term means "assembly, a called out assembly of free people." It occurs 115 times in the Greek New Testament. It has a secular usage three times and is translated as "assembly" (Acts 19:32, 39, 41). It has an institutional usage three times in reference to the church as an institution in human society as the home, the state, or the school (Matthew 16:18; 18:17). There is no question but that in ninety occurrences it refers to a local congregation of Christians because the congregation is named seventeen times, the term is plural thirty-five times, and the context shows a local meaning thirty-eight times.

In the other appearances of the word in the New Testament

(primarily in Ephesians and Colossians) it could have a broader meaning, but its primary application is still to the local assembly. That is why our Doctrinal Statement reads, "The church is a local congregation . . . ."

The church is a believing assembly. Only those who are believers in Jesus Christ can be members of an assembly of believers. The book of Acts suggests that a candidate for church membership must confess his faith in Jesus Christ by the ordinance of water baptism (Acts 2:41, 47; 8:36, 37; 19:1-5). An unbeliever may have his name on the membership roll of a church, but he is not a true member.

The church is a baptized assembly. There is no record of conversion without baptism in all the New Testament except the thief who trusted Jesus just before he died on the cross (Luke 23:39-43). Christian baptism is prerequisite to membership in a Baptist church. When a person comes for baptism, the traditional motion made in Baptist churches states, "I move we receive this person as a candidate for baptism, and after baptism into the full fellowship of the church."

The church is a covenanted assembly. There is no stated covenant recorded in the New Testament to which the members must subscribe. But there must be a commitment of each to the others to form a congregation. A group of believers getting together does not constitute a church. (An associational meeting does not constitute a New Testament church, for there is no commitment among them to be a church.)

When a person joins a church, he commits himself to function as a member of that body. Covenant is essential.

The church is a visible assembly. As a local congregation of baptized believers in Jesus Christ, of course she is visible. How could she be otherwise? She is called a body (Ephesians 1:22, 23), a building (Ephesians 2:19-22), a flock (Acts 20:28), a bride (Revelation 19:7-9); and each of those is visible and tangible.

God made the church visible that she might be a picture of invisible spiritual realities, just as the tabernacle in the wilderness was a picture of "a greater and more perfect tabernacle" than that which Moses built (Hebrews 9:11).

People should be able to look at each church and see spiritual realities demonstrated by her love, fellowship, ministry, devotion to God, and message.

THE AUTONOMY OF THE CHURCH

Jesus is the head of each church. God instituted the church in such a manner that Jesus is her head and she is His visible representation on earth.

Associations, conventions, boards, or councils cannot control one of the Lord's churches because He alone is her head.

The Bible is her guidebook. She is not bound by decisions of councils, synods, or associations. She believes and behaves according to the instructions of that Book. The congregation votes to determine details of her program, but it is limited to teach and support ministries which biblical principles would approve. The church is bound by the Book.

Pastors are the leaders, the human heads of the church, appointed by the Lord Jesus himself. They are the "shepherds of the flock," the "overseers of the body," the "rulers of the congregation" in biblical terminology. They are not dictators, of course, but they are assigned by the Holy Spirit to lead the churches under the headship of Jesus Christ.

THE PERPETUITY OF THE CHURCH

The first church was established in Palestine during the personal ministry of Jesus on earth. His statement, "I will build my church" (Matthew 16:18), was declarative of what He would do during His incarnate ministry, not what He would do through the Holy Spirit after His ascension and coronation.

His promise that "the gates of hell shall not prevail against it" (Matthew 16:18) has proven true, for true churches have continued to exist in every age since that time to present.

Churches which are true to Jesus will be here when He returns. They will continue in spite of apostasy and persecution as they have continued to this day. When the Lord returns, He will find faith on the earth!

THE OFFICERS OF THE CHURCH

Pastors are the shepherds of the church. Deacons are the servants of the church.

When faithful men of God fulfill the functions of the offices of pastor and deacon, the church will be strong and her witness will have an impact for Christ. God appoints the pastors (Acts 20:28), and the church selects the deacons (Acts 6:1-6); but both are accountable to God for faithful service.

THE MINISTRY OF THE CHURCH

How effective is your church in evangelizing sinners? How much does your Gospel message reach beyond your church building? How many did your church lead to Christ and baptize in the last twelve months? How well are members of your church growing through the educational program of your church? How consistent is your church in keeping herself pure by the discipline of erring members? The answer to those questions will reveal how faithful your church is to the ministry which Jesus assigned to her.

THE FELLOWSHIP OF THE CHURCH

Baptist churches form local, state, and national associations in "furthering the faith." In all those associational relationships, each church is equal to every other church. There is no "big I and little you" among the Lord's churches. Since each is the body of Christ in her community, each body is equal to every other body.

Jesus loves each church. He gave himself for sinners and redeemed them. Then the Holy Spirit brought redeemed saints together in local churches. If we love Jesus, we must love His churches also and show it by participating in their instruction, fellowship, worship, and witness. "Unto him be glory in the church by Christ Jesus, throughout all ages, world without end" (Ephesians 3:21).

THE CHURCH ORDINANCES

A church ordinance is a ritual or ceremony with a spiritual meaning which Jesus ordained to be observed by a New Testament church. It does not convey saving grace, but testifies by demonstration the fact of God's saving grace which He has offered and the believer has received.

We believe there are two ordinances which Jesus set in His churches. The initial ordinance is baptism. It is the declaration that one has become a Christian by faith in Jesus. It is to be received one time by the believer and need never be repeated. The continuing ordinance is the Lord's Supper. It is to be observed over and over as a reminder of the Lord's death and a prophecy of His return. The order of the ordinances must ever remain the same: baptism first and the Lord's Supper after baptism.

Some have put a misplaced emphasis on the ordinances. Rather than the rituals being a testimony to grace already received, some have declared them to be the means by which we receive God's grace. Not so. Baptism does not save. The Lord's Supper does not sanctify. They testify, in turn, that one has been saved and is growing in the Lord Jesus Christ.

THE ORDINANCE OF CHRISTIAN BAPTISM

Baptism is immersion in water. That is its mode. The English word baptize is a transliteration of the Greek word baptizo. The word means "to dip; to plunge; to submerge." It occurs ninety times in the New Testament, seventy-five times as a verb and fifteen times as a noun. There are other distinct Greek words which means "to pour" and "to sprinkle." Those are never used in the New Testament in reference to baptism. To baptize is "to dip, to plunge, to submerge." Baptism is immersion.

Immersion was the only form of baptism known among Christians for a full century after the ministry of Jesus. When other forms appeared, they were considered a heresy.

The Bible describes baptism in terms of immersion. John the Baptist baptized where there was "much water" (John 3:23). Baptism is a going down into the water, a burial in the water, and a coming up out of the water (Acts 8:36-39). It pictures a burial and resurrection (Romans 6:4).

That was the kind of baptism Jesus received (Matthew 3:16) and which He commanded us to receive and practice (Matthew 28:19).

Baptism is immersion in water of a believer in Jesus Christ (Acts 8:36-38; 19:4, 5) who has repented of sin (Matthew 3:1-8; Acts 2:38) and has received the word of God (Acts 2:41) and the Holy Spirit (Acts 10:44-48; 19:1-7). That is a description of a proper candidate for baptism.

Who may be baptized? Only a person who believes. Philip responded to the Ethiopian's request for baptism, "If thou believest with all thine heart, thou mayest." Only when the man responded, "I believe that Jesus Christ is the Son of God," did Philip baptize him (Acts 8:37, 38). To baptize an unbeliever (whether an infant not yet capable of faith or an adult not willing to trust Jesus) is a perversion of the Lord's ordinance. A person receives the Holy Spirit the moment he believes (Romans 8:9), and he who has not received the Spirit is not a candidate for baptism because he is not saved (Acts 19:1-9). What was your condition when you were baptized?

Baptism is immersion in water of a believer in Jesus Christ as a confession of his personal faith in Jesus and forgiveness of sins already received. Every example in the New Testament shows that personal faith precedes baptism. By faith we become children of God (Galatians 3:27). In baptism we confess to what we have received. Baptism, therefore, is not necessary to receive salvation. It testifies to grace already experienced.

Baptism is by the authority of a New Testament church. The Great Commission which Jesus gave to His churches has three elements: (1) evangelism, (2) baptism, and (3) discipleship training. So we say the Lord gave His churches the authority to administer baptism.

But the church's authority goes further than authorizing the act of baptism. She has authority to validate baptism—to confirm the validity of a baptism which has already been performed. For instance, if a person comes to your church and desires membership based on the baptism he has already received, your church has the authority to investigate and confirm that his baptism is valid or to declare that baptism invalid. Thus the church can deal with baptisms which she does not administer. The church validates the baptism of candidates who come to her because she witnesses the ordinance. But to keep from error she must also exercise authority on those coming by transfer of membership from another church. Your church has that authority.

Baptists believe that baptism is a prerequisite to church membership and participation in the Lord's Supper. The proof of that statement is that there is no record in the Bible of any person being admitted to membership in a church or to the Lord's table apart from a confession of faith in baptism. While we cannot produce book, chapter, and verse which lays down that rule, we can feel confident about it on the basis of the practice of New Testament churches.

THE ORDINANCE OF THE LORD'S SUPPER

What is the proper name for this ordinance? It is not a sacrament, if that means it confers saving grace. It is a sacred and solemn ceremony, of course. It is a eucharist because it is a time of thanks and grateful praise. It is communion because it permits special fellowship with Jesus and with fellow Christians in a very sacred ceremony. It is an ordinance since it was ordained (instituted, commanded) by Jesus. It is the Lord's Supper because the emphasis is on the Lord. He instituted it and commanded its observance "in remembrance of me" (I Corinthians 11:24, 25). Baptists commonly call the memorial the Lord's Supper.

How did it begin? Jesus and His twelve apostles gathered in an upper room of a private home in Jerusalem to observe the Jewish Passover. After the Passover meal had ended, Jesus took the unleavened bread and the cup which was left over and instituted the Lord's Supper. The Supper is not a meal. It used only the remnants of a meal. Its purpose is not to satisfy hunger or thirst but to remember the sufferings of the Lord Jesus on our behalf.

How is it administered? The Lord's Supper was instituted as Jesus and His disciples were assembled in a private home. The early churches must have observed it in private homes also, since that was the meeting places of the first Christians. The ordinance was observed in a meeting of believers, not as a private family affair.

The assembled believers ate the bread and drank from the cup as a testimony to the death of the Savior. It was never intended as a meal to satisfy hunger; and when it was made so, it ceased to be the Lord's Supper that was observed (I Corinthians 11:20-22).

Churches observe the ordinance today by eating the broken bread and drinking the fruit of the grape (which looks much like the color of blood) in remembrance of the broken body and shed blood of Jesus. It is always a most solemn observance.

What is the purpose of it? The biblical statements concerning the Supper indicate three great purposes in it.

(1) It is a memorial of Jesus. He said to do it "in remembrance of me."

(2) It is a testimony to the world. Its proper observance will "shew the Lord's death."

(3) It is a statement of faith. Since we do it in remembrance of Jesus "till he comes," the observance is a statement that we expect His return.

Why do you partake of the Lord's Supper? While no saving grace is conferred in the ordinance, it is a unique and special time of fellowship with Him. Do not neglect the observance of the Supper with your church.

Who may partake of it? Christians are greatly divided over this question. There are three common opinions current today.

(1) "Open communion" means the invitation is open to anyone who wishes to share. Some would limit the participants to confessed Christians, regardless of their denomination or doctrine; while others would open it to anyone, whether he has confessed Christ or not.

(2) "Close communion" means the invitation is extended to those who are in doctrinal agreement with the observing church. Those of "like faith and order" may participate.

(3) "Closed communion" (also called "strict communion") means only a member of the local congregation may participate. Some churches limit that further to active members, not including any negligent members present.

The Bible sets forth three absolute standards to govern those with whom we eat.

(1) One must be saved. We eat at a table where those who do not trust Jesus have no right to eat (Hebrews 13:10).

(2) One must be baptized. There is no text in the New Testament which clearly states this, but the example of New Testament Christians indicates that they practiced this rule.

(3) One must live an orderly lifestyle. One is excluded if he causes "divisions and offences contrary to the doctrine which ye have learned" (Romans 16:17). One is excluded if he "walketh disorderly, and not after the tradition which he received of us" (II Thessalonians 3:6). One is to be excluded if he is "a fornicator, or covetous, or an idolater, or a railer, or a drunkard, or an extortioner" (I Corinthians 5:11). One is to be excluded if he holds false doctrines as a "heretic" (Titus 3:10). One is to be excluded if he is out of fellowship with the Lord or with the people of the Lord in doctrine or practice.

How do I prepare to receive it? The Supper must be received after self-examination, self-judgment and self-discipline (I Corinthians 11:28-34). The church should not have to judge a person. He should have such a sense of awe at approaching the Lord's table that he would examine himself most carefully. Come, then, to the Lord's table.

Baptism and the Lord's Supper have been ordained (appointed and established) in New Testament churches. Each member should be careful to participate in both ordinances as a testimony of his faith and obedience to the Lord. The ordinances testify to what you have received in Jesus.

CIVIL GOVERNMENTS

Is there a biblical doctrine concerning civil government? Yes, indeed. The four basic institutions of human society are home, state, church, and school. God gives principles governing each in Holy Scripture. This week's study deals with Bible principles concerning civil government.

GOD AND GOVERNMENT

God instituted human government. It has been said that "God made man capable of governing everything except himself." That is why He instituted human government. Since each person cannot govern himself, God set up a system by which each would be governed by other people.

When Romans 13:1, 2, calls for each person to be subject to the governing authorities, it gives two great reasons why. (1) The authority residing in human government has been ordained (instituted, set up) by God himself. (2) To resist duly constituted government is to resist what God has ordained. And that is sin!

There are no exceptions to that requirement. "Every soul" means each person. "Let each one obey the governing authorities." No one is exempt from that requirement.

But what if the government is not a Christian government? What if the officer of government is not a Christian person? That does not change the requirement. The Roman government was pagan, with the Caesar calling himself a "god," when Paul wrote these words. God instituted government. To submit to government is to submit to God.

God intends government to maintain order in society. That is why we should pray for all who are in positions of authority (I Timothy 2:1-4).

God placed great authority in the institution of human government. Genesis 9:6 establishes capital punishment as a function of government. Romans 13:4 speaks of the "sword," using a term which means the executioner's sword. God gave governments the authority to enforce obedience and punish disobedience on the part of those who harm the welfare of society.

It is surprising to hear Romans 13:4 speak of the officer of government as "the minister of God to thee for good." That term "minister" is used elsewhere in Scripture referring to Jesus, the apostles, other Christians, and even of you. A minister is one who does the will of God in the place assigned to him. Since the officer of government is doing the will of God by maintaining an orderly society, he is the servant (minister) of God. Therefore, respect the officials of your government, whatever their political party.

CITIZENS AND GOVERNMENT

Citizens are to pray for good government (I Timothy 2:1, 2). This is more than saying, "God, bless our nation." It is to include the whole scope of praying: "supplications, prayers, intercessions, and giving of thanks." Is that the way you pray for your rulers? Pray for good government in your land. It is particularly important for us to pray in those years when public officials are elected by vote. Did you pray before you voted? Did you ask for Christian men and women with high moral and ethical standards to be elected? Christians could change the course of our nation if we would only pray as God calls upon us to pray.

Citizens are to submit to the officers and the requirements of government. Romans 13:1, 2, 5 is especially strong in teaching that requirement. First, there is a call for submission to duly instituted authority. Then, there is an explanation that civil authority is a reflection of God's authority. Next, there is a warning that to rebel against civil authority is to rebel against divine authority. Finally, there is a warning that to resist duly constituted authority will bring one under wrath and judgment by that authority.

But there is more involved than fear of punishment. We are to be submissive to civil authority, not only because we fear the penalty, but also as a matter of conscience which testifies that it is the right thing to do.

There is another reason for civil obedience. Not only will you escape punishment and have a clear conscience, but you will also be a witness and "put to silence the ignorance of foolish men" (I Peter 2:13-17). That is, you will be a witness for Jesus. That is the greatest reason of all, isn't it? The Christian citizen should be the best citizen in the nation.

Citizens are to pay the taxes required by government. Jesus said, "Render therefore unto Caesar the things which are Caesar's; and unto God the things that are God's"

(Matthew 22:21). Paul wrote, "Render therefore to all their dues: tribute to whom tribute is due; custom to whom custom; fear to whom fear; honour to whom honour" (Romans 13:7). Because the officer of government is the minister (servant) of God, we must pay taxes to support him in his God-assigned duties (Romans 13:6).

But what if the government squanders my tax money on programs with which I disagree? I must continue to pay taxes and work to elect officers of government who will be good stewards. Because someone else misses the will of God, I have no excuse to disobey Him also.

Jesus put the "render unto Caesar" and "render unto God" in the same sentence. I am as much obligated to meet the requirement to pay taxes as I am to give to the work of God.

Citizens are to have a higher allegiance to God than to human government. There may be occasions when officers of government will rebel against God and try to require a Christian citizen to disobey God in order to obey the government. In such a case the Christian must always have supreme allegiance to God. Like certain of the first Christians, we might have to say to officials, "Whether it be right in the sight of God to hearken unto you more than unto God, judge ye. For we cannot but speak the things which we have seen and heard" (Acts 4:19, 20). "We ought to obey God rather than men" (Acts 5:29).

Christian disobedience should be for religious convictions. The Christian is not to engage in riots or other forms of breaking the law by violence. He should simply walk with the Lord in a calm spirit and let the occasion be a testimony to his faith in Jesus Christ.

CHURCH AND GOVERNMENT

The state needs the input of the church. The church needs to keep reminding the citizenry and its rulers of the ethical/moral principles of revealed religion. It should be the conscience of a nation, calling awareness to abuses and seeking their correction. Our founding fathers never thought of a strictly secular government, as is being promoted today.

The church and state are separate institutions. Each is to respect the areas and ministries of the other, recognizing the contribution each makes to society. But neither is to interfere in the ordinary affairs of the other.

Church and state can contribute each to the strength of the other. The church can support the state by prayer. The state can support the church by protection. But the church is to receive no subsidy from the state, and the state is to set no requirement on the church. The church should be freed from taxation on property used for worship, education, or benevolence. Such use contributes to the welfare of society and the strength of the state. Since the good done reflects back upon the state, it loses nothing by exemption from taxes. However, the churches should not own commercial property or engage in business without paying the same taxes which all other businesses are required to pay. In that case they are in competition with tax-paying businesses and should not be exempt.

For the church to receive a tax subsidy from the state, there must be some element of control by the state. That would violate the autonomy of the church under her Head, Jesus Christ. So the church should receive no such financial support. A religious institution that receives public funds should not complain when it is asked to follow guidelines set by public officials.

The Christian should make every effort to be an exemplary citizen. It would be a great witness for Jesus Christ if every Christian would obey the laws, respect the officials, vote in elections, serve in the military, hold public offices, pray for the peace of the nation, and otherwise seek to influence government for the good of society and the glory of God apart from sectarian interests.

It is not asking too much to expect Christians to be the best citizens. Stop and take an inventory of your citizenship. Use the principles of this study as a measurement. In any area you appear weak, work to strengthen yourself there. Remember that Christian citizenship is obedience to God.

1. Why should Christians pray for their government?

2. In what sense are officers of government servants of God?

3. How is paying taxes an act of obedience to God?

THE SECOND COMING OF CHRIST

"Jesus is coming!" Does that announcement quicken your pulse and arouse your emotions with glad anticipation? It is called "the blessed hope" for every child of God (Titus 2:13). What is your response to it?

The return of the Lord Jesus is a basic theme which runs through all the New Testament. It is the continuation of the promises in the Old Testament of a coming Messiah. He came. He is coming again.

This thrilling doctrine has been abused by the exaggeration of its friends. Some have foolishly set dates for His return, even though the Bible says no one knows the date. Others have developed hair-brained schemes of events related to His return. But in spite of all the confusion, the saints glory in the fact that the Lord is coming soon.

The Bible is so clear in its statements on the subject that it must be accepted by everyone who believes that the Bible is true.

JESUS WILL RETURN

The patriarchs of the Old Testament believed the Savior would come to earth. Job testified, "I know that my redeemer liveth, and that he shall stand at the latter day upon the earth" (Job 19:25). When do you suppose are those "latter days" which Job foresaw? They are the days in which we live, the days which seem to be the end of this age. "Enoch also, the seventh from Adam, prophesied, . . . saying, Behold the Lord cometh with ten thousands of his saints, to execute judgment upon all" (Jude 14, 15). It is amazing that within seven generations of the creation of mankind there was a prophecy of the coming of the Savior. Apparently, God placed it in the consciousness of the race, and so it passed to all persons.

The prophets described the return of the Savior. Isaiah saw the blessings of the Messianic kingdom when the natural animosity between the animals would be removed and the hostility between people would cease because the Lord would reign. That time has not come, so it must be yet future. Daniel saw a stone cut without hands which crushed the kingdoms of the world and grew until it filled all the earth—a prophecy of the coming kingdom of God when "the kingdoms of this world are become the kingdoms of our Lord, and of his Christ; and he shall reign for ever and ever" (Revelation 11:15).

Jesus foretold His return. He said it would be witnessed worldwide like the lightning flashes in the east and is seen even in the west (Matthew 24:27). He said it would be with power and in the clouds of heaven (Matthew 26:64). He said it would be to receive us to himself, that where He is we would be also (John 14:3). He said it would be quickly, suddenly, and without warning (Revelation 22:20). He would not have told it and repeated it if it were not certain. You can take His word for it.

The apostles preached His return. One promised that "unto them who look for him shall he appear the second time" (Hebrews 9:28). They looked for His coming to be soon, feeling it was near at hand (James 5:8). It would be "the Lord himself" who would come, indicating they expected a bodily and personal appearance (I Thessalonians 4:16). He would come to judge the living and dead and to institute His kingdom (II Timothy 4:1). They expected Christians to look forward with glad anticipation to the appearing of the Savior (Titus 2:13).

The clear and repeated testimony of Holy Scripture is that Jesus is coming. He came in fulfillment of many Old Testament prophecies. He comes to fulfill other of the Old Testament and all of the New Testament prophecies. His coming is certain.

JESUS MAY RETURN AT ANY TIME

The Bible describes the conditions at the time when Jesus returns. It will be a time of social unrest (II Timothy 3:1-5). It will be a time of amazing changes in the international affairs of nations (Luke 21:25; Ezekiel 3, 39; Daniel 11; Revelation 13). It will be a time of religious revolution. Apostasy will appear in the form of scoffers at the promises of God (II Peter 3:3, 4), heretics in religious doctrine (I Timothy 4:1-3), coldness of devotion among professed people of God (Matthew 24:12), and many deceivers in the field of religion (Matthew 24:5, 24-27; II Timothy 3:13).

There will be a movement toward an apostate one-world church (Revelation 13:12, 16) at the same time there is a great evangelistic harvest around the world (Matthew 24:14). A witness to His return is a spiritual yearning among the saints of God (Hebrews

10:25; Luke 21:28).

Do not try to set events which must transpire before the Lord can appear. That would deny the repeated Bible statement that His return is imminent, even at the door. There is no prophecy which must be fulfilled before His return that would keep Him from coming this minute if He so chose. Live as if He might come before you sleep tonight or before you awake in the morning. Be as the servant who looks for his master. Be ready at the instant in which He may return, whenever it may be.

JESUS WILL RETURN TO CONCLUDE THE AGE

The Jews thought of time in two divisions: the present age and the age to come. That age to come was to them the age of the Messiah. It is the same to us. The return of Jesus will end the present age and usher in another age called the day of the Lord.

His coming will be audible. A trumpet blast will announce His arrival. He did not cry or lift up His voice that it might be heard in the streets when He was here in His incarnate ministry (Isaiah 42:2). But a trumpet blast heard around the world will announce His return. The only time the Bible mentions that Jesus lifted up His voice was when He commended His spirit to God at His death on the cross (Luke 23:46). But everyone will hear when He returns.

"Our God shall come, and shall not keep silence . . . . He shall call to the heavens from above, and to the earth, that he may judge his people. Gather my saints together unto me; those that have made a covenant with me by sacrifice. And the heavens shall declare his righteousness: for God is judge himself" (Psalm 50:3-6).

His coming will be personal. It is "the Lord himself" who shall descend from heaven with a shout (I Thessalonians 4:16). The very same Jesus who went up into heaven at His ascension will descend from heaven at His appearing (Acts 1:11). He said, "I will come again, and receive you unto myself" (John 14:3). How much He must love us!

His coming will be glorious. "Power and great glory" shall attend His appearing (Matthew 24:30). Why would it be otherwise? He will appear as God, not as man when He came before. We cannot imagine the glory that will be revealed in Him. But when the apostle John saw Him in a vision, he fell at His feet as if dead because he was so overcome by the Lord's glorious majesty (Revelation 1:10-20). What a day that will be!

He will come in the air. The

dead saints will be resurrected in glorified bodies and the living saints will be translated in glorified bodies (both happening in an instant of time), and all will be caught up to meet the Lord in the air. And so shall we be forever with the Lord (I Thessalonians 4:17).

He will come with resurrection power. Old Testament prophets foretold how He would redeem from the power of the grave and the hold of death (Hosea 13:14). Jesus announced that He would call and all the dead would come forth, both saved and unsaved, to stand before Him in judgment (John 5:25, 28, 29). Bodies that have been buried corruptible, dishonorable, weak, and natural will be raised incorruptible, glorious, strong, and spiritual (I Corinthians 15:42-44). The same body which was buried will be raised in the same way that the same seed that is planted will be harvested (I Corinthians 15:35-38). God gives each one of us a body as He is pleased to give. We do not know just what the resurrection body will be like. But we are sure it will not be subject to age, sickness, pain, and death to which the present body is subject. We can testify with the psalmist concerning our resurrection body, "I shall be satisfied, when I awake" (Psalm 17:15). As we have borne the image of the earthly here (looking like our parents), so we will bear the image of the heavenly there (looking like our Lord). Glory!

Caught up from earth into heaven. Caught up to the personal presence of the Lord. Caught up to be forever with Him. No wonder that is called "the blessed hope" of the believer.

JESUS CALLS US TO BE READY

The doctrine of the return of the Lord is intended to do more than to inform us of end-time events. It is designed to direct us in daily living now.

We must watch and be ready because Jesus is coming. Jesus said, "Watch therefore: for ye know not what hour your Lord doth come" (Matthew 24:42). His coming may be at evening, at midnight, in predawn, or at daybreak. We must be ready whenever His appearing might be (Mark 13:33). We should be ready every hour, for He may come at any hour.

We must work and be faithful because Jesus is coming. Jesus compared His departure and return to a master who went on a journey and assigned certain responsibilities to each of his servants. When he returned, he called them each to account for his stewardship. And Jesus said that is what He has done and will do when He returns (Mattthew 25:14-30).

His command to us is, "Occupy till I come" (Luke 19:13). We must be busy.

We must walk and be bold because Jesus is coming. John wrote of our amazement at the love of God that He would make us His sons and call us by that title. He said it contained a hope beyond this world, which included being like Him when He shall appear. Then he wrote, "Every man that hath this hope in him purifieth himself, even as he is pure" (I John 3:3). Purity of life is directly related to our hope of the return of Jesus. "The very God of peace sanctify you wholly; and I pray God your whole spirit and soul and body be preserved blameless unto the coming of our Lord Jesus Christ" (I Thessalonians 5:23).

We must wait and be patient because Jesus is coming. The anticipation might tend to make us impatient. But God commands patience in the light of the soon return of the Lord Jesus (James 5:7, 8). The certainty of His coming is an incentive to our waiting, working, and watching with a calm spirit. He will certainly appear one day.

"It may be at morn, when the day is awaking,/ When sunlight thro' darkness and shadow is breaking,/ That Jesus will come in the fulness of glory,/ To receive from the world His own . . . ./While hosts cry hosanna, from heaven descending,/ With glorified saints and the angels attending,/ With grace on His brow, like a halo of glory,/Will Jesus receive His own" (H. L. Turner).

1. What is the second coming of Jesus?

2. Why is it a theme in the Bible?

3. How has the doctrine been abused?

4. What does the Old Testament say of it?

5. Why do we believe He could come at any time?

6. Why will His coming conclude this present age?

7. How can you live so as to be ready for His coming?

THE COMING JUDGMENTS

God "hath appointed a day, in the which he will judge the world in righteousness by that man whom he hath ordained; whereof he hath given assurance unto all men, in that he hath raised him from the dead" (Acts 17:31).

Judgment is demanded by the very nature of God. He is just. Justice means all people, whether good or bad, must receive their due. You are headed for judgment the same as I am. Paul said, "Every one of us shall give account of himself to God" (Romans 14:12). That word "every" means "the entire group taken one at a time." What a solemn thought. The wise person will prepare for death and for the judgment to follow.

We distinguish between two parts of divine judgment. The saved will appear before the judgment seat of Christ to receive rewards for their service for God. The unsaved will appear before the great white throne judgment to be punished for their sins and rejection of God's offer of grace in Christ. What you do with Jesus in this world, trusting Him or rejecting Him, will determine at which judgment you will appear. At this point

in your spiritual life, where will you stand? If there is any question, settle it with the Lord right now.

THE JUDGMENT SEAT OF CHRIST

When will it occur? The judgment seat of Christ will be held immediately upon His return in the air. He will appear in the air, and the saints will be resurrected/translated and caught up to meet Him there. The Bible says He will "judge the quick and the dead at his appearing and his kingdom" (II Timothy 4:1). "The Son of man shall come in the glory of his Father with his angels; and then he shall reward every man according to his works" (Matthew 16:27). One of the first things that will happen upon the return of the Lord is for the saints to stand before His judgment seat to be rewarded.

Who will be judged there? The saints of God will appear before the judgment seat of Christ. Paul speaks of "we" and "us" in discussing this judgment in Romans 14. Believers are included in that pronoun, but not unbelievers. They are "the rest of the dead" who do not live (are not raised from death) until after the saints have ruled with Christ for a thousand years (Revelation 20:4, 5). Second Corinthians 5:1-10 discusses the Christian hope at death and the judgment. Paul speaks of our desiring to go to be with the Lord and our confidence in being absent from the body and present with the Lord. He concludes the discussion with these words: "We must all appear before the judgment seat of Christ; that every one may receive the things done in his body, . . .whether it be good or bad" (II Corinthians 5:10). It is evident that the same persons who will be absent from the body and present with the Lord are those who will appear before the judgment seat of Christ. Yes, this is the judgment of the saved.

What is the purpose of this judgment? It is not a judgment to determine who is saved and who is lost. That is determined by one's relationship to Jesus in this world. This is a judgment of works for the purpose of rewards, and salvation is not a reward for good works (Ephesians 2:8, 9).

This judgment will bring believers into complete unity with Christ and one another. That is when we are made to "see eye to eye" (Isaiah 52:8).

Rewards for faithful service will be conferred at the judgment seat of Christ. "Verily there is a reward for the righteous" (Psalm 58:11). Jesus said He was coming to reward everyone according to his works (Revelation 22:12). One of the aspects of that reward will be the place assigned each saint in the millennial kingdom of Christ. Jesus spoke of one having one scope of authority and another having a larger scope (Luke 19:11-28). Each will be rewarded according to his labor for the Lord. Paul wrote, "If we suffer, we shall also reign with him" (II Timothy 2:12).

THE GREAT WHITE THRONE JUDGMENT

The Bible seems to make a distinction between the judgment seat of Christ and the great white throne judgment. They are never mentioned together as if they are the same. References to the judgment seat of Christ seem to always be to the judgment of the saints for the purpose of rewards. Reference to the great white throne judgment seems always to refer to the judgment of sinners for the purpose of punishment. These comments follow the premillennial order of events at the end of this age and the return of Jesus.

When will it occur? Revelation 20:1-15 refers to two resurrections of the dead. First, there is a group who participate in what is called "the first resurrection." It includes people who were martyred for their loyalty and witness to Jesus. "They lived and reigned with Christ a thousand years" (verse 4). They stand distinct from a group referred to as "the rest of the dead." This benediction is pronounced upon those saints: "Blessed and holy is he that hath part in the first resurrection: on such the second death hath no power, but they shall be priests of God and of Christ, and shall reign with him a thousand years" (verse 6). Without doubt, these are the saints of God. No lost person is blessed or holy or will reign with Christ. We understand that these are the ones who appear before the judgment seat of Christ. On the other hand, "the rest of the dead" are those who appear before the great white throne judgment. Notice that they lived after the thousand years in which the blessed ones reigned with Christ (verse 5). So the judgment seat of Christ comes before the millennial reign of our Lord and His saints, while the great white throne judgment comes after the millennial reign.

What will it be like? Note how this judgment is described. (1) It will be "great" in the number who appear there and the solemn verdict pronounced there. (2) It will be "white" in view of the purity of the Judge and the correctness of His decisions. (3) It is a "throne" because of the authority of Him who sits as Judge there. (4) It is a "judgment" because a legal decision based on true evidence will be given there, and the proper sentence will be executed upon those who appear there.

There is no biblical evidence that the court will follow our judicial system on earth. Here we have a prosecution and a defense. Evidence is presented and witnesses are examined. The case is argued back and forth. Sometimes justice prevails, and sometimes the courts err. But the evidence at the great white throne judgment will be indisputable. There will be no arguments. Evidence will be presented and the verdict will be given.

Who will be the judge there? Deity will be the judge, whether God the Father or God the Son. That is evidenced in the statement that heaven and earth fled away from the face of Him who sat upon the throne. However, the Bible is more specific.

Acts 17:31 states that God has "appointed a day, in the which he will judge the world in righteousness by that man whom he hath ordained; whereof he hath given assurance unto all men, in that he hath raised him from the dead." Whom has God raised from the dead? Jesus Christ, His only begotten Son. Therefore, Jesus will be the Judge upon the throne to judge sinners.

Who will be judged there? If the saints have been before the judgment seat of Christ before they reign with Him for a thousand years, and if the rest of the dead (the sinners) were not raised until after the thousand-year reign, it must be the sinners who appear before the great white throne judgment. Note that there is no word of approval or rewards at that judgment. It is rather a judgment where condemnation and punishment are paramount. Yes, this is a judgment of the doomed.

What evidence shall be presented there? One part of the evidence will be the accusations of a guilty human conscience. Remember how Herod, because of his guilt over having John the Baptist killed, thought Jesus was John, risen from dead (Matthew 14:1, 2). Many believe that everything you ever thought, felt, heard, saw, desired, or did is written in your subconscious mind, ready to be brought to the surface in vivid remembrance.

The divine remembrance will be a part of the evidence. God takes note of His people. A record of the doings of each is written before Him. As it identifies those who are saints, so it identifies those who are sinners (Malachi 3:16). That record must be present at the great white throne judgment.

Human remembrance will be a witness also. Jesus said the rich man in hell was able to remember his circumstances on earth and the brothers he had left behind (Luke 16:25). Just so, memory will testify that God's verdict is just.

There will be books of divine records. Revelation 20:12 speaks of "the books" being opened without identifying them. They may be the records of daily conduct, or they may be the books of Holy Scriptures. Either way, they will testify against the sinner's rejection of God's offer of grace in Jesus. Of course, the Book of Life is the primary witness. One whose name is not written in the Book of Life is cast into the lake of fire. That is the second death.

What will be the outcome of the judgment? There is no hope of salvation for the sinners who appear before the great white throne. They are judged in order to determine the degree of punishment they must suffer. Jesus said some will suffer more than others (Matthew 10:15; 11:22). The degree will be in intensity, not duration, because each one assigned to hell will be there eternally.

Next week's study will deal with the eternal states—the heaven to be inhabited by the saints and the hell to be endured by the sinners. What a tragic end to go into eternal hell fire, eternal punishment, torment, separation from God and all good, and to have no hope of ever escaping that suffering! What a motive for evangelism! What a call to Christ!

God has set before you the way of life and the way of death. Your eternal destiny is determined in this life. As death finds you, so will the judgment. As the judgment finds you, so will all eternity. Prepare to meet God.

THE ETERNAL STATES

Everybody has to live somewhere, and everybody has to live somewhere forever. There are but two destinies: heaven and hell. The wise person is careful about his address while on earth and will be doubly careful about his address hereafter. One may change his address in time at will, but he can never change his address in eternity.

Here are the two alternatives: To which of those two destinies are you headed?

How can we know what heaven is like and what hell is like? How can we know whether they are real or not? How can we know what it will be like to dwell in either place? The only answer to those questions is in the Bible. We must take the Bible descriptions of heaven and hell as the literal description of real places. It teaches that heaven is a place of bliss for the saints, and hell is a place of punishment for sinners.

HEAVEN, HOME OF THE SAVED

Isn't it interesting that we speak of heaven as a home and of hell as a destiny? It is because of the bliss of the former and the tragedy of the latter.

Where is heaven? The Bible uses the term heaven in three applications. First, heaven is the realm of the atmosphere where the birds fly and the clouds float (Genesis 1:20). Second, heaven is the expanse where the stars are located (Psalm 19:1, 2, 4). Third, heaven is the place where God is revealed in His fullness and is worshiped by angels (II Corinthians 12:2-4; Revelation 21, 22). But that is not all that is said of heaven in the Bible.

One day the present heaven and earth will pass away. There will be a new heaven and a new earth, wherein dwells righteousness. The city of God will come down from God out of heaven and will be joined to the new earth. Then will come to pass the saying, "Behold, the tabernacle of God is with men, and he will dwell with them, and they shall be his people, and God himself shall be their God" (Revelation 21:3). What a blessed prospect! (To read the biblical account of those amazing events, see Romans 8:19-23; II Peter 3:10-13; Revelation 21.) That new heaven and earth will be the home of the saved.

Who inhabits heaven? God is there. You would expect that, of course. Without the blessed presence of God, even a heaven would be a hell. The Bible speaks repeatedly of God being in heaven, looking down from heaven, and of our going to heaven to be with Him.

The angels of God are there. Their great ministry is to worship Him (Revelation 5:11, 12; 7:11, 12) and to serve His will. They know what is happening on earth and rejoice when sinners are saved (Luke 15:7, 10).

The redeemed saints are there. Heaven is the "Father's house" to them (John 14:2). They are before the throne joining in the worship of God.

What is heaven like? Heaven is a place, not a state or condition or feeling. It is a place as definite as your house on earth. It is a place of complete freedom from sin. Natural evil will no longer be there: "there shall be no more curse" (Revelation 22:3). Satanic influence will no longer be experienced there because Satan and his cohorts will be cast into the lake of fire before this (Revelation 20:10). What a wonderful place of no more evil!

Heaven is a place of perfect union with God. He will dwell personally with us, and we shall see His face with love and without fear (Revelation 21:3; 22:4). We will have been made like Jesus in our glorious resurrection bodies (I Corinthians 15:49). And there we will enjoy unceasing and unhindered fellowship with God (Revelation 22:1-6).

Heaven is a place where we will receive our inheritance which is "incorruptible, and undefiled, and that fadeth not away, reserved in heaven" (I Peter 1:4). It will be like a room in our Father's house (John 14:1-3). What a glorious home!

Heaven is a place of fellowship with our redeemed kindred. Those of our loved ones in the flesh who have preceded us into eternity will be there, and we will be joined with them in the presence of our Lord (II Samuel 12:18-23). Those of our loved ones in the Spirit—saints of all ages and locations and situations—will be there to share our fellowship (Matthew 8:11). What a glad reunion that will be! Imagine talking with Moses, Abraham, Isaiah, John the Baptist, and especially with Jesus. Glory!

Heaven is the realization of the ultimate goal of our redemption. Only then will we enter the fullness of the eternal life which we already possess by faith in Jesus. We will know God more and more perfectly, never exhausting His divine person. We will enjoy endless development as we keep learning of Him and enjoying fellowship with one another. Thank God for salvation in Jesus which makes heaven our home.

How is heaven described in the Bible? It is a tabernacle where God is worshiped (Revelation 21:1-8). It is a city where God dwells with His people (Revelation 21:9-27). It is a garden where God fellowships with His people and they serve Him (Revelation 22:1-5). Worship, companionship, and fellowship will all be enjoyed at the same time in the tabernacle of God, the city of God, and the garden of God.

Come on. Let's all go to heaven by faith in Jesus.

HELL, DESTINY OF THE DOOMED

Many people admit the reality of heaven but deny the existence of hell. Yet, Jesus spoke more of hell than He did of heaven. Be warned. Hell is real.

Hell is a place. It is definitely a place as is earth or heaven. It is a place prepared for the devil and his angels, not for humans (Matthew 25:41). People who go to hell do so by their own choice in rejection of salvation in Christ. It is a place of suffering pangs like burning in a fire that is never quenched and where death never comes (Matthew 10:28; Mark 9:43, 44; Revelation 20:10). It is an eternal place of endless suffering (Matthew 25:46; Isaiah 33:14; Revelation 20:10). No person in his right mind would want to go to such a place. Every person who is not deceived by the devil will prepare to go to heaven.

Hell will be inhabited. The devil and all his angels will be there because hell is prepared for them (Matthew 25:41; Revelation 19:20; 20:10). All fallen angels will be there. The wicked and impenitent

people of earth will be there because of their own choice to reject God's offer of grace in Jesus (Psalm 9:17). All persons whose names are not written in the Lamb's book of life will be in hell (Revelation 20:15).

I would not want to be in a crowd like that for a little while, would you? I certainly would not want to be in a crowd like that for eternity. I'm glad to have assurance that I am going to heaven to be with the Lord and His redeemed children.

Hell is the very opposite of heaven. Heaven is a place of light; hell is a place of darkness. Heaven is a place of peace; hell is a place of torment. Heaven is a place of reward; hell is a place of punishment. Heaven is a place of joy; hell is a place of sorrow. Heaven affords fellowship with God; hell produces companionship with Satan. Heaven is enjoyed with saints; hell is endured with sinners. Who in his right mind would choose to go to hell and miss heaven? No one. But the person who rejects Jesus Christ has been blinded by Satan and is not thinking logically about spiritual things (II Corinthians 4:3-4).

Hell is eternal. The terms everlasting and eternal are used fourteen times to refer to the duration of the righteous and seven times of the retribution of the wicked. (See Matthew 18:8; 24:42, 46; II Thessalonians 1:9; Hebrews 6:2; Jude 6.) "For ever and ever" occurs seventeen times concerning God's people and three times concerning the devil and his servants. (See Revelation 20:14; 21:8). The wicked shall be punished the same duration as the righteous shall be blessed. Hell will last just as long as heaven. A denial of the eternal sufferings of the wicked is a rejection of the clear statements of Holy Scripture and a wistful desire rather than a Bible truth.

Someone has observed that if once every thousand years a bird came and took away one grain of sand, the earth would eventually be removed. But the words "for ever and ever" break the heart. Do you catch the seriousness of your loved ones being without Christ? Do you see the destiny to which your friend or business associate is headed? How can you love a person who is bound for hell and not give him warning? Speak to someone today about security in Christ.

Hell is a place of conscious suffering as punishment. Some think that a person is like a chunk of wood which is cast into the fire, soon consumed and existing no more. Not so. Others think the fires of hell purify and one is finally transferred to heaven. Not so. Hell is a place of perpetual suffering from which there is no release.

'There is the punishment of separation. Jesus' words describe the ultimate doom: "I never knew you: depart from me" (Matthew 7:23). The fires of hell are less suffering than the exclusion from the presence and favor of God. What a sense of loss must lay upon the mind of the condemned. He can remember all the privileges he had on earth, all the opportunities to make peace with God through Jesus Christ. Now they are gone forever. What remorse! What self-condemnation! What indescribable punishment!

There is the punishment of pain and torment under the wrath of God. The fierceness of the wrath of the Almighty God is awesome beyond words. The Bible speaks of torment, the smoke of their torment, tormented in flames, and wailing and gnashing of teeth. The suffering will be felt in the body as well as the anguish felt in the spirit. There is no experience on earth to come close to the distress endured by those who reject Christ and go to hell. Be warned. Be warned!

Hell can be escaped. But the only escape is to receive Jesus Christ. Those who trust Him are delivered from condemnation of sin and set free (Romans 5:1; 8:1). To be in Christ is not to be condemned, but to be out of Christ is to be condemned already (John 3:36). Where are you?

God has set before you the way of life and the way of death, the way to heaven and the way to hell. Choose life. Choose heaven. Choose Jesus. Enter the grace He offers you by repentance from sin and personal faith in Jesus. Today!

THE EXISTENCE OF GOD

I approach this quarter of studies with great apprehension. We are dealing with the greatest subject ever considered by the human mind: the person of God. Who is He? What is He like? Those questions are beyond our understanding.

I feel like a child reaching out to grasp a star in trying to express correctly and clearly the attributes of our God. My heart is thrilled as I prepared to write. My concern is that I might not be able to make clear to you these divine doctrines.

What is your response to the doctrine of God? The atheist says that there is no God. The agnostic doesn't know whether there is a God or not. The materialist declares that he needs no God. The fool hopes there is no God. The Christian knows there is a God who is his heavenly Father in Jesus Christ.

God is! The Bible affirms that great truth without attempting to prove it. The sacred record begins, "In the beginning God" (Genesis 1:1). That means that when the beginning began, God already was (John 1:1). He was first

and alone. Only a fool will say in his heart, "There is no God" (Psalm 14:1).

The God who is has revealed Himself. What God has revealed about Himself is recorded in the Bible. What God has revealed in the Bible was recorded by divine inspiration and is completely true and totally reliable. Bible study will reveal to us what God has shown about Himself.

BELIEF IN GOD

Belief in God is universal among all people. Every culture, race, nation, and location has a religion of some sort. Those people who have never seen a Bible, who do not know that there is such a book as the Bible, have a religious system. The religion may be crude or perverted, but it is the recognition of the existence of a supreme being to whom man must respond.

Belief in God is not based on reason, argument, tradition, or even the Scriptures. It is based on a witness in the human spirit. "That which may be known of God is manifest in them; for God hath shewed it unto them" (Romans 1:19). There is what someone has called "a God-shaped blank" within each person which makes him know that God is and that he must respond to Him.

Only a very small part of the human race has ever denied the existence of God. The reason for that denial is spiritual, not intellectual or cultural. It is because "they did not like to retain God in their knowledge" (Romans 1:28). Spiritual rebellion is the basis on which all atheism rests.

Wise people can look objectively at nature and see evidence of God's person and power (Romans 1:19, 20). We have evidence that He is. We must respond to Him who is God. Therefore, we need to know who He is and what He is like.

ARGUMENTS FOR THE EXISTENCE OF GOD

Philosophers have thought through the subject and found several reasons to believe in the existence of God apart from the testimony of the Holy Scriptures. A person who does not accept the Bible as authoritative should be persuaded by these arguments.

The argument from cause: How do we explain the existence and order in the universe? Was it by accident or was it planned? The Bible says, "Every house is builded by some man" (Hebrews 3:4), and we agree with that. Who, then, built the earth and the universe of which it is a part? God!

The argument from design: Can we have such an intricate universe without an originating and superintending intelligent power overseeing it? No, not any more than we can have a watch without a designer and maker, or a book without a writer and a printer. God designed our universe.

The argument from being: Man recognizes himself as an imperfect being, but he has an inner awareness that there is a perfect being somewhere. Who is that being? God. Whence came man's idea of Him? From God himself.

The argument from morals: Whence came our sense of right and wrong? What is the basis of such judgments? It is because there is a God who rewards right and punishes wrong. So morality becomes obligatory, not optional.

The argument from the Scripture: It asserts, assumes, and declares that the knowledge of God is universal truth, not a deception. It reports God's work in history and proves that He is by what He does. But more than that, it tells who He is and what He is truly like.

The **God who is is** our heavenly Father in Jesus Christ. Glory!

WITNESSES TO THE EXISTENCE OF GOD

Nature witnesses to the existence of God. Read Romans 1:19-32. The changing of the seasons, the rotation of the planets, the symmetry and color of flowers all speak of a Creator and Preserver of our earth. A seminary professor said to a class of preachers, "Gentlemen, if you drive from home to school without seeing a sermon illustration, you do not have your eyes open." He meant that God is to be seen everywhere.

Psalm 19:1-6 describes most beautifully the revelation of God through nature. (1) It testifies to His glory and the work of His hands. (2) It is a continuous testimony which speaks forth day and night. (3) It is a silent testimony, not given through the human voice or language. (4) It is a universal testimony which goes out through the whole earth. It is a testimony that God is and that He is involved in our world.

History witnesses to the work of God. Psalm 78 reports of God's work in the history of Israel at her exodus from Egypt. Things that happened then can be explained only as the work of a sovereign God.

The restoration of Israel to Palestine, the revival of her long-forgotten and unused language, and her reestablishment in the community of nations is amazing. Such a thing has never been known in human history. It is explained only as the work of God drawing human history toward its consummation.

The Bible is a witness to the existence of God. A person who believes the Bible will have no question that God is and that He is at work in our world. There you will find ample proof of His person and work. And its message is true.

"All scripture is given by inspiration of God" (II Timothy 3:16), even though it was written by mortal men. What was reported of the Ten Commandments may be said of all Scripture, "The writing was the writing of God" (Exodus 32:16). Jesus said that by searching the Scriptures we could know what God is like because they testify of God (John 5:39).

It is by the purpose of God that the Bible has come to us in its purity. It is the very Word of God today as it was when it was first written by Moses, Isaiah, Paul, John, and others. It gives us details of God's person and work which we could know by no other agency.

Jesus, the Living Word, testifies of God. He is Deity who came in human flesh to show us what God is like (John 1:1, 14, 18) and to perform the work of redemption for sinners.

His miracles show the glory of God (John 2:11). His words show the love of God (John 3:16; 16:27). His person shows the nature of God (John 14:9; 10:30). We see the revelation of God in Jesus and fall before Him confessing, "My Lord and my God" (John 20:28).

THE NATURE OF GOD

We agree that God is. The question arises, "What is He like?" That is the subject of this entire quarter of studies. At this point, however, we can make some helpful observations.

He is the living God. He calls Himself by the name "**I AM THAT I AM**" (Exodus 3:14). He lives. Because He is living, He hears, sees, feels, knows, wills, purposes, and acts (Exodus 3:6-10; Jeremiah 10:10-16). He is distinct from the works of His hands, not a part of His creation. He is distinct from the works of men's hands, not an idol. As the living God, He is the source and sustainer of all the life in the universe.

He is a person, not an impersonal force. It is difficult for us to think of personality apart from a physical body. God does not have a physical body because He is Spirit. He cannot be confined to the limitations of matter which would result from inhabiting a body of flesh and bones. But

neither is He a vague misty spirit which has neither form nor substance. He is a living person with characteristics which we call attributes.

His attributes are many. We will discuss some of them in the next twelve lessons. Do not be turned off by theological terms as you read that God's attributes include the following: life and personality; self-existence; immutability and unity; truth; love and holiness; eternity and immensity; omnipresence, omniscience, and omnipotence; veracity and faithfulness; mercy and goodness; justice and righteousness; and the list could continue. There are attributes of God which we do not know because we are not able to comprehend them. One of the glories of eternity will be that we will know God more personally, intimately, and thoroughly than we could ever know Him in this world.

He is the Creator of all that exists. "It is he that hath made us" (Psalm 100:3). "All things were made by him" (John 1:3). "By him were all things created, that are in heaven, and that are in earth, visible and invisible, whether they be thrones, or dominions, or principalities, or powers: all things were created by him, and for him " (Colossians 1:16). That settles the issue for one who believes the Bible. He made everything according to His own design and for His own purpose. He is God!

CONCLUSION

History reports that no people have ever risen higher than their religion. No religion has ever been higher than its idea of God. What one understands of God's nature and work, therefore, is of paramount importance in life.

It is of greatest importance that we know God as He truly is. It is not just a concern that our theology be correct; it is a concern that our lifestyle reflects His will for us. Every error in doctrine or failure in conduct could be corrected by a clearer understanding and a humble response to the person we call God. Who is He? What is He like? How are we to respond to Him? Those are the most crucial questions of human existence.

The person who does not recognize God and yield to Him will go into idolatry. He may not bow before an image or stand in awe before a "sacred" tree, but he will make a god of himself (giving primary allegiance to his own desires) if he does not recognize the one true and living God. Things which receive our invisible adoration (wealth, power, fame, sensual pleasures) are idolatry as much as bowing to a graven image is. To know God is to recognize Him as God, be thankful that He has made himself known, and yield to Him as sovereign over all of life.

The great need of Christians today is to understand God as much as human intelligence will enable them to do so. Then we will worship Him, pray to Him, and serve Him as His dear children.

The chief end of man is to glorify God and to enjoy (love) Him forever.

THE ETERNITY OF GOD

God is; He has always been; He will always be. God never changes from past to present through future. He is the eternal God.

The Bible testifies, "Thy years are throughout all generations. . . Thou shalt endure. . . Thou art the same, and thy years shall have no end" (Psalm 102:24, 26, 27).

What practical effect does that have on us? The Bible explains, "The eternal God is thy refuge, and underneath are the everlasting arms" (Deuteronomy 33:27). The eternity of God is a firm foundation of assurance for those who trust Him.

God is eternal. We are creatures of time. There was a time when we were not, and there will be a time when we are no more upon this earth. But, God remains forever the same. There never was a time when God was not, not even in the measureless eternity before time began. There will never be a time in the future when God is not. He is the eternal God. Think of that!

The amazing truth of the Christian Gospel is that the eternal God is He whom we call "Father" in Jesus Christ. And He delights to call us His sons and daughters in Christ. This study is very practical since we often speak of our Heavenly Father.

THE ETERNAL GOD IS REVEALED

He is "I AM." He is never "I WAS" or "I WILL BE." The name of God is always present tense because He is forever the same. He is unaffected by past, present, or future.

God revealed himself to Moses by the name, "I AM THAT I AM" (Exodus 3:14). That is a strange sounding name to us. Various translators have expressed His name as "I am Who I Am," "I AM WHAT I AM," "I am The I am," "I am, that is Who I am," "I am the God who is." It is difficult to convey the full meaning of His name into our English language. The Torah (the Hebrew Scriptures) gives His name as Ehyeh-Asher-Ehyeh, which means "the living God."

We worship before Him with the words of the psalmist,

"From everlasting to everlasting, thou art God. ... A thousand years in thy sight are but as yesterday when it is past, and as a watch in the night" (Psalm 90:2, 4).

God can be eternal because He is self-existent. He depends on nothing outside of Himself for His welfare. He fared perfectly well before there was an earth. We do not provide for His benefit, but He provides for ours.

God is everlasting. There was no yesterday when He was not. There will be no tomorrow when He will not be. He is from everlasting the Lord God, the Holy One, and shall always be the same. Do you feel a sense of comfort in knowing that "the eternal God is thy refuge, and underneath are the everlasting arms" (Deuteronomy 33:27)?

God is not a creature of time. He has no beginning or end. His is a life without birth or death. He takes an oath saying, "I live forever" (Deuteronomy 32:40). He only has immortality of all the creatures in heaven or on earth (I Timothy 6:16). He is "the King eternal, immortal, invisible, the only wise God" (I Timothy 1:17). He is free from all succession of time. He was never younger than He is now, neither will He ever be older than now. His life is an eternal "now." He is "I AM."

I stood on a hill and watched flood waters rush through a narrow valley below. It carried bushes and some useful items on its bosom. I thought how God, standing outside and above time, must watch it pass without being touched by it. The difference is that He is involved with the creatures of time — you and me. He is involved because He loves us.

Do not let such teaching leave you with a feeling that you are somehow separate from the eternal God. Habakkuk addressed God as, "O Lord my God, mine Holy One" (Habakkuk 1:12). The eternal God is my Father and your Father in Jesus Christ.

THE ETERNAL GOD OUTLASTS PEOPLE

He was before us. He had to predate us in order to be our Creator. The psalmist testified, "It is he that hath made us" (Psalm 100:3). In divine counsel He determined within Himself to make humans, male and female, and give them dominion over all the earthly creation.

Before there were people, there was God. Before man lived, God was the eternal and living God. When the beginning began, God already was. It was He who caused the beginning.

He governs throughout our lives. He gives us strength or makes us weak, takes us away or permits us to stay (Psalm

102:23 , 24). He does according to His will among the beings in heaven and the inhabitants of earth.

James rebuked those who made great plans for their future, saying, "We will go into such a city and continue there a year, and buy and sell, and get gain." Instead, we should say, "If the Lord will, we shall live, and do this, or that" (James 4:13, 15). Why bring God into plans for the future? He governs the future of all people. "If the Lord will" must be written across all the plans of finite man.

His government in life is indicated by His discipline. He rewards the right and punishes the wrong, both in this life and in that which is to come. He blesses or punishes because He is the governor and judge of all the earth.

He controls the time and circumstances of our deaths. He sets the number of our days upon the earth. He calls us through death into eternity when those days are ended (Ecclesiastes 12:7). The end of our lives effects no change in His life. Our life span is used up. His years never fail.

THE ETERNAL GOD OUTLASTS CREATION

God existed before the material universe. Genesis 1 makes that very clear. When the beginning began, God was already active. He brought into existence the expanse of space, the waters, dry land, all air and water creatures, all vegetation, land animals, and mankind. He did it all because He was there before anything else was.

Psalm 90:1, 2 states very beautifully, "LORD, thou hast been our dwelling place in all generations. Before the mountains were brought forth, or ever thou hadst formed the earth and the world, even from everlasting to everlasting, thou art God." He was here before the mountains arose, even before the earth existed, and before human population covered the world.

God produced the Creation. "All things were made by him; and without him was not any thing made that was made" (John 1:3). Everything that exists, animate creatures or inanimate objects, came from the creative hand of God. Every creature that exists, whether on earth or in the heavens, came from the creative hand of God.

God is greater than His creation as the artist is greater than his painting. That is why it is impossible to represent God in the form of any creature of earth. That is why it is wrong to give to another the allegiance due to God only.

God changes the Creation. The material universe is not eternal. Both the Old Testament (Psalm 102:25-27) and the New

Testament (Hebrews 1:10-12) speak of the end of the universe as we know it. As a worn-out garment, God will fold it up and lay it aside. But He does not change with changing objects. His years grow no fewer because of those that are passed.

THE ETERNAL GOD GIVES ETERNAL LIFE

You would not expect Him to give any other life, would you? He is the eternal God who lives eternally. The life He gives is His own divine life; so it is eternal. He is the source of eternal life. He has given to Jesus, His only begotten Son, the power to give eternal life to all who trust Him. He who hears the Gospel and believes on God has eternal life, according to Jesus' testimony recorded in John 5:24.

Eternal life is not a gift that God gives apart from Himself. It is a gift of God but not like a gift you select and send to a distant friend. He is our life. Eternal life is Christ Himself living the life of God in you. "Christ liveth in me" (Galatians 2:20) is the explanation of eternal life.

Eternal life refers to the quality of life (the life of God) and the quantity of life (a life that never ends). God has committed Himself in the person of His only begotten Son, Jesus the Christ, to give you eternal life the instant you trust Him.

"The eternal God is thy refuge," so flee to Him for protection. "Underneath are the everlasting arms," so lean constantly on Him (Deuteronomy 33:27). Eternal life is in God's Son; so trust Him only. The eternal God pledges His everlasting care over you.

THE TRIUNITY OF GOD

This is holy ground! This week's study deals with the essential nature of all three persons of the Holy Trinity. It is concerned not with what God is like but rather with who He is.

It is possible to get so involved with trying to understand the doctrine of the triunity of God (how three can be one) that it becomes a mere intellectual exercise. It must not be so. This doctrine has been called "food for the heart, not just for the mind." Our sense of reason must seek to understand. But it must kneel in reverence before this awesome and incomprehensible doctrine whether it understands it or not. This study is a call to worship as well as to understand.

There are three basic positions that one might take concerning the doctrine of the Trinity. (1) Some deny that God is a trinity and insist that He is one. (2) Some teach that God is one and has simply identified himself at different times as Father, Son, or Spirit. (3) Some teach that God is truly three persons who are of one essence, each distinct from the other and yet neither separate from the other, who are one God. That third position is taken in these lesson comments. That is the position most in agreement with the teaching of the Holy Scriptures.

COMPREHENDING TRIUNITY

Here is mystery but not confusion. Some people reject all that they cannot explain, so they deny God's triunity. They insist that what man cannot understand must not be truth. Thus, man is thought to be superior to God's revealed Word. What a monstrous sin!

If we do not accept what we cannot explain, think about this: A black cow eats green grass and gives white milk which makes yellow butter. How? An electrical impulse is sent out on sound waves which are invisible yet are picked up by an electronic device and provide pictures from around the globe. How is it possible?

Some day we shall see God and be astonished. We will be as a man who, having been reared in a dark cave, finally comes out and sees the sun, the grass, and the blooms of the flowers. It is wise to go to the Bible today, discern its teachings, and believe what it says about God.

The Bible says that God is one. The great Shema, recited countless times by ancient Israel, says, "Hear, O Israel: The Lord our God is our Lord" (Deuteronomy 6:4). God is referred to as "he," a singular masculine pronoun. We Christians agree with that. We do not worship three Gods, but one. We believe, "There is one God, and one mediator between God and men, the man Christ Jesus" (I Timothy 2:5). Our God is one. That truth is affirmed fifty times in the Bible.

God is plural. He is more than one. We might say that He is plural unity, compound unity, if that would help us understand Him.

The Hebrew language of the Old Testament has two words which are translated "one" in English. The word yachid means "absolute one; the one and only one." It is never used of God in the entire Bible. The word echad means a compound unity and is always used of God as one. God is one and yet He is more than one.

One can be plural. Jesus prayed that all believers might be one (John 17:22, 23). Paul said that Jew and Greek, bond and free, male and female, all become one in Christ Jesus (Galatians 3:28). One can be many in Bible usage.

God used plural pronouns in speaking to Himself and of Himself. He said, "Let us make man in our image" (Genesis 1:26). Notice the plural pronouns "us" and "our." Yet, God was speaking to Himself in that statement. Check each usage in Genesis 3:22; 11:7; and Isaiah 6:8.

God intimates that there are separate persons in the Godhead. Some of the Messianic prophecies deal with God sending God to earth to effect redemption or establish the kingdom. The clear indication of Scripture is that there is one God who is three persons.

How can God be three, yet one? We think of a person as having a physical body. The three persons of the Holy Trinity do not have bodies like yours and mine. God is spirit. Numbers belong to created beings. God is infinite and beyond numbering. We are finite and must have numbers to understand. He is above the laws of the natural world or the spiritual world. He is God.

Various attempts have been made to illustrate the Trinity. We say water is fluid, vapor (steam), and hard substance (ice); yet it remains water. We point to an egg having a shell, an albumen, and a yoke. We speak of a man being a teacher, a husband, and a father. But none of those adequately illustrates the divine nature of the Trinity. All human illustrations fall short of adequately describing divine things.

CONFESSING TRIUNITY

Triunity is indicated in the Old Testament references to God. The most common Hebrew name for God is the word "El." It derives from a word which means "strong." That name occurs more than two hundred times in the Bible, chiefly in Job, Psalms, and Proverbs.

The plural form of the Hebrew word for God is Elohim. (See the El in its spelling?) That name occurs more than 2,500 times in the Hebrew Bible, scattered throughout its books. It is a plural word, yet it is not translated "gods" and is commonly used with a singular verb.

There are three explanations for the plural in God's name. (1) Some say it is a holdover from an ancient belief in many gods. We reject that outright. (2) Others say it is a reference to the plural of majesty and simply emphasizes the greatness of God. (3) Others see in it a foreshadowing of the Trinity which is more clearly revealed in the New Testament.

The third position seems preferable.

Plural pronouns are used of God in Genesis 1:26-28. It appears that the Holy Trinity were taking counsel with themselves in accord with their eternal plan for mankind. That also may be a foreshadowing that God is three who are one.

Triunity is declared in the New Testament. What the Old Testament intimates, the New Testament declares plainly. (1) Jesus declared unity with the Father. He said, "I and my Father are one" (John 10:30). The Jews took up stones with the intent of stoning Him to death. When He asked them why they were doing it, they replied, "For a good work we stone thee not; but for blasphemy; and because that thou, being a man, makest thyself God" (John 10:33). They were correct in that He did claim deity in that statement. Had He not been God, He would have spoken blasphemy.

Jesus was one with the Father. He was a person of the Holy Trinity. His relationship with the Father and Spirit remained valid, even when He came to earth in a human body.

Jesus distinguished between Himself and other members of the Godhead. In John 14:16, He said He (second person of the Trinity) would ask the Father (first person of the

Trinity) to send the Holy Spirit (third person of the Trinity). It seems evident that Jesus understood the nature of God as being the unity of three divine persons. He did not make a mistake in that, did He?

The work of God is ascribed to each person of the Godhead. Creation is ascribed to the Father (Genesis 1:1), the Son (Colossians 1:16), and the Spirit (Job 26:13). The incarnation of Jesus is ascribed to the overshadowing of the Spirit, the power of the Father, and the birth of the Son (Luke 1:35). Atonement for sinners was effected when the Son offered Himself to the Father by the Spirit (Hebrews 9:14). The resurrection of Jesus from death is ascribed to the Father (Acts 2:23), the Son (John 10:27,28), and the Spirit (Romans 1:4). The salvation of sinners is attributed to the election by the Father, the sanctification of the Spirit, and the cleansing by the blood of Jesus (I Peter 1:2). Is that sufficient evidence? What is attributed to one person of the Holy Trinity is attributed to others as well. The best explanation is that three persons were working as one. That is triunity.

We refer to the "first person, second person, and third person" of the Holy Trinity. That is a mistake if by "first, second, and third" we refer to

rank of importance and power. The Athanasian Creed reads, "In this Trinity, nothing is before or after, nothing is greater or less: but all three Persons are coeternal, together and equal." They are undivided and indivisible. What one is, all are. What one does, all do. What one purposes, all purpose. There is perfect unity in God.

CONFIRMING TRIUNITY

Walk with me through the New Testament and notice texts where three persons of the Godhead are evidently identified.

At the baptism of Jesus, the voice of the Father spoke from heaven as the Spirit descended upon the Son who was in the water (Matthew 3:16, 17). That record is more confusing than enlightening unless the doctrine of the Trinity is true.

Jesus gave us a baptismal formula when He gave the Great Commission. He told us to make disciples, then to baptize those converts "in the name of the Father, and of the Son, and of the Holy Ghost" (Matthew 28:19). The triunity is indicated in that the term name is singular but Father, Son and Spirit are three. It is an emphatic indication of the three who are one.

The apostle Paul gave an apostolic benediction when he concluded his second letter to the Corinthian believers. The blessing he pronounced upon them was, "The grace of the Lord Jesus Christ, and the love of God, and the communion of the Holy Ghost, be with you all" (II Corinthians 13:14). Why did he name the three unless he meant to represent them as distinct persons in the divine nature?

Deity is applied to the Father (Romans 1:7), to the Son (Hebrews 1:8), and to the Holy Spirit (Acts 5:3, 4). All three are God. Each one is fully God, not one third of God. Each has a distinctive ministry in the work of God, but no one works apart from the others. They are three who are one.

Someone might object, "But I don't understand it." A proper reply would be, "If you could understand the person of God, you would be God and not man," or, "God would be like a man instead of God." He is infinite; we are finite. No one of us can even grasp the total scope of human knowledge. How can we expect to grasp the full meaning of divine things?

The triunity of God is a proper subject for study. It is also a subject for worship. How great a God He is! Please do not miss out on the wonder of it by trying to understand the nature of it.

I remember awaking early in Tiberias, Israel, that I might see the sun rise over the Sea of Galilee. The cloud formation that day was spectacular. I marveled at the beauty of it without thinking of the scientific aspects of it. So I worship before the Triune God without fretting over my inability to comprehend Him.

THE IMMUTABILITY OF GOD

A pastor was visiting on a farm and noticed a weather vane the farmer had set on top of his barn. It bore an inscription, "God is love." The pastor was a little offended by it.

"Do you mean that God's love is as fickle as the wind?" he inquired.

"No, indeed," the farmer replied. "I mean that 'God is love' whichever way the wind is blowing."

That is the essence of the immutability of God. He never changes. Do not let the theological terminology keep you from this wonderful truth. Our hope is built upon the blessed truth that God does not change.

Suppose God did change. He might have changed since the Bible was written. He might have changed since Jesus died for sinners. He might have changed since He forgave us. We could have no certain confidence at all if God were changeable.

But God himself says, "I am the Lord, I change not" (Malachi 3:6). We stake the destiny of our eternal spirits on that truth. We live in confidence day by day because of that truth.

Study this lesson on the immutability of God very carefully. You can come away from it knowing Him better and having your faith greatly strengthened.

IMMUTABILITY DEFINED

Your dictionary will say that to be immutable means to never change or vary. That is a satisfactory definition.

To say that God is immutable is to say that He, in His nature and character, is absolutely without change. He is the essence of perfection. For Him to change would be to contradict himself and be less than the perfect person He is. It means He would differ from himself, which He can never do.

Change would mean that God would move (1) from better to worse, (2) from worse to better, (3) from immature to mature, or (4) from one type of being to another. But God is perfect in every aspect of His being. For Him to change would make Him less than He is. That He cannot do.

His perfection makes change impossible. Can omniscience get any wiser? Can ultimate holiness become any purer? As one has said, "All that God is He has always been, and all that He has been and is He will ever be." He will never be any better or any worse, for He is already absolute perfection. Believe it and rejoice.

Man does change; it is impossible for him not to do so. He is finite. But God is infinite and has no need to change.

It is good for man to change when he changes to be more like God, "changed into the same image from glory to glory" (II Corinthians 3:18). At the same time man's physical body grows older and weaker, his immortal spirit grows stronger and more like his Lord.

IMMUTABILITY DECLARED

The Bible states repeatedly that God is unchanging and unchangeable. Psalm 102:26 speaks of the temporariness of this present world. It will grow old, and God will fold it up like a worn-out garment and lay it aside. Compared with the temporariness of man, the earth seems very permanent. Compared with the immutability of God, the earth is quite temporary. When the universe is worn out and run down, "Thou art the same, and thy years shall have no end" (Psalm 102:27). That is amazing, isn't it?

The immutability of God is the basis for our hope in times of judgment. Malachi 3 records God's warning of coming punishment upon sin. God draws a fearful picture of the dreaded day of judgment. Then in the midst of those dreadful statements He declares, "I am the Lord, I change not; therefore ye sons of Jacob are not consumed" (verse 6).

Do you catch the significance of it? God's purpose to use Israel to produce the Savior did not change. He may have had to punish her for her sins, but He would not consume her. He would keep her to perform His purpose in her.

Apply that to God's purpose for you in Christ Jesus. His purpose is to present you perfect before His presence with exceeding great joy (Jude 24). His purpose will never change because He does not change. So whatever trials you may endure, you know the glorious end to which you are traveling.

James declares that God is so certain to remain the same that there is not even the slightest shadow caused by turning in Him (James 1:17). That is the basis of our assurance of ultimate salvation. Believe it and rejoice in it.

Man finds it necessary to change. He makes promises he cannot keep. He finds health failing or strength waning. He faces death, financial reverses, and other common calamities of life. He changes even when he does not wish to. He grows older. He dies. But look at God. "God is not a man, that he should lie; neither the son of man, that he should repent: hath he said, and shall he not do it? Or hath he spoken, and shall he not make it good?" (Numbers 23:19). Of course, He will keep every promise and fulfill His will.

IMMUTABILITY CHALLENGED

If God does not change, what is meant by saying that He repented? "God saw their works, that they turned from their evil way; and God repented of the evil, that he had said that he would do unto them; and he did it not" (Jonah 3:10).

To repent means to change the mind and thus to change the actions. Change is the essence of the meaning of the word. The Bible says that God does not change. Then it reports that God repented (changed). What is the meaning?

Repentance on God's part is only the change of a judicial action, not a change in His person. God would have overthrown Nineveh because He had decreed judgment upon sin. But He also had decreed mercy for those who would turn from their sins. When the people of Nineveh turned from their sins, God sent His mercy and grace upon them instead of His anger and judgment.

God did not change; the people of Nineveh did. He who judges sinners is also He who forgives sinners. He does not change in doing so.

Repentance is but one of the many methods by which God manifests His immutable truth and wisdom in creation. It is a way to state God's unchanging attributes in the changing circumstances of human history. It is a sign of God's grace as He turns threatened judgment from penitent sinners who turn to Him in faith. It magnifies Him rather than detracting from Him.

God said that the soul that sins shall die. You sinned. You were under the penalty of eternal death by the decree of God. Then you heard the Gospel and responded in faith to its announcement of salvation from sin. God did not mete out the death penalty upon you, but He forgave you and gave you eternal life instead. Did He change in that act? No, you changed. He remains forever the same.

IMMUTABILITY APPLIED

Immutability is applied to changing people. How temporary we appear in view of the unchanging nature of God. How we change toward one another, though God does not change toward us.

Others forget us, or we forget them. Attitudes toward us change. We revise our opinions of others at the slightest cause. But through all those changes in human relationships, God remains the same.

Immutability is applied to faith in God. We can come to Him with confidence that He has not changed toward us. He does not keep office hours, available at some times and unavailable at others. He does not accept us on the basis of our performance, accepting us one time and rejecting us another. He is the same toward us as He was when we first met Him.

This moment God feels toward you as He did when His only begotten Son died for your sins. He has not changed moods. He has lost none of His affection toward you. His invitation still stands for you to come to Him and He will give you rest. He will meet you now just as He has met you before.

All our efforts and desires to find God, to please Him, to fellowship with Him, require changes on our part. He is always perfect and need never change. But when we repent of what took us away from Him, and return to Him that we might be healed, we always find Him faithful.

THE OMNIPOTENCE OF GOD

"Thou canst do every thing" (Job 42:2) is a summary of the blessed Biblical doctrine of the omnipotence of God. That doctrine means that God has all power so that He can do anything He wills to do.

Why study a subject like this on the day we commemorate the resurrection of our Lord Jesus? Because His resurrection is the greatest demonstration of God's power ever witnessed in human history. Paul spoke of "the exceeding greatness of his power to us who believe, according to the working of his mighty power, which he wrought in Christ, when he raised him from the dead" (Ephesians 1:19, 20). The lesson comments will deal with the power of God. As you read, think especially of His power demonstrated in the resurrection of our Lord.

Here is a doctrine which, if truly understood, will strengthen your faith and magnify your heavenly Father. Do not let the unfamiliar word omnipotence scare you away from this blessed truth. Think of its wonderful encouragement to us.

When you have been through the testing and come forth with Job's testimony, "I know that thou canst do every thing" (Job 42:2), you will have a living witness to the omnipotence of God. How that will strengthen your faith for whatever is ahead for you. How that will magnify your heavenly Father to whom the Bible bears witness by this testimony, "Power belongeth unto God" (Psalm 62:11).

WHAT IS OMNIPOTENCE?

The word omnipotence is a compound word. Omni means "all;" potent means "power." Omnipotence means "all power." One who is omnipotent has total power over all persons and things.

The dictionary lists several shades of meaning for the term omnipotence: ability in every respect and for every work; indefinite greatness in power, ability, and authority; a potency that is absolute; almightiness. The fact that so many attempts are made at stating its meaning indicates that the concept of one person having omnipotence (all power) is almost beyond our understanding. But we do not have to understand it. We must only believe it that we may trust Him who is omnipotent.

God's omnipotence is His power to do all things, without the diminishing of strength, without means. Think about that.

God has the power to do all things. The skeptic might ask, "Does that mean that God can create a rock so heavy He cannot lift it?" Such questions are irreverent and absurd. It means that God is able to do all that it is His will to do. Though He can do all things, God will do nothing which is inconsistent with His created universe. He will not make two plus two equal five, for instance. He set the laws which govern nature; and He might supersede them, but He will not break them.

God exercises His power without diminishing His strength. That is amazing. We humans use our strength for a while and must stop and rest. We exhaust our strength as we work. That is not so with God! He uses His power and has no less than when He began. He never gets tired. He is never less than He is at this moment.

God exercises His power to accomplish His purposes with or without means. He sent a strong wind to open the waters of the Red Sea (Exodus 14:21); that involved the use of means.

He stilled the storm on the Sea of Galilee by a spoken word (Matthew 8:26); that did not involve the use of means. He is unlimited in the exercise of His power.

He raised Jesus from the dead with no use of means. His divine purpose was sufficient for that miracle. Before such a demonstration of power, we can do nothing but stand in awe and worship Him.

HOW DO WE KNOW THAT GOD IS OMNIPOTENT?

The names of God testify to His omnipotence. Remember the significance of a person's name in Bible times. Each one was given a name which had a meaning. It spoke of a point in history, a faith in God, an experience of the parents, an indication of one's nature, etc. God named Himself. He told us His names because His names speak of His person.

His most common name in the Hebrew language is El or Elohim. (Those are the singular and plural forms of the word.) It means "strong; plenteous in might." That name is used over 2,500 times in the Old Testament to testify that He is a God of power.

El Shaddai is a common Old Testament name for God. It means "God of overflowing might." God called himself

"Almighty God" (El Shaddai) when He promised to make the ninety-year-old childless Abraham the father of nations of people. When he and Sarah had a problem believing that promise, God asked, "Is any thing too hard for the Lord?" (Genesis 18:14). Of course, nothing is too hard for Almighty God.

El Elyon means "most high God." It is related to His name "Jehovah of Hosts." Power and supremacy over all is the essential meaning of His name. The psalmist wrote, "The Lord most high is terrible; he is a great King over all the earth" (Psalm 47:2).

"The name of the Lord is a strong tower: the righteous runneth into it, and is safe" (Proverbs 18:10). "Fear this glorious and fearful name, THE LORD THY GOD" (Deuteronomy 28:58).

The works of God testify to His omnipotence. Where can you see the works of God? You can see them in nature, in human history, in His miracles, in the saving of sinners, and in the spirit world. Behold the power of your God!

God's power is seen in nature. He made all that exists. He upholds it all and keeps it operating. He causes the seasons to follow their regular cycle and the harvests to come. He even feeds the birds of the air and the wild beasts of the forests. God is involved in His creation. You can see His control over all. It all reflects the work of His hand.

God's power is seen in human history. No nation rises or falls without His raising it up or putting it down. He exercises full control over all nations, even those who do not recognize Him (Habakkuk; Daniel 4:34, 35). But God is concerned about individuals, also. It is by His will that you live in a certain place, do productive labor, and receive a sufficient return that you can have the livelihood you need (James 4:12-15). History is His story, the record of His work in human affairs.

God's power is seen in His miracles. Who but an omnipotent person could have created the heaven and the earth by His spoken word? Who could have opened the waters of a sea and made the sea bed to be dry land? Who could have healed the sick, raised the dead, stilled the storms, multiplied food, and done all the amazing miracles that occurred in the earthly life of Jesus? Who could have raised one from the dead?

God's power is seen in His saving of sinners. From Acts 9, read the record of the salvation of Saul of Tarsus. There was a man whom people would say was most likely not to be converted. But in a moment Jesus changed that vicious persecutor into a devout disciple and fervent witness of the Gospel of Christ. It is a miracle of grace when He saves a sinner. Jesus was raised from death that the salvation of sinners might be possible. So there is a double miracle involved.

God's power is seen in His control of the spirit world. God raised Jesus from the dead, "and set him at his own right hand in the heavenly places, far above all principality and power, and might, and dominion, and every name that is named, not only in this world, but also in that which is to come: and hath put all things under his feet" (Ephesians 1:20-22). That is why Jesus cast out demon spirits and set free those people who were bound by them.

Demons are terrified of His power. Angels delight in doing His bidding, recognizing His authority over them. What a lesson that is for humans to reverence Him also.

WHAT IS THE SIGNIFICANCE OF OMNIPOTENCE TO US?

God's omnipotence is the basis of our faith. If we can say, "The Lord is my strength and song" (Psalm 118:14), we have great assurance. When He works for us, no one is strong enough to overthrow His work or thwart His purposes.

He is God! When His infinity is applied to His ability, we recognize that He is omnipotent, all powerful. We can know a God who has power to do whatever He promises and to enable us to do whatever He commands.

God's omnipotence provides assurance of answered prayers. Jeremiah 33:3 is a precious prayer promise which has encouraged my faith once and again: "Call unto me, and I will answer thee, and shew thee great and mighty things, which thou knowest not. " I would like to see God's "great and mighty things, " wouldn't you? He not only promises them, but He also has the power to perform them.

His power is "able to do exceeding abundantly above all that we ask or think" (Ephesians 3:20). What a basis that is for confident prayer! His power is already resident in each of His dear children. He is already working in us; so we should ask and reach out for whatever we need. He is willing and able to give. We shouldn't worry about asking for "little" things. God encourages us by saying, "I am the Lord thy God, . . . open thy mouth wide, and I will fill it" (Psalm 81:10).

God's omnipotence gives motive to our worship. He is "Our Father which art in heaven" (Matthew 6:9). We come before Him in love, but with a deep spirit of love and awe. We come before His presence with singing in full recognition that He is the God who has made us and to whom we belong. We thank Him and bless His name because He is our Lord (Psalm 100). "O come, let us worship and bow down: let us kneel before the Lord our maker. For he is our God" (Psalm 95:6, 7).

We recognize the importance of showing respect for those in authority over us in civil and in religious matters. Then how much more should we bow in worship before an omnipotent God? His power gives impetus to our worship.

God's omnipotence shows reason for our obedience. Military service has taught multitudes of men and women the importance of submitting to duly constituted authority. It is an important lesson to learn.

What a reason we have to obey the Lord God in whom all power finds its source! To disobey Him is the ultimate treason. To say, "No, Lord," is a contradiction of terms.

What grace we see when He who could command us invites us instead. Such a loving Father deserves our loving obedience.

God is truly omnipotent. He has all power. He gives power to those who need it (Isaiah 40:27-31). He has no less power when He makes another powerful. He does all His works without effort. One deed is done as easily as another.

His omnipotence enables His sovereignty (absolute power) and His infinity (limitless power).

To the lost person, His omnipotence says salvation is possible. To the saved person, His omnipotence says service is possible.

"Alleluia: for the Lord God omnipotent reigneth" (Revelation 19:6).

THE OMNISCIENCE OF GOD

It has just occurred to me that nothing just occurs to God! I can learn new truths or new insights into former truth, but God never learns anything new. He already knows all things about all persons and things.

God knows all things, has never learned any new thing, and can never know anything He does not already know. We say He has "all knowledge." In theological language we say that God is omniscient.

God's knowledge was not acquired in some remote time past. He knows everything by nature and without learning. If there ever had been a time when there was something God did not know, He would not be a perfect God. In that one area, at least, He would be imperfect. But He is perfect and infinite in knowledge as in other attributes.

God knows all things actual and possible. He knows what we do and what we could have done. He knows the consequence of this action or that action on our part. He knows what He will do in response to our needs and our actions. He is infinite, without limit, in His personal knowledge.

A god who must be taught is not the God of the Bible. The Lord God is omniscient! He knows all things past, present, and future — from the one end of time to the other. What a God is He!

BIBLE STATEMENTS ON OMNISCIENCE

God knows all things of a general nature. The Bible speaks of His being "perfect in knowledge" (Job 37:16). If we try to comprehend His limitless knowledge, we learn that there is "no searching of his understanding" (Isaiah 40:28). We worship before Him, realizing "how unsearchable are his judgments" (Romans 11:33). He knows everything about every person and thing. "Known unto God are all his works from the beginning of the world" (Acts 15:18).

Do not argue with God's omniscience just because you do not understand it. Do not demand that you must understand it before you will believe it. Do not follow philosophical reasonings which question it or raise questions about it. Believe it because the Bible says it.

God knows all things in nature. He created the stars, counted their number, and calls each of them by name (Psalm 147:4). Not even a little sparrow in the fields falls to the ground without His knowing of it (Matthew 10:29). He causes the rains to fall, the seeds to sprout, the plants to produce, the sun to shine, and the seasons to rotate in proper order. He is the Lord over all nature. And He answers prayer when His dear children pray about storms, droughts, earthquakes, and other affairs of nature.

God knows all persons. Meditate on the words of Proverbs 5:21, "The ways of man are before the eyes of the LORD, and he pondereth all his goings. " Each person's way is directly before God's eyes, and He knows the truth about each thing. He ponders each one's way by observing it, considering it, carefully examining it, and evaluating it. No wonder the Bible says, "All things are naked and opened unto the eyes of him with whom we have to do" (Hebrews 4:13). Nothing is hidden from Him.

Read Psalm 139. Every word, deed, act, and thought is known to God.

He knows us intimately in every place and under every condition. There is no way to get away from Him.

God knows each one so personally and totally that He has numbered the very hairs of each head. That is omniscience.

God knows all events in human history. He knows the past, the present, and the future. His total knowledge of human events is related to every prophetic statement in the entire Bible. That is amazing, isn't it?

Read Daniel 2 and 8 to see God's knowledge of future history revealed. God revealed to Daniel what kingdoms would arise, what would be the nature of each kingdom, and in what order they would come in human history. "I have even from the beginning declared it to thee; before it came to pass I shewed it thee" (Isaiah 48:5). From the beginning God declared what the end would be. From ancient times He has told things which are yet future. He announced that He would do as He pleased in human history, and none could turn aside His plan (Isaiah 46:9-11).

From eternity before time, through time, to eternity beyond time, God knows every detail about every person and thing. That is omniscience! "Such knowledge is too wonderful for me; it is high, I cannot attain unto it" (Psalm 139:6). Let us worship before our omniscient God.

THE NATURE OF OMNISCIENCE

God's knowledge is underived and independent. No one needs to report in order for Him to be informed. He never learns anything He did not already know. "The Lord is a God of knowledge" (I Samuel 2:3).

Certain people exercised a superficial faith in Jesus. They believed on the basis of their senses, but there was no heart-deep trust in Him. Jesus did not receive them as true disciples, "because he knew all men, and needed not that any should testify of man: for he knew what was in man" (John 2:23-25).

God knows us just as intimately today. There is no searching of His understanding. He depends on no person or thing outside of himself as a source of knowledge.

God's knowledge is instant and perfect on every matter. He does not increase in understanding as events transpire. His knowledge is total and complete at every moment, even concerning those events which have not transpired. It takes no effort for Him to know, to think, or to remember. He knows everything that exists or could have existed in the whole universe in every period of its existence.

Try to grasp the extent of God's knowledge. He knows all persons, every spirit, each thought, every mind, all laws, all causes, all mysteries, all feelings and desires, every secret, each thing visible and invisible, all things present and future as well as past, every item in earth, in heaven, or in hell. He never discovers anything new, is never surprised by new knowledge, and never wonders about anything. He does not seek information or ask questions to learn. Grasp that and you understand omniscience! Worship before the God of infinite knowledge.

God foreknows the free acts of man as well as his potential acts. Man's ways are known to the Lord, but He does not decree every deed a person does. Man is a responsible person, not a robot under divine sovereignty, and is accountable for his decisions and acts.

How should we describe the nature of divine omniscience? (1) It is immediate, not coming by experience. (2) It is simultaneous, not by successive observations or by a process of reasoning. (3) It is true, corresponding to absolute fact. (4) It is clear, free from vagueness or confusion. (5) It is eternal, all things comprehended in one timeless act of the mind without successive thoughts. (6) It is complete, knowing all things as they are as well as what they would have been if circumstances had been different. (Some call that God's "double knowledge" since it includes what is and what might have been, Isaiah 48:18.) God even knows the free acts of His creatures. Think about that!

We can say with the psalmist, "Such knowledge is too wonderful for me; it is high, I cannot attain unto it" (Psalm 139:6). If we could completely comprehend omniscience, we would have a mind like God. That could never be.

THE APPLICATION OF OMNISCIENCE

The doctrine of God's omniscience is a terror to one who has something to hide. The secret sin or hidden fault is neither secret nor hidden from the all-knowing God. Psalm 90:8 testifies, "Thou hast set our iniquities before thee, our secret sins in the light of thy countenance." Job testified, "His eyes are upon the ways of man, and he seeth all his goings. There is no darkness, nor shadow of death, where the workers of iniquity may hide themselves" (Job 34:21, 22). Let the sinner settle his account with the Lord now, before it is too late.

The doctrine of God's omniscience is blessed assurance to one who trusts Him. No sudden discovery on His part will ever change His attitude toward the believer (Isaiah 54:8-10; 48:8-11). He knows His own and keeps them secure. He knows every trial, tragedy, and temptation they face. He knows and prepares in advance to enable His dear children to enjoy victory over them all. Glory!

The doctrine of God's omniscience is the explanation of Biblical prophecy. Prophecy is pre-written history. God knows what is and what will be. He declares in advance what will be the outcome. Prophecy would be but a poor guess concerning future events if it were not for God's omniscience. But it is the sure and certain announcement of what shall come to pass.

Prophecy is God's announcement of what He purposes to do in human history. From the beginning He has declared what the end shall be. From ancient times He announced things that have not yet transpired, but will certainly come to pass. He plans and performs, doing all His pleasure. He uses persons and things in working His purposes in the world. He declares, "I have spoken it, I wilt also bring it to pass; I have purposed it, I will also do it" (Isaiah 46:11). Behold the miracle of prophecy.

The doctrine of God's omniscience inspires awe in all who understand the nature of such a person. Let us say one to another, "O come, let us worship and bow down: let us kneel before the Lord our maker. For he is our God" (Psalm 95:6, 7).

We can worship Him with these words of praise: "Great is our Lord, and of great power: his understanding is infinite" (Psalm 147:5). He is worthy of worship, isn't He? A previous study of the infinity of God underscored the truth that He is absolutely without limits. That is also the extent of His knowledge.

Do you feel your mind reeling in your effort to grasp the full implication of God's infinite knowledge? Great! It will help you understand better the majesty of Him whom we call "Father" through Jesus Christ. It will encourage your faith in Him and inspire your worship of Him.

Pride of intellect is a stumbling block for many who do not come to Jesus in humble faith. But who can be proud of his knowledge in the light of God's knowledge? Such pride in man is a sign of his foolishness. It is wisdom to know and trust God who is the source of all true wisdom. "If any of you lack wisdom, let him ask of God, . . . and it shall be given him " (James 1:5).

THE OMNIPRESENCE OF GOD

An atheist was trying to implant his unbelief in his little child. He wrote the sentence, "God is no where," and required her to copy it. In her inexperience, she put a space between the "w" and the "h" instead of between the "o" and the "w." Her sentence read, "God is now here."

God is now here! He is personally present now (at this moment) here (in this place) with me. At this same moment He is personally present with you in your place. He is in Boston and Bombay, San Antonio and Sao Paulo, Texas and Thailand at the same moment. He is fully, continuously, personally present in every place and with every person at the same moment of time. That is omnipresence!

A Hindu worshiper was moving about, tapping on trees and stones whispering, "Are you there? Are you there?" He was trying to find his god. We need never ask. Our God has revealed Himself as Immanuel, which means "God is with us."

The doctrine of omnipresence is that God is always present and He is everywhere present. You do not have to wait for God to come; He is here. You do not have to wonder where God is; He is here. That is omnipresence.

It is difficult for us to grasp such a doctrine. Our experience has been confined by time and space. We know that if a person is in the next room, he is not in this room. If he is in this room talking with another person, he is not talking with me. How is it possible to be personally present in all places and conscious of every person? Only God can do it. That is His omnipresence.

THE MEANING OF OMNIPRESENCE

Omnipresent is a compound word made up by the union of two words. Omni means "all." Present means to be "at hand, in attendance." Omnipresent means to be everywhere; close to everything; next to everyone.

We say God is immanent. That is another term meaning He is present throughout the universe.

We say that God is infinite.

That means He is without bounds or limits. Apply that to His presence and it means His being has no limits. Therefore, He can be everywhere present at the same time.

An ancient believer whom we know as Hildebert of Lavardin wrote, "God is over all things, under all things; within but not enclosed; without but not excluded; above but not raised up; below but not depressed; wholly above, presiding; wholly beneath, sustaining; wholly within, filling."

He is more than near to you. It is not enough to say He is with you, beside you, before you, or behind you. You must say He is within you (as a believer) and surrounds you as the air.

God is present universally and simultaneously. There is all of God with me here at the same time there is all of God with you there. His center is everywhere; His circumference is nowhere. He is present in His ultimate being, not just in His power or in His influence. It is God Himself who is omnipresent.

A god who is confined by the boundaries of time and space is not the God revealed in the Holy Scriptures. The ancient pagans believed Jehovah was the God of the hills but not the God of the valleys (I Kings 20:28). But we who know Him, know that He is the God of the whole earth.

THE STATEMENT OF OMNIPRESENCE

God testifies, "Am I a God at hand, saith the Lord, and not a God afar off? ... Do not I fill heaven and earth? saith the Lord" (Jeremiah 23:23, 24). He cannot be confined to the scope of the earth. All of heaven and the heaven of heavens cannot contain Him (I Kings 8:27). He is so far beyond His created universe that we cannot comprehend His limitless presence. Heaven is His throne; the earth is His footstool. Can you even begin to grasp the majesty of your God?

Psalm 139 bears witness to the omnipresence of God. He is in heaven and in the realm of the dead (called hell in verse 8). He is at the uttermost parts of the sea. He is in the darkness the same as in the light (Psalm 139:7-16).

Read the great sermon preached by the apostle Paul on Mars' hill in Athens, Greece (Acts 17:22-31). It is the finest summary of the doctrine of God to be found in the New Testament. One point of emphasis is the omnipresence of God. Paul spoke of "all nations of men ... on all the face of the earth" (verse 26) and applied to them the omnipresence of God. He said that God is "not far from every one of us: for in him we live, and move, and have our being" (verses 27, 28). He is with every one of His creatures, but He is with His dear children in a special relationship.

Jesus referred to the omnipresence of God in the Great Commission for world missions. He promised, "I am with you alway, even unto the end of the world" (Matthew 28:20). How can He be with each missionary, personally alongside him, when one goes to one part of the world and another goes to the other? His omnipresence makes it possible. What a blessed doctrine!

What are your circumstances at this moment? God is there with you. Where have relatives or friends gone? God is there. The Bible confirms with positive statements the truth of God's personal presence with all persons and in all places at the same time. Believe it and rejoice in it.

THE APPLICATION OF OMNIPRESENCE

God's omnipresence explains the nature of the world. Is it running by itself, or does God control it? Is it like a machine which has been turned on and runs until it is out of fuel, governed by blind fate, or is there a sovereign, benevolent power in control? Bless God, He is in control by His sovereign power and is involved by His universal presence.

God's omnipresence offers deep comfort and steadfast assurance to the saints of God. God is with us. He really is! Not in some vague and general way, but in personal presence, loving interest, and actual involvement. He is closer to us than our thoughts. He is more intimately within us than our breath. From every point on earth we are equally near to God. Christians should gather with other Christians for worship and study. But God is no more at church than He is any other place. He is everywhere present.

God's omnipresence warns sinners. Psalm 139 is a classic statement of God's personal presence and involvement in our lives. Because He is here, He knows every place we go, every deed we do, every thought we think, and every word we say. If a person wanted to get away from God, where would he go? God is in heaven, the realm of the dead, the remote regions of the earth, and He sees in the darkness as well as in the light. He even sees the baby yet developing in the mother's womb. How then can any sinner expect to hide his sins from God? He cannot. God warns, "Mine eyes are upon all their ways: they are not hid from my face, neither is their iniquity hid from mine eyes" (Jeremiah 16:17). Again He cautions, "They consider not in their hearts that I remember all their wickedness:

now their own doings have beset them about; they are before my face" (Hosea 7:2). The doctrine of God's omnipresence is a call to repentance.

God's omnipresence assures of protection and help. A great message of comfort is given in the second half of the book of Isaiah. His message of comfort is related to the omnipresence of God. "Fear thou not; for I am with thee: be not dismayed; for I am thy God: I will strengthen thee; yea, I will help thee; yea, I will uphold thee with the right hand of my righteousness" (Isaiah 41:10). His presence keeps us safe and gives us victory when we go through trials (Isaiah 43:2).

Someone may say, "I understand the teaching of God's presence with me, but I see no evidence of it." That is a valid observation. Here is the solution.

Distinguish between God's presence and the manifestation of His presence. He is there when you do not see Him because He is unseen by the human eye. He is there when you do not feel Him, because He does not always deal with human emotions. Do not accept His presence because you see Him or feel Him but because you believe His Word.

"Speak to him then, for He hears, and spirit with spirit can meet; Closer is He than breathing, and nearer than hands and feet" (Tennyson).

THE SOVEREIGNTY OF GOD

Why should we study a lesson entitled "The Sovereignty of God?" The words sovereign and sovereignty do not occur in the Bible. Is this study of significance to Christians today? Indeed it is!

Though the terms relating to the sovereignty of God are not written in Biblical vocabulary, the truth of His sovereignty is everywhere evident. We must study His sovereignty to know Him more perfectly.

A study of the sovereignty of God is important also because there is such a gross misunderstanding of the doctrine. Just its mention causes some people to think of a blind fate which condemns some people to hell without their choice and others to heaven without their consent. That is a perversion of the doctrine. It should be understood correctly.

There is a great consolation in the doctrine of the sovereignty of God, when it is understood. It arouses faith. It gives courage in trials. It explains mysteries. It assures that He who is sovereign will vindicate righteousness and deliver His people.

The doctrine of God's sovereignty magnifies Him. You will come away from this study rejoicing that He is in control. He reigns! None can thwart His plans. He does according to His will among the armies of heaven and the inhabitants of the earth. He reigns in sovereign authority and power. Glory!

THE DEFINITION OF SOVEREIGNTY

To be sovereign means to be the supreme ruler over all. It means to have total and absolute authority.

When sovereignty is applied to God, it means He is free to do whatever He wills. None can stop Him or compel Him to change. He has total authority over all persons and things seen and unseen, material and spiritual, past, present, and future.

The names given to God in the Bible indicate His sovereignty. He is "God most high" (Psalm 57:2). Who can be higher than He who is "most high"? No one can. He is called "Almighty God" or "God Almighty" (Genesis

17:1; 28:3). Who is mightier than He who is "almighty" (all-mighty)? No one. He is called the "most high" and the "Almighty" because there is none higher than He or with greater might than His. That is God's sovereignty.

The Bible repeatedly ascribes power to God. "There is no power but of God: the powers that be are ordained of God" (Romans 13:1). Do you catch the significance of that statement? There is no power (authority) but that which resides in God. Those who exercise power do so only because God enables them to do so. Would you take God's word for it? Then hear this statement: "God hath spoken once; twice have I heard this; that power belongeth unto God" (Psalm 62:11).

Do not be afraid of the doctrine of the sovereignty of God. It means that God is supreme over all persons and things. He is in control of all situations. He is God!

THE DECLARATION OF SOVEREIGNTY

God has power over all nations. He puts a hook in the nose and a bridle in the lips of a rebellious nation and turns it to His will (II Kings 19:28). The hearts of rulers are in His hand and He directs them as He wills (Proverbs 21:1). He told Habakkuk that He would raise up the great Babylonian nation to discipline Judah for her sins, then judge the Babylonians for their sins after He had performed His purpose in them. That is sovereignty.

Early Americans met to form the government of their new nation. Wrangling and regional preferences blocked every move. Finally Benjamin Franklin arose to remind the delegates that God governed the affairs of mankind. They could not expect to raise up a new nation without His aid. So each session was begun with prayer and the new union was formed. Yes, God is sovereign over nations, even today.

God is sovereign over all persons. He chose Jacob over Esau (the younger chosen over the elder of the twins) for no obvious reason except His own will (Romans 9:11-24). He raised up Pharaoh of Egypt, who rejected Him and considered himself a god, for the sole purpose of showing His power through him (Exodus 9:16). He named Cyrus as the king who would free the Hebrews from their bondage more than a century before Cyrus was born. That is the sovereign God working His irrefutable will among the people of earth.

Why am I a minister of the Gospel? God chose me. I had an experience like Jeremiah, claiming to be too young and unable to speak. But, God called me just the same. I intended to go into space technology as my life's vocation. God changed that. I am where I am by His assignment, not my prior choice, though I have learned that the place He assigns is truly best.

God is sovereign over all circumstances. He gives riches and honor, enabling people to gain wealth (I Chronicles 29:12). He gives and He takes away (Job 1:21). No one can turn Him from His chosen purposes or make Him change His acts (Job 9:12). No circumstance ever arises which is beyond God's power to control or outside His awareness. He who sees when a sparrow falls to the ground certainly knows the situation concerning His dear children.

God does whatever He wills. His control includes all that is in heaven, in earth, in the seas, and in secret places (Psalm 135:6). He declares "the end from the beginning, and from ancient times the things that are not yet done, saying, My counsel shall stand, and I will do all my pleasure: ... I have spoken it, I will also bring it to pass; I have purposed it, I will also do it" (Isaiah 46:10, 11). As He works His will among the inhabitants of heaven and earth, none can stop Him, challenge Him, or demand an explanation of His acts (Daniel 4:35). According to His will, He works among the affairs of mankind.

Our appropriate response to the sovereignty of God is humility and reverent awe. We should pray with the psalmist, "Keep not thou silence, O God: hold not thy peace, and be not still, O God. . . . That men may know that thou, whose name alone is JEHOVAH, art the most high over all the earth" (Psalm 83:1, 18). Let us worship before Him now.

THE DIFFICULTY OF SOVEREIGNTY

If God is sovereign, how do we explain the presence in creation of things which God cannot approve? Why are there evil, pain, death, and injustice in the world? Could it be that God is sovereign but not good, hence He permits it? Or could it be that God is good but not sovereign and unable to do anything about it? The answer is, "Neither." God is both good and sovereign. There must be another explanation.

God permits pain, death, sickness, and various calamities in carefully restricted areas. Remember how He permitted Satan to attack Job's possessions but not his body. Then God permitted Satan to touch Job's body (his health) but not to take his life. So God permits and restricts evil today.

Evil and its consequences are permitted to show man

his frailty, his need of God, the seriousness of his sin, the grace of God in forgiving sin or relieving distress, the vindication of God for judging sin, and the government of God over the created universe. Its presence does not deny His sovereignty.

If God is sovereign, how can man have a free choice, or why is he held responsible for his sins? The question indicates that the sovereignty of God makes man a robot who is controlled by God's decrees without the consent of His will. That is not so. Man is still able to make responsible choices and is held accountable to God for the choices he makes.

God sovereignly decreed that man should be free to exercise moral choice within prescribed limits. Man is free to choose between good and evil, for instance, as indicated by Adam's choice of the forbidden fruit in the Garden of Eden (Genesis 2:8, 9; 3:1-19). God did not lose His sovereignty because He permitted the man to choose. Neither was Adam freed from responsibility for his choice because God is sovereign. The two doctrines are not opponents. It is difficult for us to understand them and to reconcile them by human reasoning. But the Bible teaches both.

Think of the alternative to God's sovereignty. If God is not in control of the universe, we are in desperate danger. The world is running wild without a superior power to govern it. We hope things will work out right, but we have no assurance of it unless God is truly sovereign over all. What blessed assurance rests in that doctrine! God is in control and will make all things work out best.

THE DEMONSTRATION OF SOVEREIGNTY

Ephesians 1 contains one of the classic statements of the sovereignty of God in relation to the saving of sinners. It raises questions we cannot answer now, but will know fully when we see Him. Review verses three through fourteen and see His sovereignty declared.

God chose us in Him before the foundation of the world (verse 4). That means He chose us before the earth was formed, the human race began, or we were ever born. Astounding, isn't it?

God predestinated us to the adoption of children by Jesus Christ (verse 5). That means He planned that we should be accepted as His own dear children through Jesus Christ. He wanted us to be His children and chose us as His own. Glory!

God works according to a plan which He purposed in himself. He did not ask our consent or cooperation in the making or the executing of His plan. "He hath purposed in himself" and worked "all things after the counsel of his own will" (verses 9, 11). We were not brought into the planning or the executing of His divine will.

God works all things toward a worthy goal. That goal is twofold. (1) He works all things to our good. Read verses 1, 4-12, and make a list of the good things which come to believers. Each was purposed of God in eternity before time. Each was manifested in time for our good. God's sovereign decrees work out what is best for us.

God works all things to His glory. Verses 6, 12, and 14 speak of the praise of the glory of God. We were elected by the Father to the praise of His glory. We were redeemed by the Son to the praise of His glory. We were sealed by the Holy Spirit to the praise of His glory.

The sovereign purpose and work of God is to accomplish man's good and God's glory. Do not fear the doctrine. Rejoice in it.

The doctrine of the sovereignty of God is that He is in control. His control is not that of a resistless power which treats us like pawns but of a loving Father who treats us like children. God knows all, controls all, and is devoted to our best interests in His eternal plan. It is safe to trust Him. Believe it and rejoice.

THE HOLINESS OF GOD

Have you ever stood in the conscious presence of the blinding white light of God's holiness until you saw yourself as you truly are? If not, you have not yet experienced the fullest wonder of worship or the deepest awe of His divine person.

Holiness takes first place among the moral attributes of God. Above, before, and permeating all else is God's holiness.

God's greatest glory is His holiness. That is what God most wants us to see about Him. When He reveals Himself, His holiness always stands out in glorious radiance.

If we fail to see God as holy, we will not reverence Him as we should. If we fail to see God as holy, we will not shun sin as we should. If we fail to see God as holy, we will not follow the standard of Godly conduct as we should. God's holiness is a key to Christian living.

God's holiness is the standard by which all is judged to be right or wrong. A thing is right because it agrees with the holy nature of God. A thing is wrong because it disagrees with the holy nature of God.

Man's opinions about right and wrong are totally unreliable, but God's holiness never varies. In every generation and situation, right is right and wrong is wrong.

Holiness in God includes separation from evil and perfection in purity. Holiness in people means that we are made pure and kept pure. Holiness in God demands purity in us.

THE STATEMENT OF GOD'S HOLINESS

The psalmist says it best. "Exalt ye the LORD our God, and worship at his footstool; for he is holy. . . . Exalt the LORD our God, and worship at his holy hill; for the LORD our God is holy" (Psalm 99:5, 9).

One of God's greatest prophets, Isaiah by name, reported his vision of seraphim flying about the throne of God as they cried out, "Holy, holy, holy, is the Lord of hosts" (Isaiah 6:3).

The newly redeemed Hebrews saw God's power as He opened the Red Sea for them to pass and destroyed the enemy army that attempted to follow them. Then they sang a song of praise which declared God to be "glorious in holiness" (Exodus 15:11).

The inspired psalmist wrote in another of his songs, "Thou art holy, O thou that inhabitest the praises of Israel" (Psalm 22:3). And He is!

Is there any need for other Scripture references to be noted? How many times must God say it for us to understand and accept it with joy? One time is enough, of course. But God stated it and repeated it that there may be no question in our minds. The fact is certain. Our response is required. How will you respond to the revelation of the holiness of God?

THE DEFINITION OF GOD'S HOLINESS

God's holiness has a passive and an active application. On the one hand, holiness is the absence of evil or anything that defiles. On the other hand, holiness is the active sum and total virtue of all His justice, truth, love, and other attributes. In practical terms, the holiness of God, like new-fallen snow, is pure (but inactive). It is right in action. It is holiness manifested by what it does and refrains from doing.

The terms holy and holiness occur more than 830 times in the Old Testament. They are used to refer to God and the persons or things which are dedicated to God. Even an object (like the candlestick in the tabernacle) dedicated to God partakes of His holiness because it belongs to Him.

God is not making an impossible demand when He says, "As he which hath called you is holy, so be ye holy in all manner of conversation; because it is written. Be ye holy, for I am holy" (I Peter 1:15, 16). As the fragrance of a lovely perfume is passed by shaking hands with a lady who is wearing it, so the holiness of God is conferred upon those who are truly His by repentance from sin and personal faith in Jesus Christ.

THE DESCRIPTION OF GOD'S HOLINESS

God's holiness is intrinsic. It belongs to Him by nature. It is so much a part of His nature that He would not be God if He were not the Holy God. As light and heat are the essence of the sun and as numbers are the essence of mathematics, so holiness is essential to the very nature of God.

Isaiah called God "the holy one" thirty times in his book. Job called Him "the Holy One" (Job 6:10). God described Himself in these words, "Thus saith the high and lofty One that inhabiteth eternity, whose name is Holy; I dwell in the high and holy place, with him also that is of a contrite and humble spirit " (Isaiah 57:15). Do you feel a sense of awe as you think of Him whose very nature is holy, whose holiness permeates every attribute of His being? That is our heavenly Father.

God's holiness is original. He did not derive His holiness from any other person or thing. He did not work it up and develop it within Himself. He is eternally the Holy One. He has never been more holy or less holy than He is now. He is the origin and source of holiness, wherever it appears. "Holy and reverend is his name" (Psalm 111:9). Do you hold His holy name in awe? He alone is holy. Christians are holy only because they are made holy in Him. "Who shall not fear thee, O Lord, and glorify thy name? for thou only art holy" (Revelation 15:4).

God's holiness is transcendent. His holiness is higher, broader, deeper, and purer than any other. "There is none holy as the LORD" (I Samuel 2:2). Compare Isaiah 6:3 with Revelation 4:8 and you will find that the heavenly host never ceases to ascribe threefold holiness to our God. Day and night, century after century in human time, they cry out, "Holy, holy, holy." It befits the saints of God to join that song of the angels, for we are the children while they are the servants of God.

God's holiness is efficient. It is the source of holiness in others. It is the standard for life and conduct. His holiness is unique. We receive holiness by grace. He has holiness by nature. We who were sinful are made holy. He was never less holy than He is today. Our holiness is but a dim reflection of His glorious holiness.

THE APPLICATION OF GOD'S HOLINESS

God never does anything wrong. To do wickedness or to commit iniquity is far from God (Job 34:10). All He does is perfect, without blemish, the expression of absolute holiness. What a God is He!

God shares no fellowship with unholy persons. That is why He requires repentance from sin, confession, and forgiveness to be accepted before Him in peace. Over and over He says, "You shall not defile yourselves; you shall sanctify yourselves; you shall be holy because I am holy." (See Leviticus 11:43-45.)

God has no pleasure in wickedness. He hates the workers of iniquity. He will destroy those who speak lies and practice deceit. (See Psalm 5:4-6.) Our sins will turn away His ears from hearing our prayers and His hands from helping us, unless we come in repentance before Him (Isaiah 59:1, 2).

The Bible summarizes God's attitude toward sin by the symbol of light and darkness. First John 1:6 reads, "If we say that we have fellowship with him, and walk in darkness, we lie, and do not the truth." There can be no fellowship with God unless there is first a cleansing from sin and the possession of true holiness.

God's holiness shows our sins to be exceedingly sinful. When Isaiah saw the Lord, he cried out, "Woe is me! for I am undone; because I am a man of unclean lips, and I dwell in the midst of a people of unclean lips: for mine eyes have seen the King, the Lord of hosts" (Isaiah 6:5). A vision of God's holiness was sufficient to convince him of his sin. The person who is unconcerned about his sin indicates that he has no understanding of the holy nature of God. God hates sin and delights in right. You must settle the sin problem to share fellowship with God.

God can be approached only through His holy Son Jesus. He is "the way, the truth, and the life," and no one can come to the Father except through Him (John 14:6). Man can approach God with confidence, but never with self-confidence. Israel trembled at the revelation of God on Mount Sinai. How much more should we "serve God acceptably with reverence and godly fear: for our God is a consuming fire" (Hebrews 12:28, 29).

First John 1:8-10 teaches that every person has sinned and no person is without sin. It is necessary, therefore, for us to confess our sins to God and come to Him through our advocate Jesus Christ. There is no other way to cleansing and holiness.

God's holiness demands the punishment of sin. He would not be a holy God if He permitted sin to go unpunished. A holy God will make sure that every transgression and disobedience receives a just recompense of reward (Hebrews 2:2). God's eyes are too pure to look with favor upon evil, and He cannot bear to approve iniquity (Habakkuk 1:13). Yet He sees and knows all the sins of people all over the world. The only alternative is judgment upon sin and those who persist in their sins. God is a strict judge toward sin. The only way to find refuge from God is in God. You are safe from His justice when you are covered by His grace, for Jesus Christ has paid the penalty for those who trust Him. Knowing the truth of it, enter into the good of it.

God's holiness has a holy influence on Christians. That is true in several respects.

God's holiness produces humility in us. Like Moses before the burning bush, we can only remove our shoes and fall with our faces to the ground in reverent awe before the perfection of His holiness (Exodus 3:4, 5). To hear of Him is one thing; to see Him is another. To see Him in perfect holiness is to abhor self and to repent in dust and ashes (Job 42:5, 6).

God's holiness produces reverent awe in us. That is the "reverence and godly fear" spoken of in Hebrews 12:28. Look at the people who had a vision of God in Bible times. They hid their faces, covered their faces, fell to the ground, became weak in bodily strength, and sometimes fainted. Such is the majesty of His glory.

God's holiness produces a change in lifestyle for us. It warns us against defiling our temple (the physical body) because it is the holy temple of God's indwelling Spirit (I Corinthians 3:17; 6:19, 20). It makes a person desire to put on the graces of mercy, kindness, humility, meekness, long- suffering, forbearance, and divine love (Colossians 3:12-14). That makes the believer more like Jesus in conduct as well as character.

Some Christians seem to ask, "How close can I come to sin and still be a Christian?" That is not the question a Christian should ask. He should rather say, "How can I be as far from sin as possible, to be more like my Savior?"

Learn to ask of everything, "Is it holy? Will it help me be more like my Lord?" That will please God because it imitates Him.

"As he which hath called you is holy, so be ye holy in all manner of conversation; because it is written. Be ye holy; for I am holy" (I Peter 1:15, 16).

THE JUSTICE OF GOD

Last week our study dealt with the holiness of God. This week's lesson is a companion to it. Holiness and justice complement each other in the divine attributes. Holiness refers to God's character (who He is), while justice refers to God's dealings with people (what He does). Actions are influenced by character; so justice is the natural outflow of God's holiness.

We might not have a clear appreciation of the justice of God because of a confusion of terms in our English language. The Hebrew word for justice in the Old Testament and the Greek word for justice in the New Testament are sometimes translated *justice* and sometimes *righteousness.*

When Paul preached of God, "He will judge the world in righteousness" (Acts 17:31), he was saying, "He will judge the world in justice." The two terms are like two sides of the same coin. They refer to the same virtue in the divine person.

Justice does not contradict the Christian doctrine of grace. On the contrary, the Gospel is the good news that through the Savior the requirements of divine justice have been met. The law demanded the death penalty for sin. Jesus came and took our sin upon Himself, even though He was innocent of any sin, and died the death we should have died. Justice was satisfied in Him, and grace makes salvation available to us.

If God were not just, right could never reign, wrong would never be punished, sinners could never be saved, and we could have no assurance whatever. But we rejoice in Jesus Christ because God is just and deals justly with us.

THE DEFINITION OF JUSTICE

Your dictionary will define justice as the quality of being right and correct; rightfulness. It is related to being upright, legitimate, and equitable. A person who lives justly is upright, honorable, and noble. He is ethical and moral, honest and truthful. We call such an individual a good person.

Multiply those virtues of right, correct, legitimate, upright, ethical, honest, truthful, and correct by an infinite number and you have a partial idea of what we mean by saying that God is just.

The Bible teaches that God is equitable, acting fairly and rightly with all people. Psalm 19:9 declares, "The judgments of the Lord are true and righteous altogether." And they are! Moses worshiped Him as "the Rock." He proclaimed that what God does is perfect, that He is right, that He is fair, and that there is no iniquity in Him. (See Deuteronomy 32:4.) That is the God whom we meet in the pages of the Holy Scriptures and in the person of Jesus Christ.

The New Testament takes up that theme and declares that God is "no respecter of persons" (Acts 10:34). That means that He shows partiality to no one. He deals justly with each of His creatures, showing favoritism toward none.

God never does wrong, because He is just. Ancient Israel learned, "The just Lord is in the midst thereof; he will not do iniquity: every morning doth he bring his judgment to light, he faileth not" (Zephaniah 3:5). He who is just and does no iniquity treats each of His creatures according to the purity of His nature. Because He is just, He deals in justice with all. Observe how God exercises justice in human affairs.

God sets out a just and right law. His law is summarized in the Ten Commandments. The apostle Paul wrote of them, "The law is holy, and the commandment holy, and just, and good" (Romans 7:12). Look at the list of those commandments. Suppose every person on earth kept every one of them. All human conflict would cease and peace would reign. The best thing a person can do is to live according to God's principles revealed in the Bible. Keeping the law will not save you, but those who are saved should live by the principles of God's law. Try it.

God blesses obedience and punishes disobedience to His law (Psalm 11:4-7). His blessing or punishing is not the act of a capricious and unpredictable will. It is according to the solemn rule of right and wrong. He applies an evenhanded justice in the world of human affairs. God Himself would sin if He were any thing other than just in all His ways.

God acts free from passion in the exercise of His justice. His judgment is always according to truth. He judges the world in righteousness. He does not change His principles according to the way He feels about a particular person.

The Bible speaks of God being angry with the wicked.

But His anger is not a selfish temper like human anger. God's anger is the revulsion of His holy nature against any form of moral or spiritual evil. It was His anger against sin which caused Him to pronounce the death penalty upon mankind. But it was His anger toward sin and love for sinners which caused Him to give His only begotten Son as a sin offering by which sinners are saved. God never gets mad or acts unjustly.

The justice of God means that He is right in who He is and what He does. Stop for a moment and meditate on that. Because of who God is, He will never do anything that is unjust. Because of what God does, He is always right in every action. You can depend on the just God to deal justly with you.

THE DECLARATION OF JUSTICE

In justice, God reveals Himself in the Bible. Sin must be punished and righteousness must be rewarded. But it would not be just of God if He suddenly appeared without warning and applied the principles of divine justice to human affairs. We would be judged without having been given light.

So God gave us the revelation of Himself in the Holy Bible. He revealed Himself as a just God who will call people to account for their personal lifestyles. That is an act of justice.

Ezra, a priest/scribe who set his heart to know the Word Of God, to obey it and to teach it, testified of God, "O Lord God of Israel, thou art righteous" (Ezra 9:15). Ezra discovered from the Bible that God is just. God had revealed it there.

Moses joins in that testimony, saying of God, "His work is perfect: . . . a God of truth and without iniquity, just and right is he" (Deuteronomy 32:4). David wrote, "The LORD is righteous in all his ways, and holy in all his works" (Psalm 145:17). The New Testament witnesses of Christ that He has "loved righteousness, and hated iniquity" (Hebrews 1:9).

Why does the Bible make such an emphasis that God is righteous and just? Because we are accountable to such a God and will be judged by Him. We must know that He is just in order to live our lives justly and righteously.

In justice, God loves right and hates wrong (Psalm 11:4-7). He will accept into His presence in peace only the person who is right in character and does right in conduct. If one has committed sin, it must be forgiven before he can approach God in peace. Justice demands it.

God hates the sin while He loves the sinner. Does that

sound like a contradiction? It is not at all. A mother might be disgusted with the dirt while at the same time she lovingly washes it from her precious child. Because God hates sin, salvation from sin is required. Because God loves the sinner, salvation from sin is provided. God is just in hating sin and in loving sinners. There is the basis of your hope for peace with God.

In justice, God visits proper punishment upon sinners. God's grace offers forgiveness in love, but it does not cancel punishment in justice. God offers forgiveness to a sinner after having provided it through the sacrifice of His only begotten Son, The sinner refuses God's offer. He deserves the punishment he will receive. Justice demands it, and God is just when He executes it.

Daniel declared that God was just when He brought the Babylonian captivity upon Israel (Daniel 9:12). The nation had forsaken God. "Therefore hath the LORD watched upon the evil, and brought it upon us: for the LORD our God is righteous in all his words which he doeth: for we obeyed not his voice" (Daniel 9:14).

Even the angels in heaven declare that God is righteous (just) when He pours out His judgment upon wickedness (Revelation 16:5, 6). Judgment is not an indication of God's harshness, but of His justice.

God would not be just if He did not punish sin. He must judge sinners if He is the God of Holy Scripture.

Be warned. Flee to God for forgiveness. A day of judgment is coming. It has already been set. God will judge the whole world of mankind through Jesus Christ on that awesome day. Settle the sin issue before the judgment falls on you.

In justice, God rewards the faithfulness of the obedient. He gives a crown of righteousness to those who love Him and desire His appearing (II Timothy 4:8). His acts of judgment not only involve "condemning the wicked, to bring his way upon his head" but also "justifying the righteous, to give him according to his righteousness" (I Kings 8:32). That is the way you would expect a God of justice to act, isn't it?

Hebrews 6:10 assures you that "God is not unrighteous to forget your work and labour of love, which ye have shewed toward his name, in that ye have ministered to the saints, and do minister." For God to fail to reward the good done by His dear children would be as much an injustice as for Him to fail to punish the wicked for their rebellion and sin. He promised to reward and to punish. He is able, willing, and certain to do all that He has said.

In justice, God protects and

delivers His people. His people know His promises to protect and deliver them. They trust Him to do so and rejoice as He does what He has promised (Psalm 98:1-3). Every promise He makes He will faithfully perform. That is His justice.

Those who have lived long with the Lord testify, "(Thou) hast performed thy words; for thou art righteous" (Nehemiah 9:8). The righteousness (justice) of God is seen in His faithfulness to His promises. No one in any generation of human history has ever found God to be unfaithful. Every word He speaks is absolute truth. Every promise He makes is certain to be fulfilled. You can trust a God like that. He is just in His words and in His ways.

In justice, God provides salvation. It is right for God to condemn the sinner. Sin is willful rebellion against the holy law of God. The person who sins deserves to die because he has defied the sovereign God. God was just in decreeing, "The soul that sinneth, it shall die" (Ezekiel 18:4).

If God is just in condemning the sinner, how can He be just in forgiving him? Romans 3:23-31 explains that God set Jesus to be the covering for sin by His death on the cross. So God can be just and the justifier of him who trusts Jesus. Confess your sins to Him, and He will forgive you (I John 1:9).

Abraham asked, "Shall not the judge of all the earth do right?" (Genesis 18:25). Indeed He shall. He is the God of justice.

THE LOVE OF GOD

The love of God is so vast that it is beyond our knowing or expressing. Trying to describe it is like a child reaching for a star. He can never reach it, but his reaching signals that it is there and indicates the direction one must look to see it.

I have never preached a sermon or taught a lesson on the love of God without ending it feeling that the discussion was incomplete. The love of God so outreaches the love of man that even the Bible must refer to it in superlative terms, saying, "Behold, what manner of love" (I John 3:1).

The love of God is unique in its nature as well as in its scope. We cannot love as much as God loves (scope); neither can we love in the manner God loves (nature). Those who translate the Bible into other languages often have a problem finding a phrase with which to express truly the love of God.

I asked Lillian Howland, who works with the Wycliffe Bible Translators in the Garifuna dialect of Central America, "What Biblical concept was the most difficult to translate into the Garifuna language?" After a moment's reflection, she replied, "The love of God. The Garifuna word for love literally means 'it pleases me.'" That is the distinction between God's love and man's love. We can join John's statement of wonder, "Behold, what manner of love the Father hath bestowed upon us" (I John 3:1).

THE LOVE OF GOD DECLARED

"God is love" (I John 4:8). That statement is not literal, of course. It is a description of God's nature, not a definition of His person. The statement indicates that an essential attribute of God is love. If God "is" love in a literal sense, we worship love when we worship God. But we do not. Instead of worshiping love, we worship the God who is love.

God's love is His desire for and delight in the welfare of those whom He loves. Many years ago a Bible translator was working among a language group in India. He could not find a word or phrase in their language which could be used to translate the concept of God's love. There was a medical station at the mission where he worked. One day a mother came from a far distant place, carrying her sick child to the physician. She had walked so far, bearing the weight of the seriously ill child, that the mission staff was amazed. "How did you do it?" they inquired. She said, "Because I____my child." The Bible translator caught the word she used and it became the word for the love of God. God's love is willing to pay any cost if it brings benefit to the object of His love. That was why Jesus went to the cross to die for guilty sinners!

God's love is that aspect of His nature which seeks the good of those whom He loves. He corrects and caresses as a loving Father. He is committed to the good of His beloved ones. That is true love.

God's love is voluntary and rational. It is based on clear reason and deliberate choice. He is not bound by that attribute to love every person and every thing, regardless of its nature or moral value. He "set his love upon you" by sovereign choice, not because of merit on your part (Deuteronomy 7:6-8). A person might say, "I just fell in love with him/her. I could not help it. It just happened." That is not so with God. He loves because He chooses to do so.

He chooses to love because He desires to help poor fallen mankind to change from sinners to saints through Jesus Christ.

I stand amazed at the thought that God chose to love me. I sing with P. O. Bliss, "I am so glad that Jesus loves me, Jesus loves even me." Thank You, Father, for loving me.

THE LOVE OF GOD DESCRIBED

These thirteen lessons of this quarter of studies deal with the attributes of God one by one. But do not think of each attribute as disjointed and separate from the others. They are interrelated. Each influences and directs the others. Therefore, the attribute of the love of God is related to every other attribute of His divine person.

God is self-existent; so His love depends on nothing outside of himself for its existence. It is not merit in us that brings God's love, but it is rather His own nature to love us.

God is eternal; so His love has no beginning or ending. He assures us, "I have loved thee with an everlasting love: therefore with lovingkindness have I drawn thee" (Jeremiah 31:3).

God is infinite; so His love has no boundary. It is not limited to one race, nation, language, generation, or geographical area. He loves the whole world of mankind in all ages.

God is holy; so His love has no imperfections. He does not (indeed, cannot) love sin. But He can and does love the sinner.

God is immense; so His love is everywhere at the same moment. It is like a bottomless, shoreless sea which encompasses all people.

God is immutable; so His love will never change. It is more lasting than the created universe. People "fall in" love and "fall out of" love. God's love never changes.

God is tri-personal; so His love is from the Father, the Son, and the Holy Spirit. When you feel deserted, unworthy, or destitute, remember that all three persons of the Holy Trinity love you with an infinite, unchanging, eternal love.

God does not love you just because you are good. Remember the little rhyme we were taught when we were children: "Jesus loves me when I'm good, when I do the things I should./Jesus loves me when I'm bad, though it makes Him very sad." A bumper sticker affixed to an automobile read, "God loves you whether you like it or not!" That may sound like a smart-aleck statement, but it is true.

Take the truth personally. Look at your reflection in a mirror. Point to yourself in the mirror and say with conviction, "God loves you!" Keep on saying it until you are convinced and respond in love to Him.

THE LOVE OF GOD DELINEATED

God's love is manifested in good will. His thoughts toward us are thoughts of peace (Jeremiah 29:11). While others may think of us with envy, malice, revenge, or deep hatred, God thinks of us with an attitude of desiring and planning our peace.

When you think of God, think of His love toward you. He is for you; He is on your side. He has sent Jesus, who served as our substitute when judgment fell. Realizing that God made the supreme sacrifice of love in the crucifixion of Jesus, have no doubt about His loving you and providing for you today (Romans 8:32). God's goodness to you day by day is proof of His love to you.

God's love is manifested in emotional identification. That expresses itself in two areas.

He hurts when we hurt. "In all their affliction he was afflicted, and the angel of his presence saved them: in his love and in his pity he redeemed them" (Isaiah 63:9). Remember the words penned by Frank E. Graeff in his hymn entitled, "Does Jesus Care?" The chorus declares, "O yes, He cares, I know He cares/His heart is touched with my grief;/When the days are weary, the long nights dreary,/I know my Savior cares." And He does because He loves you.

His emotional identification with us is indicated in the sense of possession. Even in human affection there is an element of breathless wonder which says, "You are mine!" Just so, God claims us as His own. He is our Father who calls us His children. We who are His children call Him our Father. "They shall be mine, saith the Lord of hosts, in that day when I make up my jewels" (Malachi 3:17). Aren't you glad He recognizes you as His own?

God's love takes pleasure in its object. He delights in His creation (Psalm 104) and in His people. Zephaniah 3:17 reads, "The Lord thy God in the midst of thee is mighty; he will save, he will rejoice over thee with joy; he will rest in his love, he will joy over thee with singing." "You are precious to Him. Stop and think about that.

Ephesians 1:18 speaks of "the riches of the glory of his (God's) inheritance in the saints." Some understand that to refer to the riches the saints inherit in Christ. It is better to understand it to refer to God's rich inheritance in His people.

That is, God looks upon us as His rich treasure. Oh, how much He loves those who are His in Christ Jesus!

God's love is active. It does good toward the object of His affection. Loving the world of mankind. He gave His only begotten Son (John 3:16). John, the apostle of love, wrote, "Hereby perceive we the love of God, because he laid down his life for us" (I John 3:16). Love is known by what it does. That "love" which is expressed in words only and not accompanying deeds is not true love at all. One who says that he loves but does not express it in actions is a hypocrite. You know the love of God by what He does.

God's love is sacrificial. Look at the Father sending His only begotten Son into the world to die for sinners. When Jesus came into the world in human flesh, He emptied Himself. He took a position lower than the angels which serve God. He came for the express purpose of dying, and He bore the guilt of sins He had not committed. He came to die for people who rejected Him, some of whom were instrumental in securing His execution.

Much human love is selfish. "I will love you as long as you please me. If I have to suffer on your account, that will kill the love I feel toward you." God's love is just the opposite.

THE LOVE OF GOD DIRECTED

God loves His only begotten Son. The Father loved the Son from before the beginning of the world and continues to love Him until now (John 17:24). He called Him, "my beloved Son" (Matthew 3:17; 17:5), which means "My dearly-loved Son," "My Son, the Beloved in whom I delight," "My Son, whom I love and delight in." Oh, how the Father loves the Son!

God loves those who trust Jesus. Jesus assures us, "The Father himself loveth you, because ye have loved me, and have believed that I came out from God" (John 16:27). Please do not think of God the Father as being aloof and uncaring while Jesus loves you tenderly. The Father loves you just as Jesus does. In Jesus' high priestly prayer to the Father, He expressed the desire that the world might recognize that the Father had sent Him, and that the Father loved the world even as He had loved Jesus (John 17:23). God loves us just as He loves Jesus, His only begotten Son, Glory!

God loves poor lost sinners. He loves unlovely and ungodly people who do not love Him, who even hate Him. He loves those who are "ungodly," "sinners," and "enemies" (Romans 5:6, 8, 10). He loves those who are dead in trespasses and sins, who walk according to the ways and are under the control of the present evil world, who follow evil spirits, who live in lusts and are exposed to the wrath of His righteous judgment (Ephesians 2:1-3).

God's love is personal. It includes the masses of humanity, but it is directed to individuals. A mother loves all of her family, but she loves each one of them personally and individually.

Remind yourself often that God loves you. Live in the delight of His love and direct your lifestyle to reflect it to others.

THE TRUTH OF GOD

While a student in the university, I took a course in Greek and Roman mythology. We studied about their religious systems and read stories of the exploits of their gods. I was impressed at the different gods they worshiped and the ways in which they differed from the Lord God whom we worship. The pagan gods were said to lie, cheat, kill, commit adultery, and commit other sins which people committed. Our God stands in stark contrast to that. He is a God of truth.

The Bible is quite emphatic at this point. God is a God of truth. Every word that He speaks is truth. All that He does is according to truth. God demands truth of His creatures. He will reward truth and punish error. The Bible, God's inspired Word, sets out the truth without error. We will live in truth if we follow Bible principles under the leadership of the Holy Spirit.

Think of someone you know whom you feel to be absolutely true. Think of someone you know who is marked by deceit and untruth. Which one do you trust? With which one do you feel more comfortable?

Since God is a God of truth, you can trust Him. Since God is a God of truth, you must imitate Him. Since God is a God of truth, you must obey Him. That is the way to live a happy, productive life.

THE TRUTH OF GOD EXPRESSED

The Bible is filled with statements affirming the truthfulness of our God. It seems almost unnecessary to mention them to believers. But a review of those statements will strengthen our faith in that fact and assure our hearts. Notice these selected references (out of the scores in the Holy Scriptures) which affirm the great fact that our God is a God of truth.

He is "a God of truth and without iniquity" (Deuteronomy 32:4). His truth reaches unto the clouds (Psalm 57:10). He has plenty of mercy and truth (Psalm 86:15). He keeps truth forever, never changing in that divine virtue (Psalm 146:6).

Every promise He makes is certain because He who

promises is faithful (Hebrews 10:23). Even if we do not believe Him, He abides faithful (II Timothy 2:13). He is such a God of truth that it is impossible for Him to lie (Titus 1:2; Hebrews 6:18).

Those Scripture references are sufficient, aren't they? Many others could be added to them. It seems that God was careful to make it clear and emphatic that He is a true God.

God's truth affects the person who trusts Him. The liar is made honest. The thief is made reliable. The deceiver is made trustworthy. The crooked is made straight. God changes us to be like Himself when He makes us new creatures in Christ. We should live for the God of truth by being truthful ourselves.

THE TRUTH OF GOD EXPLAINED

The dictionary defines truth very poorly. Originally the word meant "loyalty, trustworthiness, sincerity, genuineness." Today we use it to mean the quality of being in accordance with experience, facts, or reality.

Agreeing with facts or reality is the most common definition. Truth is the agreement with a standard.

The theologian has a similar problem. The statement "God is truth" carries two elements: (1) God is the one who truly knows. (2) God is the truth known. He is the source and substance of the truth. He is the standard by which all things are measured to determine if they are true.

The practical conclusion is that all truth among mankind has its foundation in the person of God. A thing is true if it agrees with God. A thing is false if it disagrees with God. Idolatry is untrue. Sin of every kind is untrue. It does not agree with Him who is "the way, the truth, and the life" (John 14:6). The apostle John wrote, "We may know him that is true" (I John 5:20).

Truth is God perfectly revealed and known. It is reality unveiled. Jesus is truth because in Him the total of the qualities hidden in God is presented and revealed to the world. To have truth is to have Him.

All truth — mathematical, logical, moral, religious — has its foundation in the divine nature, for it discloses facts in the being of God. The statement that two and two make four, or that virtue is commendable and vice is repulsive, expresses an eternal principle in the person of God.

To know the truth, one must know Him who is truth. That is why Jesus said on one occasion, "I am the… truth" (John 14:6), and on another, "Every one that is of the truth heareth my voice" (John 18:37). The more one knows the truth of God (revealed for our understanding in the Bible), the more he can live truly and worship meaningfully. Some scientists today reject God out of the pretense that their search for truth has eliminated Him. That is not so. One can never know full truth apart from Him who is truth.

THE TRUTH OF GOD EVIDENCED

God did not leave mankind to grope for the revelation of His truth. Consider these areas where the truth of God is manifested.

Truth is manifested in God's Word. If someone asks, "Which part of God's Word?" the Biblical answer is, "Every word of God is pure" (Proverbs 30:5). Open the Bible at any book. Read from any chapter. What you will read will be the inspired Word of God. It will set out the truth which God Himself has made known to us.

King David remembered God's promise of blessing upon his house. He claimed that promise as certain because, as he testified, God's words are true (II Samuel 7:28). You can claim God's promises with the same certainty as that patriarch. His words are as true today as they have ever been.

Jesus testified that God's words are true and that they exercise a sanctifying influence in our lives. He prayed for those who believe. They were left to live in a hostile, sinful world. They needed protection against the evil about them. Jesus prayed for them, "Sanctify them through thy truth: thy word is truth" (John 17:17).

If you would know the truth, know the Bible. If you would increase in the truth, increase your knowledge of Bible teachings. If you would live according to truth, live by principles revealed in the Holy Scriptures. Truth is manifested in God's Word.

Truth is manifested in God's work. Psalm 111:7 says that the works of God's hands are in agreement with truth. He never does anything which is false or deceptive. His ways are perfect, and His works are true without taint of iniquity. He is just and right (Deuteronomy 32:4).

Satan tries to copy the works of God. He empowers his agents to perform miracles like the agents of God. (Remember how the magicians of Egypt duplicated some of the miracles of Moses, Exodus 7:8-13.) But God's works are not deceptive. He shows himself in what He does, and He is the God of truth.

Truth is manifested in God's Son. Jesus laid aside all insignia and appearance of Deity when

He came as an infant born to a virgin mother. But it was only the likeness of Deity that He laid aside. He kept the totality of the divine nature, even while here in human flesh. The Bible says that when Jesus came He was "full of grace and truth" (John 1:14). And He was, for He was God in human flesh.

Jesus said of himself, "I am the way, the truth, and the life" (John 14:6). If that were not a statement of fact, He would be untrue. If He were untrue, He would not be God. If He were not God, we would be lost in our sins and without hope. But, thank God, it is true. Jesus is the God of truth, our Savior.

Jesus' words were words of truth. There was no guile (hypocrisy, deceit, untruth) found in His mouth (I Peter 2:22). Jesus' deeds were deeds of truth. Therefore, they testified of the Father, the God of truth, who was working through His Son. If you would know the truth of God, look to Jesus who is revealed to us in the Holy Scriptures.

Truth is manifested in God's Spirit. Jesus said the present ministry of the Holy Spirit is to guide believers into all truth (John 16:13). That is not surprising when you remember that the Spirit is "the Spirit of truth" (John 14:17; 15:26). He takes the things of the God of truth and reveals them to the saints who have been born again by the Word of Truth in order to enable them to walk more perfectly in the truth. Invite the Spirit to lead you into fuller truth.

Truth is manifested in God's people. That is why the Bible admonishes saints to put off the sins of the flesh, to put on the graces of the Holy Spirit, and to seek to follow the Lord Jesus. Their purpose is to shine as lights in the world so that people in spiritual darkness may learn the truth and enter into the light of life. They are to lie no longer, but each is to speak truth with the other. In that way they will represent Him who is the Truth and be directed to Him.

THE TRUTH OF GOD EXPERIENCED

Accept God's statements in the Bible as settled facts. King Solomon reviewed several centuries of the history of Israel and concluded, '"There hath not failed one word of all his good promise, which he promised by the hand of Moses his servant" (I Kings 8:56).

He will not lie or make statements about which He must repent afterward (I Samuel 15:29). Every word of God is pure. Believe it.

Trust God under all circumstances. Sometimes He delays the fulfillment of His promises. He promised to bring Israel from Egypt, but He waited four centuries to do it (Genesis 15:13-21; Exodus 2:23-25). Some will begin to doubt His promises because it seems He delays too long in fulfilling them (II Peter 3:4). But He never fails to do as He said.

Sometimes God seems to change a promise. But if it appears that He does so, keep on trusting Him. Any change He makes is only to improve the promised blessing, not to withhold it. Be always assured, "The Lord shall give that which is good" (Psalm 85:12).

Circumstances change. Human generations arise and pass on. History follows its cycles. But God's promises remain certain. Trust Him at all times.

Know that, in all conditions and subjects, God is true and faithful. Here is the Biblical witness: "Know therefore that the LORD thy God, he is God, the faithful God, which keepeth covenant and mercy with them that love him and keep his commandments to a thousand generations" (Deuteronomy 7:9). Before such a true and faithful God we kneel and worship.

Here is the Biblical witness: "Know therefore that the LORD thy God, he is God, the faithful God, which keepeth covenant and mercy with them that love him and keep his commandments to a thousand generations" (Deuteronomy 7:9). Before such a true and faithful God we kneel and worship.

God is a God of truth. We who are His children by faith in Jesus Christ have His divine nature in us. Therefore, all we are, all we say, and all we do must be according to divine truth. Flee from all that is false. Develop this blessed attribute of truth in your personal life as a child of the God of truth.

JESUS IN GENESIS

Contrary to popular belief, the Gospel of Jesus Christ is not exclusively a New Testament idea. In fact, the Gospel is first pronounced in the first book of the Bible, Genesis.

After Adam and Eve sinned, God met them in the garden. Sin had exposed their nakedness and brought shame into their lives (Genesis 3:7-10). God had already declared the penalty for sin: death (Genesis 2:17). Although they did not die immediately, their sin did eventually bring physical death, and worse, spiritual death.

As God meets with the first couple, He explains the many consequences of their sin. For instance, Eve would experience pain in childbearing, and Adam would work hard farming with very little return.

In the midst of this difficult news, God did share some good news. In fact, it is the Good News! In Genesis 3:15, God promises that Eve's offspring will defeat Satan's. In Romans 16:20, Paul refers back to this same concept.

THE CURSE

The serpent is cursed, with no hope of redemption. Adam and Eve, however, are provided for even though the consequences for their sin are dire. And remember, although the word *curse* is not used to describe those consequences, they did include physical and spiritual death! Satan is "the root of the problem" only in a carefully qualified sense: he was the source of the temptation toward evil. The commission of the sin is entirely the fault of the woman and the man. So now the root of the problem is the corrupted human nature that all humans inherit from the first Adam. God cursed Satan as the enemy who brought evil to the human race. God imposed punishment on Adam and Eve for their sin. God promised to war against Satan on our behalf.

THE SEED

God promises that a seed of woman will come forth to defeat Satan. That seed is Jesus!

Notice how the Bible intricately traces the offspring of Eve all the way to Christ. In the book of Genesis alone, the word seed is used forty-one times. At each mention, the promise of "the anointed one" or "Messiah" gets closer and closer.

Consider the following prophesies and fulfillments surrounding the coming Christ:

Isaiah 7:14: Jesus will be born of a virgin. (Fulfilled in Matthew 1:18–23)

Genesis 12:3: Jesus will be a descendant of Abraham. (Fulfilled in Matthew 1:1)

Genesis 17:19 and Numbers 24:17: Jesus will come from the line of Isaac and Jacob. (Fulfilled in Matthew 1:2)

Micah 5:24: Jesus will be born in the town Bethlehem. (Fulfilled in Luke 2:1–7)

Jeremiah 23:5: Jesus will be from the lineage of King David. (Fulfilled in Matthew 1:6)

Jeremiah 31:15: Jesus' birth will be accompanied with great suffering and sorrow. (Fulfilled in Matthew 2:16)

In Matthew 1:23, the lineage is completed as the Bible states, "Behold, a virgin shall be with child, and shall bring forth a son, and they shall call his name Emmanuel, which being interpreted is, God with us."

Two thousand years after the promise had been made, God came to earth in the flesh in order to war against Satan.

Jesus is the seed of woman promised in Genesis 3:15. How appropriate that God used the seed of the one who was deceived (woman) to battle the deceiver (Satan)! Satan sought to kill and destroy Eve through sin, but God chose to defeat Satan through her seed! But how?

THE SACRIFICE

God declared to Satan that the seed (Jesus) would "bruise thy head." What great news! Jesus would defeat sin and the grave once and for all. His work on man's behalf would allow mankind to be restored unto God.

However, the Messiah's salvation for mankind would come at a price. Verse 15 continues, "and thou shalt bruise his heal." Christ's victory over sin would come at the cost of His own life. Satan would not take Christ's life away from Him; rather, Christ would willingly lay it down. Why?

Sin, remember, deserves death. The only hope for mankind to escape eternal separation from God is if someone else will take the penalty. Christ conquered sin by sacrificing His life on mankind's behalf.

The picture of Christ's substitutionary atonement is seen at the end of Genesis 3 where God clothes Adam and Eve with the skins of animals. God killed animals in order to make a covering for them. In the same way, God sent His own Son to die in order to make atonement (a covering) for our sin. Those who have placed their faith in Christ Jesus now wear His garments of righteousness, washed white in the blood of the Lamb (Revelation 19:8).

The resurrection of Christ demonstrates both His victory over sin and the new life that is given to those who receive His salvation (Romans 6:4). The Bible even refers to Christ as the "Last Adam" to indicate the new life given to those who are born again (1 Corinthians 15:45), replacing the old life ruined by sin.

THE PLAN

The fact that the Gospel is proclaimed in the first book of the Bible may be surprising for some, but God's plan to defeat Satan actually predates Genesis. In fact, the Bible refers to Jesus as the Lamb who was "slain from the foundation of the world" (Revelation 13:8). Jesus, the second person of the Trinity, is co-eternal with the Father and the Holy Spirit. He did not begin at Bethlehem; rather, He has always existed (John 1:1). He was even active in creation (Colossians 1:16). Further, His mission, to sacrifice His life on behalf of mankind, has eternally existed! Before sin even entered into the world, God had made a way of redemption for His children.

And because Jesus rose from the grave and ascended into Heaven, we will enjoy all of eternity in His presence.

While the Bible gives us a glimpse of God's redemption plan through Christ, it by no means presents the whole picture. Deutoronomy 29:29 reminds us, "The secret things belong unto the LORD our God: but those things which are revealed belong unto us and to our children for ever, that we may do all the words of this law."

Can you imagine the wonder and awe that we will experience in Heaven as we learn more and more details from God's perspective? What will it be like to hear Jesus tell about his experiences on earth? How exciting will it be to find out how God moved through the centuries to preserve the prophesies of Scripture for generations to hear about Christ!

Perhaps we will all be overwhelmed by the understanding that at every turn of human history God was sovereignly working to redeem mankind through the gift of His Son. It is hard to imagine ever tiring of hearing that story. In the words of the hymn-writer:

> I love to tell the story, for those who know it best/
>
> seem hungering and thrsting to hear it like the rest./
>
> And when, in scenes of glory, I sing the new, new song,/
>
> 'twill be the old, old story that I have loved so long.

This series of lessons will introduce you anew to the central character of Scripture: Jesus. Throughout this quarter you will follow the "seed" through the prophecy of the Old Testament all the way to the cross. Each lesson will provide greater focus on our Savior, Lord, and King. Before next week's lesson, consider these important questions:

Why is Christ's bruising (Genesis 3:15) a victory and not a defeat?

How are the prophesies of the Messiah in the Old Testament encouraging to your faith today?

Why is it important to know that God had already planned for Jesus to be the lamb "slain from the foundation of the world" (Revelation 13:8)?

Do you know Jesus as your Lord and Savior?

THE DIVINE REQUIREMENT

The death of Jesus Christ on the cross is the finest example of self- sacrificing love the world can ever see. But it is more than an example; His death was a necessity.

The ancient Hebrews had a solemn ritual one day each year called Yom Kippur (Day of Atonement.). It was a solemn day in which sacrifice was offered for the sins of the whole nation. The term *kippur* is a Hebrew word which means "to cancel, to expiate, to effect reconciliation." The equivalent Greek word used in the New Testament means "to cause to be friendly; to restore; to make holy." We express the idea in the English language with the word *atone*, which indicates the two parties are "at-one." Here is the doctrine of reconciliation of sinners to God.

Leviticus 17:11 underlies all sacrifice for sin in the Old and New Testaments. Memorize it: "The life of the flesh is in the blood: and I have given it to you upon the altar to make an atonement for your souls: for it is the blood that maketh an atonement for the soul." (The New Testament equivalent of *atonement* is seen in Hebrews 9:22, "Without shedding of blood is no remission.") That is God's law concerning sin and forgiveness.

This week's study is concerned with the Day of Atonement in ancient Israel and the lessons it teaches us about forgiveness of sins in Jesus Christ. God forgives sin only on the basis of the sacrifice of Jesus on the cross.

NEED FOR ATONEMENT

Adam and Eve enjoyed meeting God, until they sinned. Then they hid from His presence among the trees of the Garden of Eden (Genesis 3). The result was that all who are born into the human race suffer a spiritual defect (called depravity) by which they are separated from God by nature and by conduct. The Bible calls that "death." The sinner is "dead in trespasses and sins" (Ephesians 2:1).

That essential unity between God and man can be restored through the atonement. The Bible speaks of guilt offerings, burnt offerings, sin offerings, peace offerings, etc. All those offerings in ancient Judaism were to present a picture by which we can understand the sacrifice of Jesus for sinners.

"When we were enemies, we were reconciled to God by the death of his Son" (Romans 5:10). God Himself came in the person of Jesus Christ to reconcile the world to Himself. He did it by imputing man's trespasses to His only begotten Son who paid the penalty in His substitutionary death. "He hath made him to be sin for us, who knew no sin; that we might be made the righteousness of God in him" (II Corinthians 5:21).

REQUIREMENT FOR ATONEMENT

Atonement is necessary for one to approach God. It is certain death for one to approach God's personal presence without the blood of an acceptable sacrifice (Leviticus 16:2). The place of God's presence is a holy place. Sin can never appear before Him without receiving the judgment it deserves. He who would approach God must do so with prayer for cleansing and forgiveness of all sin (Psalm 51). "Who shall ascend into the hill of the Lord? or who shall stand in his holy place? He that hath clean hands, and a pure heart" (Psalm 24:3, 4). Sin can never enter there.

Atonement must be made by one who is free from guilt of personal sin. The ancient Hebrew priest was required to wash his body, put on clean clothes, and offer a sacrifice for his own sins before he could represent the nation in sacrifice for its sins. A priest had to be "holy, harmless, undefiled, separate from sinners" in order to offer the proper sacrifice (Hebrews 7:26). Such a priest could not be found in the whole human race. That is why God sent His only begotten Son to be our great high priest and offer the proper sacrifice for us.

Atonement can be effected only by the death of an innocent substitute. That is why the ancient Hebrews offered animals, which had no personal sin, as victims of sacrifice (Leviticus 16:5, 15-19). And that is why Jesus came to suffer, "the just for the unjust, that he might bring us to God" (I Peter 3:18). If Jesus were not sinless, He could not be our Savior. He would be disqualified as both priest and victim in an atoning sacrifice. But He is our Savior because He "did no sin" in His entire life on earth (I Peter 2:22).

Atonement is needed by people of all generations and places. God said of the Day of Atonement, "This shall be a statute for ever unto you:... for on that day shall the priest make an atonement for you, to cleanse you, that ye may be clean from all your sins before the LORD" (Leviticus 16:29-34).

The sacrifices of the Old Testament were not intended for peculiar spiritual problems of that day alone. The sacrifice of Jesus was not intended for spiritual needs of that generation alone. Jesus "is the propitiation for our sins: and not for ours only, but also for the sins of the whole world" (I John 2:2). He paid the sin-debt for all people of all generations over the whole world for all of human history. "This man, after he had offered one sacrifice for sins for ever, sat down on the right hand of God" (Hebrews 10:12).

RESPONSE OF ATONEMENT

Atonement originates in God, not man. It is God acting consistently with His divine justice and expressing His divine grace in the saving of guilty sinners. He took the initiative. "Salvation is of the Lord" (Jonah 2:9). It is His revelation, not man's discovery. It is His gift, not man's reward. The announcement of salvation must always begin, "God was in Christ, reconciling the world unto himself" (II Corinthians 5:19). We can have assurance in our salvation because the very God who required the atonement has provided it.

Atonement was God's plan from eternity. Those who are saved have had their names "written in the book of life of the Lamb slain from the foundation of the world" (Revelation 13:8). For Jesus to be "foreordained before the foundation of the world" (I Peter 1:20) means His incarnation and redemptive work were not a sudden decision of God.

Before God created Calvary's hill, He had planned Calvary's cross. Before man existed, the plan of salvation was designed. Before sin came, there was deliverance from sin planned.

Such grace of God is amazing! Atonement was God's plan from eternity, for the sake of men in time, that we might be redeemed and be with Him in eternity beyond time.

Atonement in Jesus is the only way to be saved. He is "the Lamb of God, which taketh away the sin of the world" (John 1:29). All the sacrifices of the Old Testament era were but pictures of the real sacrifice He would offer. "Without shedding of blood is no remission. . . . So Christ was once offered to bear the sins of many" (Hebrews 9:22, 28).

Jesus said, "I am the way, the truth, and the life: no man cometh unto the Father, but by me" (John 14:6). The Great Commission was given by our Lord so "that repentance and remission of sins should be preached in his name among all nations" (Luke 24:47).

God confirmed the truth personally in the words penned by the apostle John, "This is the record, that God hath given to us eternal life, and this life is in his Son. He that hath the Son hath life; and he that hath not the Son of God hath not life" (I John 5:11, 12).

Atonement for sin is available now. God says, "I have heard thee in a time accepted, and in the day of salvation have I succoured thee: behold, now is the accepted time; behold, now is the day of salvation" (II Corinthians 6:2).

"Today, if ye will hear his voice, harden not your hearts" (Hebrews 4:7).

What can wash away my sin?/Nothing but the blood of Jesus;
What can make me whole again?/Nothing but the blood of Jesus.
This is all my hope and peace/Nothing but the blood of Jesus;
This is all my righteousness/Nothing but the blood of Jesus.
Oh! Precious is the flow/ That makes me white as snow;
No other fount I know,/ Nothing but the blood of Jesus.

— Robert Lowry

LOOK AND LIVE

The Old Testament has many pictures (called "types," "figures," or "shadows") which help us to understand the person and work of Jesus. Numbers 21:4-9 is such a picture. The Bible makes application of that incident to Jesus' own ministry (John 3:14, 15). It is evident that the brass serpent is a picture of Jesus Christ. We can know Jesus better by a study of those two passages.

DEATH BY SIN
(Numbers 21:4-6)

Discouragement lead to sin (verse 4). Israel had been in the wilderness many years at the time of this week's study. Instead of taking a direct route from Egypt to Canaan, they turned aside to Mount Sinai and camped there for many months. Then the way they traveled led to Kadesh-Barnea and the rebellion there. Their progress through forty years in the wilderness had been slow, toilsome, and filled with strife. "The soul of the people was much discouraged because of the way" (verse 4).

The devil knows our weaknesses. He comes to us in our times of discouragement to raise questions about God, our relationship to God, and the quality of our service for God. He will lead us into sin if we listen to his lies. Take care when you are weak, for the devil will surely attack you then.

Sin is expressed in rebellion (verse 5). "The people spake against God, and against Moses." Rebellion against God is commonly expressed in rebellion against the man God has appointed as leader. Their rebellion was expressed in three ways:

1. They opposed God's leading. "Wherefore have ye brought us up out of Egypt?" God had brought them out of Egypt to deliver them from slavery and into freedom. They forgot that.

2. They impugned God's motives. "Ye brought us up out of Egypt to die in the wilderness." Not so! God brought them out of Egypt to bring them into Canaan. They ignored His promises.

3. They despised God's provisions. "There is no bread, neither is there any water; and our soul loatheth this light bread." That was untrue. They had manna for bread and water from the rock. They had all they needed to sustain them.

Who caused that rebellion? The devil aroused it in them, and they did not resist him. Take warning. The devil can lead you to rebel by opposing God's leading, impugning God's motives, and despising God's provisions.

Rebellion brings death. God has warned, "The soul that sinneth, it shall die" (Ezekiel 18:4). Again He warns, "The wages of sin is death" (Romans 6:23).

The death which came to the Hebrews was painful. It was caused by the bite of fiery serpents. The death was widespread. Many of the people died. The death was certain. To be bitten by a fiery serpent was certain death; the presence of three to five million people scattered through the wilderness gave ample opportunity for many to be bitten.

God recorded that incident to give us warning. Sin still brings death, both spiritual and physical. Be warned. Sin brings death but Jesus Christ gives life. Which do you choose?

DELIVERANCE BY GRACE
(Numbers 21:7,8)

Deliverance came when sin was confessed (verse 7). "The people came to Moses, and said. We have sinned, for we have spoken against the Lord, and against thee." That is a good example of what confession truly means:

1. It is personal: "We have sinned."
2. It is public: "The people came to Moses."
3. It is specific: "We have spoken against the Lord."
4. It is humble: "We have spoken . . . against thee."

That is the way you and I make confession today.

Confession of sin is required for there to be forgiveness of sin. "He that covereth his sins shall not prosper: but whoso confesseth and forsaketh them shall have mercy" (Proverbs 28:13). "If we confess our sins, he is faithful and just to forgive us our sins, and to cleanse us from all unrighteousness" (I John 1:9). The sinner who prays "God be merciful to me a sinner" will go home justified; Jesus said so (Luke 18:13). Confess your sins to God and receive His forgiveness.

Deliverance came when mercy was requested (verse 7). "Pray unto the Lord, that he take away the serpents from us." Such a request for mercy directed the prayer of Moses and moved the heart of God.

God's mercy is the sinner's only hope. "Have mercy upon me, O LORD; for I am weak," always receives God's answer (Psalm 6:2). After the grievous double sin of adultery and murder, the prayer of the repenting sinner was, "Have mercy upon me, O God, according to thy lovingkindness: according unto the multitude of thy tender mercies blot out my transgressions" (Psalm 51:1). Blessed is the sinner who prays, "Shew us thy mercy, O LORD, and grant us thy salvation" (Psalm 85:7). He is our only hope; therefore, "our eyes wait upon the LORD our God, until that he have mercy upon us" (Psalm 123:2).

Is such a hope in vain? Not at all. God's ancient prophet wrote, "Who is a God like unto thee, that pardoneth iniquity, and passeth by the transgression of the remnant of his heritage? he retaineth not his anger for ever, because he delighteth in mercy," (Micah 7:18). You can safely trust such a God who is merciful and longsuffering in His grace toward sinners.

Deliverance came by the intercession of a mediator (verse 7). "Moses prayed for the people." That took a lot of grace on Moses' part. They had rejected him, opposed his leadership, and rejected God's ministry through him. Yet he was willing to pray that they might be spared the consequences of their sin. Such a spirit of selflessness shows one to be a true man of God.

More than once Moses had prayed for them. He was willing to identify with them even if it meant his death (Exodus 32:32). In that way Moses was a type of Christ who is our mediator by whom we come to God (I Timothy 2:5, 6) and by whose intercession we are saved and secured (I John 2:1, 2).

DEMAND FOR FAITH
(Numbers 21:9)

Faith in a seemingly ineffective remedy was required. What would placing a brass serpent on a pole have to do with healing people who were dying? It seemed a little silly to the skeptics. Yet, it was God's ordained way.

Faith responded to a clearly identified remedy. The brass likeness of a fiery serpent, which had brought death, was placed on a pole so all in the camp could see it. There was no secret offer to a chosen few. The opportunity was for anyone who was in danger of death to look and live. How like our Lord that is. He has decreed "that repentance and remission of sins should be preached in his name among all nations" (Luke 24:47). We are a fortunate people "before whose eyes Jesus Christ hath been evidently set forth, crucified among you" (Galatians 3:1).

Faith must be personally exercised. One was healed "when he looked." God calls for the response of the sinner in order to receive salvation. He must believe, come, call, look, and give a personal expression of faith. Salvation is not an automatic process. God offers, but the sinner must receive.

Faith was rewarded with the promised deliverance. "If a serpent had bitten any man, when he beheld the serpent of brass, he lived." The God who kills can also make alive. He who wounds will also heal (Deuteronomy 32:39). Those who trust God testify, "Lo, this is our God; we have waited for him, and he will save us: this is the Lord; we have waited for him, we will be glad and rejoice in his salvation" (Isaiah 25:9). God will keep every promise He makes. Trust Him and see His salvation in your own life.

DELIVERANCE FOR SINNERS
(John 3:14,15)

Deliverance from sin is demonstrated to make it plain. "As Moses lifted up the serpent in the wilderness, even so must the Son of man be lifted up" (John 3:14). Salvation from physical death then demonstrates salvation from spiritual death now.

The deliverance met human need, was by divine provision, required humility, demanded faith, was fully effective, and was evidently a work of God. That was true of the deliverance in the wilderness. It is especially true of salvation by faith in Jesus Christ.

Deliverance from sin is fulfilled as promised. The Son of Man was lifted up in order "that whosoever believeth in him should not perish, but have eternal life" (John 3:15). Jesus came because of human need. He was publicly displayed as a divine provision for sinners. We receive Him by faith when we come to Him humbly and ask forgiveness. His sacrifice is fully effective. The figure in Numbers 21 is ideally fulfilled in John 3.

Deliverance from sin comes to all those who trust Jesus. Read John 3:15-18, 36; 5:24; Ephesians 2:8. Those passages state over and over that salvation is in Jesus and is received by the repenting sinner through personal faith. The promise is "to all that are afar off, even as many as the Lord our God shall call" (Acts 2:39).

You can enter into the twofold benefit of Jesus' sacrifice. (1) He will keep you from perishing, according to John 3:14-18; 5:24. You will be safe in time and eternity. (2) He will give you eternal life, according to John 5:24; 10:10; 17:3.

Do not get your eyes on the cross alone. Look to the Christ of the cross. Do not make the cross a religious relic. Make the Christ of the cross the Lord of your life. You need no relic when you have the reality!

'Twas here the debt was paid,/Hallelujah, hallelujah!
Our sins on Jesus laid,/ Hallelujah, hallelujah!
So 'round the cross we sing/Of Christ our offering,
Of Christ, our living King,/Hallelujah for the cross!

-Horatius Bonar

THE SUFFERING
SAVIOR IN PROPHESY

Writers of Holy Scripture stood in wonder at the death of the Christ of God. It was almost unbelievable that the Anointed One should die. But an even greater wonder was the manner of His death. So with a touch of awe Paul testified, "He humbled himself, and became obedient unto death, even the death of the cross" (Philippians 2:8).

But the death of Christ was no surprise to God. He had decreed it to be the way by which salvation would be offered to sinners. The first reference to a coming Savior stated that the serpent would "bruise his heel" (Genesis 3:15). The suffering-servant passage in Isaiah 53 revealed that His sufferings would be in the place and on behalf of sinners. God decreed it to be so before time began, so the Christ stood as "the Lamb slain from the foundation of the world" (Revelation 13:8).

Psalm 22 is one of the most surprising of those passages which foretell the suffering of the Christ. It described in specific detail the crucifixion of the Lord before crucifixion was practiced as a method of execution! When the prophecy was given, people could not understand what it meant because it was not practiced in that age. Even so, Psalm 22 contains thirty references to crucifixion. Behold the miracle of inspired prophecy!

DETAILED PROPHECY OF CRUCIFIXION

There are eight specific references to crucifixion in Psalm 22 which were performed in exact detail at the crucifixion of Jesus. Pursue them thoughtfully through this list.

1. There was a sense of desolation as the sufferer felt Himself deserted of God and cried, "My God, my God, why hast thou forsaken me?" (Psalm 22:1; Matthew 27:46).

2. There was heartless mockery of the sufferer as the onlookers laughed at Him and reproached Him with mocking words (Psalm 22:6, 7; Mark 15:29, 30).

3. There was mockery over the sufferer's claim to trust in God and serve God. "Let him deliver him, seeing he

delighted in him," they said (Psalm 22:8; Matthew 27:39, 40).

4. Those who were closest to Him deserted the sufferer and He was left to agony and death alone (Psalm 22:11) just as the disciples forsook Jesus and fled (Matthew 26:56).

5. Terrible thirst seized upon the sufferer as the hours of the crucifixion dragged by (Psalm 22:15), which caused the Lord Jesus to say, "I thirst" (John 19:28).

6. The statement "they pierced my hands and my feet" (Psalm 22:16) indicates that the method of execution was by crucifixion and is a clear reference to the crucifixion of Jesus (Matthew 27:35; John 20:20; Luke 24:40).

7. The distribution of the sufferer's garments by casting lots was clearly prophesied (Psalm 22:18) and exactly fulfilled (Matthew 27:35).

8. The world-wide proclamation of the suffering and victory will be proclaimed to future generations (Psalm 22:31) by the direct command of our Lord (Matthew 24:14).

How can that be explained? Was it mere accident which caused the psalmist to write such a detailed description of the crucifixion of Jesus almost a thousand years before it happened? No! Not even the most gullible or unbelieving would say it was mere accident. Such a prophecy can be explained only in the sovereignty of God.

PHYSICAL DESCRIPTION OF CRUCIFIXION

Crucifixion was one of the most brutal forms of execution ever devised by man. The cause of death in crucifixion was suffocation. A person who was hung by his hands experienced a paralysis of the muscles in his chest and shoulders. Death by suffocation usually came in an hour. When the knees were flexed and a nail driven through the feet, the sufferer was able to raise his weight somewhat and take a breath. Thus life could be sustained a little longer.

The nails were driven through the wrist of the victim in crucifixion. (In medical terms the "hand" includes the fingers, hand, and wrist — all below the forearm. That is the way the word is used in the Bible.) Nails driven in the palm of the hand would rip out when weight was put on them because all the bones of the hand are parallel.

The cross which was carried was only the cross bar of the "T" cross. The upright piece had to be at least ten feet long and weigh 120-150 pounds.

The crossbar weighed 60-75 pounds. The total cross would have weighed 200 pounds or more, making it almost impossible for one man to carry it any distance.

The "T" cross had a notch at the top into which the cross bar was placed. The victim was nailed to the cross bar, it was lifted into place, and then his feet were nailed to the upright.

The most brutal thing Jesus endured before being nailed to the cross was being beaten with a scourge. The scourge was a short-handled whip with seven or more tails. One or two pieces of metal or bone were fastened to each tail. The victim was tied to a stake with his shirt removed. By the time a dozen lashes had been delivered, the skin was gone. By two dozen lashes the muscles were bare and blood was gushing from the arteries. Over one half of the people who received a full forty lashes died under the beating and three fourths died in three weeks. The rest were crippled or disabled for life, so severe was the beating. Jesus probably lost half of His blood by the time the beating was ended.

When the victim was nailed to the cross, he had to work to breathe. He would not breathe when the weight of his body was resting on his arms. He had to push up with his feet (where the nail was driven) to get a breath. The pain endured from pushing up was unbearable, so he was constantly moving up and down as he struggled to breathe. That shortness of breath may account for the brevity of each of the seven statements of Christ while on the cross.

Imagine the suffering of the Lord Jesus as He moved His raw and bleeding body up and down against the upright stake of the cross in an attempt to breathe. His face was bruised from the beating He had endured at the hands of His mockers. His back was raw — the flesh and skin gone — and the blood was flowing. The robe which was put on Him, and then taken off, must have stuck to the raw flesh and started bleeding anew as it was ripped from Him. He was on the cross for almost six hours, working constantly to breathe, before He gave up His spirit to the Father. Remember that He did it all for us!

Add to that the spiritual burden He bore as He carried our sins in His own body to the cross.

ATONING SACRIFICE OF CRUCIFIXION

Jesus was crucified though He was innocent of any sin against God or man. Who could condemn a man "who did no sin, neither was guile found in his mouth" (I Peter

2:22)? His sinlessness was not produced in the immaculate environment of a heavenly sphere, because He "was in all points tempted like as we are, yet without sin" (Hebrews 4:15). Yet they crucified as a common criminal one who is "holy, harmless, undefiled, separate from sinners, and made higher than the heavens" (Hebrews 7:26).

Since Jesus was not crucified for His own sins, there must be some other explanation for His death. It was more than a gross miscarriage of justice. There was a divine purpose involved.

Jesus bore our sins as if He were personally guilty of them. That is the doctrine of "imputation." *Impute* means to ascribe to a person something which is not his but belongs properly to another. The guilt for our sins properly belonged to us; but when they were assigned to Jesus, that He might bear the penalty for them, we say our sins were imputed to Him.

The doctrine of imputation of our sins to Jesus is stated clearly in I Peter 2:24: "Who his own self bare OUR sins in HIS own body on the tree."

Jesus endured the penalty for our sins, suffering in our place and on our behalf. Study Isaiah 53:5 and notice how the pronouns shift back and forth from us to Him. "HE was wounded for OUR transgressions, HE was bruised for OUR iniquities: the chastisement of OUR peace was upon HIM; and with HIS stripes WE are healed."

Jesus suffered for your sins and mine as surely as if He were personally guilty of them all. That is grace!

Jesus forgives every sinner who repents of sin and trusts Him. We have redemption through His blood (Ephesians 1:7). The blood of Jesus Christ, God's Son, cleanses us from all sin (I John 1:7).

We are justified by faith (Romans 5:1). He who believes in Him is freed from condemnation (John 3:15-18). Otherwise, one who does not believe in Him dies in his sins (John 8:24). But on the other hand, Jesus promises, "Verily, verily, I say unto you, He that heareth my word, and believeth on him that sent me, hath everlasting life, and shall not come into condemnation; but is passed from death unto life" (John 5:24).

BORN TO DIE

The cradle of Jesus must be viewed in the light of the cross of Jesus. He came in human flesh to make atonement for human sin. As the shadow of the cross loomed darkly over Him, He cried, "Now is my soul troubled; and what shall I say? Father, save me from this hour: but for this cause came I unto this hour" (John 12:27).

This week's lesson text traces the Lord Jesus from before His incarnation to His birth among men, through His ministry on earth, and into His glory before the Father. The text falls into four logical divisions which set forth this portrait of Jesus. Let us investigate them prayerfully.

BEFORE HE CAME TO EARTH
(Philippians 2:5, 6)

Two things are said of our Lord before He came to earth as Mary's child. (1) He was total deity, "being in the form of God." (2) He was full of grace as He "thought it not robbery to be equal with God."

Jesus was very God of very God before He was incarnate in human flesh. The word form ("being in the form of God") does not refer to external design or appearance. It refers to nature. To say Jesus is in the form of God is to say He was always God by nature; the divine nature was His from the beginning. To see Him is to see God (John 14:9). He is the "Word" who was in the beginning, who was with God, and who was God (John 1:1, 2).

Jesus recognized in His incarnate state that He bore a relationship with God which others did not know. He said to His disciples, "I and my Father are one" (John 10:30). He spoke to the Father of "the glory which I had with thee before the world was" (John 17:5). He wanted those who trusted Him to be with Him and see His glory, "for thou lovedst me before the foundation of the world" (John 17:24).

Jesus was willing to give up all the privileges He had as God to be the Savior of sinners. He acted as if He had no reputation or station to maintain. He did not cling to His prerogatives as God's equal. He willingly surrendered it all when He came as a human baby to grow up as a human man.

"Ye know the grace of our Lord Jesus Christ, that, though

he was rich, yet for your sakes he became poor, that ye through his poverty might be rich" (II Corinthians 8:9).

WHEN HE CAME TO EARTH
(Philippians 2:7)

Three things are said of our Lord's act of incarnation.
1. He emptied Himself: "no reputation."
2. He humbled Himself: "took upon him the form of a servant."
3. He changed Himself: "was made in the likeness of men."

Think about that!

Jesus emptied Himself. The statement "made himself of no reputation" literally means "He emptied Himself, laid it aside, stripped Himself of all privileges and rightful dignity." Consider how He did that.
1. He laid aside all the insignia of deity. One mark of God is His glory (Exodus 33:20); however, Jesus did not shine with God's glory except on the Mount of Transfiguration (Matthew 17:1-9). Otherwise, He looked like a common man (Isaiah 53:2).
2. He laid aside His right to act with the authority of deity. He did not do His own will, but the will of the Father (John 6:38).
3. He laid aside the full use of the attributes of deity. He no longer used all the knowledge He possessed, for instance, but "grew in wisdom" (Luke 2:52).

What a self-emptying that was! He emptied Himself of all except the divine nature. He remained very God of very God. Jesus humbled Himself. He who was in the "form of God" came to have the "form of a servant." He "came not to be ministered unto, but to minister" as a servant (Mark 10:45). He washed the disciples' feet to teach them true humility (John 13:1-17). He told them, "I am among you as he that serveth" (Luke 22:27). Here is the Creator acting as servant to the creation. That is how much He loves us.

WHILE HE WAS ON EARTH
(Philippians 2:8)

Four things are mentioned of Jesus while He was living on earth as a Man among men. Look for them in verse 8:
1. Jesus bore the human nature: "being found in fashion as a man." The term fashion does not refer to design, but nature. He who was God became flesh (John 1:1, 14).
2. Jesus filled the human station: He "humbled himself." He was "made a little lower than the angels" who serve God (Hebrews 2:9, 16). The angels came and ministered to Him in His trials here on earth because He needed their help (Matthew 4:11; Mark 1:13). He became like us in

the fullest sense, though it cost Him dearly.

3. Jesus endured the human malady:"unto death." God cannot die, but Jesus died for sinners! "We see Jesus, who was made a little lower than the angels for the suffering of death . . . that he by the grace of God should taste death for every man" (Hebrews 2:9).

4. Jesus bore the human guilt, "even the death of the cross." The cross indicates substitutionary suffering, vicarious atonement. He took our guilt in His own body and suffered, the Just One for the unjust ones (I Peter 2:24; 3:18).

AFTER HE LEFT THE EARTH
(Philippians 2:9-11)

Jesus is exalted. "God also hath highly exalted him" (verse 9). "Unto the Son he saith, Thy throne, O God, is for ever and ever: a sceptre of righteousness is the sceptre of thy kingdom" (Hebrews 1:8).

Jesus was received in heaven at His ascension and sat down on the right hand of God (Mark 16:19). He is there now "far above all principality, and power, and might, and dominion, and every name that is named, not only in this world, but also in that which is to come" (Ephesians 1:21). It is impossible to be exalted any higher than Jesus is now exalted, "angels and authorities and powers being made subject unto him" (I Peter 3:22).

Jesus is honored by all created things. "At the name of Jesus every knee should bow" (verse 10). It will be a glorious day when "every creature which is in heaven, and on the earth, and under the earth, and such as are in the sea, and all that are in them" will say, "Blessing, and honour, and glory, and power, be unto him that sitteth upon the throne, and unto the Lamb for ever and ever" (Revelation 5:13). Saints shall rejoice to see their Lord so adored.

Jesus is enthroned as Lord. "Every tongue should confess that Jesus Christ is Lord" (verse 11). God's ancient prophet wrote of the time when "all the ends of the world shall remember and turn unto the Lord: and all the kindreds of the nations shall worship before thee. For the kingdom is the LORD'S: and he is the governor among the nations" (Psalm 22:27, 28).

One day the announcement will be made, "The kingdoms of this world are become the kingdoms of our Lord, and of his Christ; and he shall reign for ever and ever" (Revelation 11:15). "All nations shall come and worship before thee" (Revelation 15:4). He will be recognized as "Lord of lords, and King of kings," (Revelation 17:14). The result will be "that God in all things may be glorified through Jesus Christ, to whom be praise and dominion for ever and ever. Amen," (I Peter 4:11).

That Jesus to whom will be awarded universal homage is the babe of Bethlehem whose birth we commemorate at Christmas. Let us not "celebrate Christmas." Let us worship before the feet of the Christ whose coming makes Christmas meaningful to Christians over the world.

"Yea, Lord, we greet Thee, born this happy morning,
Jesus, to Thee be all glory giv'n;
Word of the Father, now in flesh appearing;
O come, let us adore Him,
O come, let us adore Him,
O come, let us adore Him,
Christ, the Lord".

-John F. Wade

WATCHING JESUS DIE

A crowd of people saw Jesus hanging on the cross. The scorners looked on Him as a fanatic who claimed to be God. From heaven, God looked on Him as a man who is the only begotten Son of God.

All kinds of people were represented at the cross (Matthew 27:33-37, 38, 44, 39, 40, 41-43). You were represented there. If you are a scorner, you were there. If you are a believer, you were there. If you are generally unconcerned, your representative was there also.

The cross is not merely an event of past history; it is as current as today. Its influence and effects are still very much with us. You can no more ignore the cross of Jesus than you can ignore the fact of life itself.

PREPARING FOR JESUS TO DIE

Plans were laid to bring about the death of Jesus. The religious leaders among the Jews thought Jesus to be a dangerous man. "All the chief priests and elders of the people took counsel against Jesus to put Him to death" (Matthew 27:1). Caiaphas, the high priest, advised that it was wise to kill Jesus, though Caiaphas was supposed to be an impartial judge in such matters (John 18:12-14). For a period of time the Jews continued to seek some opportunity by which they might put Jesus to death (John 11:53).

At last, one of Jesus' disciples came to them and offered to betray Jesus into their hands for thirty pieces of silver (Matthew 26:14-16). The Garden of Gethsemane was the place of betrayal. The darkness of night was the cover. The kiss of friendship was the sign. So the Son of Man was delivered into the hands of sinners and condemned to death (Matthew 26:45-50; Mark 10:33). The fateful deed was done.

Prosecution in courts of law preceded the death of Jesus. The trials of Jesus which led to His crucifixion fall into two divisions. There were trials before the Jewish religious leaders and there were trials before the Roman civil authorities. Each of those appearances was threefold.

Jesus was accused of blasphemy in the religious

trials (a) He appeared first before Annas, the ex-high priest, who sought to make Him testify against Himself. He was abused by being struck with the fist (John 18:12-14, 19-23). (b) He appeared before Caiaphas and the Sanhedrin before dawn (Matthew 26:57-68; Mark 14:53-65; Luke 22:54-65; John 18:15-18, 25-27). The court sought witnesses to testify against Jesus. They put Jesus under oath and asked Him whether He was the Christ, the Son of God. When He said He was, they agreed, "He is guilty of death" (Matthew 26:66). (c) Shortly after dawn He appeared before the full Sanhedrin, where He was formally condemned (Matthew 27:1; Mark 15:1; Luke 22:66-71).

During those trials, Jesus was subjected to mocking, was struck with the fist, witnessed the denial by Simon Peter, and was deserted by all His disciples. Judas Iscariot left the court which condemned Jesus to die and committed suicide.

The Jews had no authority to execute a man. They had to secure that verdict from their Roman conquerors. So the religious leaders went to the Roman governor to bring about the execution of Jesus.

Jesus was accused of insurrection in the civil trials. Religious heresy would mean nothing to the Romans, but political rebellion was a serious charge. (a) Jesus was taken before Pontius Pilate, the governor, who examined Him and declared Him innocent. He would have released Jesus except for the uproar caused by the religious leaders (Matthew 27:2, 11-14; Mark 15:1-5; Luke 23:1-5; John 18:28-38). (b) Jesus was taken before Herod, who ruled Galilee. Herod wanted to see Jesus perform some miracle, but He ignored him. Herod had Jesus dressed in a beautiful robe, mocked Him, and sent Him back to Pilate (Luke 23:6-12). (c) Jesus was returned to Pilate's court where the governor sought again to release Him, but the religious leaders stirred the crowd of onlookers into a riotous mob. Pilate had Jesus beaten, but still no sympathy came from the crowd. At last, Pilate delivered Jesus over to be crucified. The Roman soldiers mocked Jesus further and took Him away to Calvary (Matthew 27:15-31; Mark 15:6-20; Luke 23:13-25; John 18:39-19:16).

Persecution by His captors preceded the crucifixion of Jesus. He had been beaten with the scourge (from which many strong men died) and was greatly weakened. They put a crown of thorns on His head. They put the purple robe on His raw back. They knelt before Him in mock respect and said, "Hail, King of the Jews." They beat Him on the head, spit in His face, and struck Him on the head with a stick (Matthew 27:27-30; Mark 15:16-19). After such abuse,

Jesus was unable to carry His cross to Calvary.

WAITING FOR JESUS TO DIE

Jesus was on the cross six hours before He died. It is amazing, humanly speaking, that He lasted that long after the physical abuse He had endured.

Pilate wrote a superscription to be placed on the cross. The sign was to state the crime for which the victim was being executed. The sign he had prepared was probably intended as a mock of the Jewish leaders who pressured him to condemn an innocent man to death. It read, "This is Jesus of Nazareth, the King of the Jews" (Matthew 27:37; Mark 15:26; Luke 23:38; John 19:19-22).

. Those who passed by mocked Jesus. (One purpose of sustaining the life of the crucified victim was to expose him to further pain and exhibit him in shame before onlookers.) Passersby called out, "Save thyself. If thou be the Son of God, come down from the cross" (Matthew 27:35-40; Mark 15:29, 30). The religious leaders mocked Him, saying, "He saved others; himself he cannot save" (Matthew 27:41-44; Mark 15:31, 32; Luke 23:35-37). Even the criminals crucified with Him cast reproach on Him. One of them said, "If thou be Christ, save thyself and us" (Matthew 27:44; Mark 15:32; Luke 23:39).

Jesus prayed to the Father, "Father, forgive them; for they know not what they do" (Luke 23:34). He also promised the repenting criminal who was crucified with Him, "To day shalt thou be with me in paradise" (Luke 23:43).

Jesus spoke to His mother, Mary, and to His disciple John, saying, "Woman, behold thy son! . . . Behold thy mother!" (John 19:26, 27). How like Jesus to be thinking of others at the hour of His greatest personal suffering!

During the final hours on the cross there were unusual events.

Darkness came on all the land, beginning at noon and continuing until 3:00 p.m. (Matthew 27:45; Mark 15:33; Luke 23:44, 45). It seemed that God was showing the enormity of the crime that was taking place.

Jesus spoke four times during this period.

1. The first cry came about noon. Jesus spoke with a loud voice, which is strange considering the shallow breath of a victim of crucifixion. He said, "My God, my God, why hast thou forsaken me?" (Matthew 27:46; Mark 15:34). Some tried to give Him vinegar (probably sour wine) to drink, but others kept them from giving Him any help.

2. The second cry was

concerning His physical anguish: "I thirst" (John 19:28, 29).

3. The third cry was a word of victory: "It is finished" (John 19:30).

4. The fourth cry consisted of His final words: "Father, into thy hands I commend my spirit" (Luke 23:46). He surrendered His spirit and died.

Great demonstrations of nature occurred at the death of Jesus. The great veil in the temple was torn from top to bottom. An earthquake rent the rocks. The sky turned from darkness to light again. The price for sinners had been paid.

REACTIONS TO JESUS' DEATH

Those who witnessed the death of Jesus stood in awe. Some of them "feared greatly, saying. Truly this was the Son of God" (Matthew 27:54). (See Mark 15:39; Luke 23: 47, 48.) It was often necessary to break the leg bones of one on the cross to make him die by suffocation; however, Jesus died of His own will.

God did unusual things following the death of Jesus. The earthquake broke open the tombs. After the resurrection of the Lord, "many bodies of the saints which slept arose, and came out of the graves after his resurrection..." (Matthew 27:52, 53). The rending of the veil of the temple showed that God had opened the way into His presence for all people. The appearing of the once-dead saints showed that Jesus had atoned for the sins of all, even those who lived and died before He paid the redemptive price.

Those who know of the sufferings, death, and resurrection of Jesus have the privilege of telling it to people everywhere.

FATHER, FORGIVE THEM

The most amazing prayer Jesus ever prayed was offered as He hung on the cross. He cried out, "Father, forgive them; for they know not what they do" (Luke 23:34).

That prayer was no sudden burst of good will. That was His attitude toward humanity the whole time He was on the cross. That was His attitude toward sinful human beings before He went to the cross. That is His attitude toward sinful people today. That is the expression of the love of God toward sinners.

A study of this first petition by our Lord on the cross should teach us a valuable lesson about our attitude toward those who oppose us. No one of us will ever undergo what He endured. He could forgive His enemies; so can we, if we let Him love others through us.

CIRCUMSTANCES OF THE PETITION

Never before had Jesus prayed under circumstances like those. We seek a quiet time and private place for prayer. It is good to be alone with God. Jesus preferred that, also (Mark 1:35). But prayer is possible in any place and in order at any time.

Jesus prayed on His cross. He prayed while an outrage was happening. He prayed while the grossest miscarriage of justice in human history was transpiring, and He was its victim.

The enemies of the Lord thought to be rid of Him. They thought He, once dead, would bother them no more in their devious schemes and self-seeking ambitions.

Jesus knew the truth of what was happening. He had predicted it long before (Matthew 16:21) and recognized He had come into the world for that very purpose (Hebrews 10:5; John 12:27). He knew that resurrection would follow death. He knew that the redemption of mankind would be effected by His death and resurrection. And He was willing to suffer for sinners.

CONTENT OF THE PETITION

The petition recognizes that God is "Father" in all circumstances. Jesus could rejoice and say, "I thank thee, O Father, Lord of heaven and earth," when things were going well (Luke 10:21). He did not hesitate to call God "Father" with equal assurance when a horrible death awaited Him (Luke 23:34).

The petition recognizes that God offers forgiveness. The term forgive means "to take away; to lift up and bear off." In practical terms it means to hold a person responsible no longer for his wrong-doing. If I forgive a person, I surrender the right to hold his offense against him ever again. Forgiveness is an act of the will, not a certain emotion. I choose to forgive or I choose to hold a grudge.

God forgives us when He chooses to hold us no longer liable for our sins. The only way to forgiveness is through personal faith in Jesus Christ (Acts 10:42, 43; Colossians 2:13).

The petition recognizes the blinding effects of sin. Our Lord prayed, "They know not what they do." Sins of ignorance can be forgiven (Leviticus 5:15, 16; Numbers 15:22-25). The sinner is blinded by the devil (II Corinthians 4:4) and lives in spiritual ignorance until he is enlightened by the conviction of the Holy Spirit. He can be forgiven.

Sins committed in full knowledge receive the judgment of God (Hebrews 10:26-31). Sinners live on in sin because they do not know its seriousness. But woe to the person who knows and persists in his sin.

CHARACTER OF THE PETITION

Jesus' petition was a prayer of intercession. He was suffering untold agony in His body. His face was bruised by the soldiers' fists. His scalp was bleeding from the crown of thorns. His arteries were gushing blood each time His heart beat from the scourging He received. His hands and feet were throbbing from the nails which supported His weight. His back scrubbed against the cross as He raised himself to breathe. Yet in all that, He did not pray for Himself. His petition was not for His relief, but for the forgiveness of His enemies. What an exhibition of grace! What an example to us!

Jesus' petition included all men. Who was included when He said, "Father, forgive THEM!"? His petition must have included Judas Iscariot, His deserting disciples, the chief priests who had brought about His crucifixion, Pilate and Herod, the soldiers who did the gruesome deed, the thoughtless crowd which witnessed the event, and even you and me. He was suffering in behalf of all mankind, so His petition for forgiveness included all people.

CONSISTENCY OF THE PETITION

The prayer for forgiveness is consistent with the teachings of Jesus on that subject. He taught it and He practiced it.

Jesus taught us to forgive one another. "Love your enemies, bless them that curse you, do good to them that hate you, and pray for them which despitefully use you, and persecute you; that ye may be the children of your Father which is in heaven" (Matthew 5:44, 45). He taught us to pray, "Forgive us our debts, as we forgive our debtors," and warned us further, "If ye forgive men their trespasses, your heavenly Father will also forgive you: but if ye forgive not men their trespasses, neither will your Father forgive your trespasses" (Matthew 6:12, 14, 15).

Jesus taught us to forgive without measure, "until seventy times seven" (Matthew 18:22). He taught us to forgive repeatedly, seven times in one day if necessary (Luke 17:3-5). He taught us to forgive unselfishly, "hoping for nothing again" (Luke 6:35).

CURIOSITY OF THE PETITION

Jesus forgave sins while He was on earth. He spoke forgiveness to a man crippled with palsy so that others might know that "the Son of man hath power on earth to forgive sins" (Mark 2: 10). His words "Son, be of good cheer; thy sins be forgiven thee" (Matthew 9:2) were the statement of fact. The man's sins were forgiven immediately and totally. To a sinful prostitute Jesus said, "Thy sins are forgiven. . . . Thy faith hath saved thee; go in peace" (Luke 7:48, 50), and it was so.

People in Jesus' day denied that He had that power, saying, "Why doth this man thus speak blasphemies? Who can forgive sins but God only?" (Mark 2:7). But that is no problem with us. We know Jesus was God in human flesh then, and is God now.

Jesus asked the Father to forgive those who brought about His death. He did not give direct forgiveness as He had in other instances. Why? The Bible does not say, but two suggestions are made for your consideration.

1. Jesus may have asked the Father to forgive because He was bearing the guilt of mankind's sin and did not act in His forgiving power under that circumstance. Or

2. Jesus may have asked the Father to forgive because the people were rejecting the gift of the Father, His only begotten Son, and were

thereby sinning against the Father.

CONTINUATION OF THE PETITION

We are to follow the example of Jesus and be forgiving in our own hearts. "Let this mind be in you, which was also in Christ Jesus" (Philippians 2:5). We need the same attitude and purpose of mind which Jesus had. He should be our example in humility. "Christ also suffered for us, leaving us an example, that ye should follow his steps" (I Peter 2:21).

Here is the principle under which the Christian lives: "Be ye kind one to another, tenderhearted, forgiving one another, even as God for Christ's sake hath forgiven you" (Ephesians 4:32). What a witness it would be for Christ if Christians would follow the example of the Lord in forgiveness.

We are to forgive with the forgiving spirit of God. That means we will forgive any person, of any offense, under any circumstance, forever. Does that sound impossible? If so, it is because you are thinking as a natural person and not as a spiritual person. "The love of God is shed abroad in our hearts by the Holy Ghost which is given unto us" (Romans 5:5). "God is love; and he that dwelleth in love dwelleth in God, and God in him" (I John 4:16). A forgiving spirit as the expression of God's love in us is a powerful witness to those who are not trusting Jesus (John 13:35).

Let us love, bless, and pray for our enemies (Luke 6:27-38). Let us wash one another's feet in total humility (John 13:1-15). Let us be kind and forgiving as Christ forgave us (Ephesians 4:28-32). As a result, others will know we are truly God's children.

The ultimate prayer of Christian compassion is to say of one's persecutors, "Father, forgive them; for they know not what they do."

TODAY, WITH ME

Jesus said, "All that the Father giveth me shall come to me; and him that cometh to me I will in no wise cast out" (John 6:37).

That statement contains hope for every sinner who has ever considered his need of God. It invites the best and the worst of people, without restriction or limitation, to come to Jesus. It invites with the promise, "Him that cometh to me I will in no wise cast out."

What Jesus promised, He has proven. The repentance and forgiveness of one of the criminals who was crucified at the same time as Jesus proves the promise, "Him that cometh to me I will in no wise cast out." Jesus responded to the humble request of that penitent sinner with words of assurance that he was accepted, forgiven, and secured to a glorious destiny.

Why did the Holy Spirit direct Luke to write that account in his record of the life and work of Jesus? God wanted people in future generations to know that they have hope. If Jesus would receive a criminal at the hour of death, He will receive you also. The record is a Gospel invitation to every sinner to seek the Lord. It is God's appeal to you!

THE PREDICAMENT INVOLVED

Examine the circumstance under which this demonstration of salvation of a sinner was given. The location was a place of execution. Three men were there to be killed. The courts of the land had tried them and sentenced them to the most painful form of death possible. They had been treated as if they were the worst of criminals.

The companions in suffering were three men. One was innocent of any crime. One of the criminals said to the other, "We receive the due reward of our deeds: but this man hath done nothing amiss" (Luke 23:41).

Jesus was placed on a cross with a criminal on either side. That may have been done purposely to identify Him with their crimes and shame Him the more. But so fixed there, He had one hand extended to a man on either side. One turned to Him and the other turned from Him. It is a picture of people's response to Him in all generations. In that strange situation, one of the criminals turned to Jesus in repentance and faith, asking for grace.

THE PETITION OFFERED

The prayer was offered by a confessed sinner. He had said to his companion in crime, "We suffer justly, receiving the due reward of our deeds" (verse 41). At one point he rejected Jesus as did all the rest (Matthew 27:44), but his attitude changed when he heard Jesus pray, "Father, forgive them; for they know not what they do" (Luke 23:34). The prayer could be heard because in that very hour Jesus was making atonement for sinners. The sinner could be "justified freely by his grace through the redemption that is in Christ Jesus: whom God hath set forth to be a propitiation through faith in his blood" (Romans 3:24, 25).

That Jesus would respond to a confessedly guilty sinner is great encouragement to all sinners. It proves that "whosoever will may come," as the Bible says (Revelation 22:17).

The prayer was offered to Jesus. "Lord, remember me." What an act of faith that criminal displayed! Jesus was fastened to a cross to die the same as the guilty man. How did the thief think Jesus would come into a kingdom? How could Jesus "remember" him and do any good for him, when Jesus was soon to die also?

The criminal accepted by faith that Jesus is God. The term *Lord*, which he used in addressing Jesus, is used to translate an Old Testament word which means "God." That repentant sinner was acknowledging Jesus as God. What a step of faith! Others did not see God suffering on the cross, but that man did.

The prayer asked for mercy. "Remember me when thou comest into thy kingdom." It asked a place in the Lord's thoughts, "remember me." It did not ask a place in the kingdom, "exalt me, honor me;" only "remember me." The humble petition for mercy is answered in the blessings of grace.

The prayer was offered humbly. It was a simple request. The criminal could not kneel, fold his hands in prayer, submit to a ritual of religion like baptism, go to church, do good deeds, or any other act of merit. Affixed to the cross as he was, he could only ask for remembrance. It was enough!

The prayer was offered in faith. Jesus seemed to have lost all things, even His life, as He hung on the cross. But that criminal believed it was not ended for Him. He believed Jesus would come into a kingdom. He believed Jesus would come into that kingdom following His death. He believed Jesus could remember then what was happening now. He believed Jesus could make a difference in things after He came into His kingdom. So he prayed in faith, "Lord, remember me when thou comest into thy kingdom." What faith!

THE PARDON EXTENDED

Jesus responded to the criminal's request, "Verily I say unto thee, Today shalt thou be with me in paradise." It was a statement of fact, not a question of uncertainty, which our Lord made. "This very day you will be with Me in paradise."

The time of pardon was immediate: "today." There was no delay. There were no requirements to be met. "He believed in the Lord; and he counted it to him for righteousness" as Abraham had done (Genesis 15:6; Romans 4:1-25). God does not put a repenting and trusting sinner on probation. He gives full and free forgiveness immediately!

The essence of pardon was acceptance: "with me." When Jesus died, He took a criminal

to heaven with Him. How like our Lord! That criminal was no longer a sinner. He was suddenly and miraculously transformed into a saint of God. He was washed from all his sins the moment he placed personal faith in Jesus. He experienced what Paul afterwards described: "Being justified by faith, we have peace with God through our Lord Jesus Christ" (Romans 5:1).

The Bible uses many terms to describe that truth of acceptance before God. One is said to receive the "atonement," meaning he is made at-one with God. One is said to be "reconciled" to God, meaning he is accepted in peace before Him. One experiences personally the promise of Jesus, "Him that cometh to me I will in no wise cast out" (John 6:37).

The person who pardons is Jesus. He is the Savior. He is the only Savior. He is ready to save, able to save, and willing to save each one who comes to God by Him. He came "to seek and to save that which was lost" (Luke 19:10). He rejoices to bring home on His own shoulders one who has wandered away (Luke 15:4-7). He will welcome you.

THE PROMISE EXPLAINED

Two parts are to be seen in

the promise Jesus made to that trusting sinner. (1) He promised His personal presence: "with me." (2) He promised a glorious inheritance: "in paradise."

Jesus promises His personal presence to the saints. The essence of being saved is to know Him personally. "This is life eternal, that they might know thee the only true God, and Jesus Christ, whom thou hast sent" (John 17:3). Jesus requested of the Father, The ultimate glory of heaven will be to see His face (Revelation 22:4).

Jesus promises a heavenly inheritance "in paradise." Paradise is a Persian word which referred to the parks of kings and nobles in that culture. The Septuagint version of the Old Testament used the equivalent Greek word to refer to the Garden of Eden. It was used by the apostle Paul to refer to the third heaven, the personal presence of God (II Corinthians 12:2-4). It is the place of the location of the tree of life of which saints shall eat in eternity (Revelation 2:7). Paradise speaks of the sum of all possible blessedness. It is our concept of heaven today. That criminal went directly from his cross to the paradise of God in the personal presence of Jesus. Glory!

THE PRINCIPLES TAUGHT

The way of salvation is repentance, faith, and receiving. The convict on the cross could do nothing else, but he found it was enough. "By grace are ye saved through faith; and that not of yourselves: it is the gift of God" (Ephesians 2:8).

The prayer of a penitent sinner receives an answer. That man realized his need, admitted his helplessness, believed in the deity of Christ, accepted the idea of a future life, humbled Himself, and asked for forgiveness. Since God saved him on that basis, He will save you and me the same way.

WOMAN...
SON, BEHOLD

The fifth of the Ten Commandments reads, "Honour thy father and thy mother: that thy days may be long upon the land which the Lord thy God giveth thee" (Exodus 20:12).

Jesus kept that commandment to the fullest possible extent. But what does the commandment involve? It involves obedience, of course. The Bible records Jesus' relation to Joseph and His mother, "He went down with them, and came to Nazareth, and was subject unto them" (Luke 2:51). But honor means more than obedience.

This week's study deals with Jesus' act of honor toward His mother. He was concerned about her during the time He was on the cross. He was concerned about what would happen to her after He was no longer personally present with her. He was concerned, and made provision for her before He died. Jesus' concern for Mary reminds us that He is "touched with the feeling of our infirmities" (Hebrews 4:15).

This was the third statement of Jesus on the cross. The first was a prayer to God requesting forgiveness for those who opposed Him. The second was the word of forgiveness to a repenting sinner who was facing certain death. The third was a word to Mary and John, His mother and His disciple, concerning her provision for the rest of her life. This third statement reveals a wonderful sympathy in the heart of our Lord.

THE PROPHECY FULFILLED

"There stood by the cross of Jesus his mother" (John 19:25). There is a surprising amount of meaning bound up in that one sentence. That Mary "stood" by the cross of Jesus indicates her strength. A mother would suffer greatly seeing her son rejected, falsely accused, unjustly condemned, and then to see his agony as he suffered the tortures of crucifixion. Mary was a loving mother who kept Her son's sayings in her heart (Luke 2:51). She suffered much as she saw Him suffer.

Mary stood "by the cross of Jesus," indicating her identification with Him, even in the hour of His rejection by mankind. She was a witness to His sufferings. That she was "his mother" only compounded her sorrow.

That was a fulfillment of prophecy. The prophecy had been uttered by an aged saint named Simeon when Joseph and Mary had brought the baby Jesus to dedicate Him to God. Simeon had said, "Behold, this child is set for the fall and rising again of many in Israel; and for a sign which shall be spoken against; (Yea, a sword shall pierce through thy own soul also,) that the thoughts of many hearts may be revealed" (Luke 2:34, 35). As He hung on the cross, He was a "sign" against whom men spoke. And a sword pierced through Mary's soul, also. Behold the miracle of fulfilled prophecy.

THE PATTERN SHOWN

Each child is commanded of God to honor both his parents. The Bible is quite explicit, saying, "Honour thy father and thy mother" (Exodus 20:12). The idea that men and women are equally valuable and equally worthy of respect as parents is being taught by God 1,500 years before Jesus was born.

Ephesians 6:1, 2 shows that honor goes further than mere obedience. A soldier may obey an officer without honoring him. A slave may obey his master without honoring him. Honor carries the element of respectful attitude and honest concern rather than slavish obedience.

Honor is shown to parents in many ways. Jesus was expressing honor for His mother when He made provision for her livelihood.

There is a strange question unanswered in the Biblical account, however. Jesus had several brothers and sisters. His brothers (half-brothers as children of Joseph and Mary) were named James, Joses, Simon, and Judas; the names of His sisters are not given (Matthew 13:55, 56). Why did not one of them take care of Mary upon the death of Jesus? The Bible does not say. We can guess that because they did not believe in Jesus, Mary felt more at home with John than with them. It is evident that Jesus was not ready to die until provision had been made for His mother's welfare.

THE PERSONS INVOLVED

Mary, the mother of Jesus, was the primary person involved in that exchange. Little is known of her except what is revealed concerning her as the mother of Jesus. It is evident that she was a woman of faith and humility before God from her girlhood. She kept the words of Jesus in her heart and thought on them, even from the time He was but a lad (Luke 2:51).

Jesus referred to Mary as "woman." There is no place in

the Gospel record where He called her "mother." It was not a sign of disrespect. Some think it was to keep her from being elevated to a high position in the minds of people that He referred to her so. More likely, it was because Jesus related everything to spiritual things. He said, "Whosoever shall do the will of my Father which is in heaven, the same is my brother, and sister, and mother" (Matthew 12:50).

Mary was probably a widow at that time. (We assume that because there is no mention of Joseph after Jesus' childhood.) We do not know the situation of her other children.

John, the disciple of Jesus, was the one to whose care Jesus entrusted Mary. He was a former "son of thunder" (Mark 3:17) who had become "the disciple whom Jesus loved" (John 13:23; 20:2; 21:7, 20). He had deserted the Lord with the rest of the disciples upon His arrest in Gethsemane (Matthew 26:31, 56). But John had returned and was standing at the cross. There he received this commission.

THE PRINCIPLES TAUGHT

From this solemn incident there are several practical lessons to be learned. Examine the following and make your own list of truths which God shows you.

Spiritual responsibility does not cancel family responsibility.

Jesus warned that religion cannot be used as an excuse for the neglect of one's aged parents (Mark 7:11-13). Though He looked on all believers as members of His family (Matthew 12:46-50), He did not neglect His mother's needs even in the hour of His own death.

True religion must be practiced through all of life. "Pure religion and undefiled before God and the Father is this. To visit the fatherless and widows in their affliction, and to keep himself unspotted from the world" (James 1:27). Jesus' provision for His widowed mother was a part of His practice of "pure" and "undefiled" religion. Even death did not relieve that spiritual obligation.

Commitment to Jesus involves personal responsibility. Notice Jesus' words on the cross, "Woman, behold thy son! . . . Behold thy mother!" That was a form of expression common in ancient Hebrew weddings. "Son" and "mother" were substituted for "husband" and "wife." In that sense, Jesus put Mary and John under a binding obligation to each other.

Spiritual relations are more binding than physical relations. That is probably the reason Mary was committed to John, not a member of her physical family, rather than to one of her own children. Jesus' brothers did not believe in Him at that time (John 7:5), and this may have been a time when a man's foes were those of his own household (Matthew 10:36). A common faith in God forms a permanent relationship.

Love is willing to assume responsibility, even if it is not convenient. John was not only the disciple whom Jesus loved, but also the disciple who loved the Lord dearly in return. It was no burden for him to take the responsibility for Mary's welfare. Love lightened the load.

One who has erred can return and be useful in the service of the Lord. John was among those disciples who forsook Jesus and fled at His arrest in Gethsemane (Mark 14:50). Simon Peter drew near during the trials of Jesus only to deny Him in a moment of weakness (Mark 14:66-72). John returned by the time they had reached Calvary and stood firm there. All the disciples who fled were afterward used of God in great evangelistic and missionary ministries. Thank God for a second chance. John returned in time to be commissioned of the Lord with the care of Mary.

Here our Lord shows us what real love is. It is more than romantic emotion or passing sentiment. It is commitment to a person. It is the practical expression of thoughtful kindness in meeting human needs.

Jesus set the example of love in providing for His mother. "Beloved, let us love one another" (I John 4:7).

MY GOD, WHY?

"My God, my God, why hast thou forsaken me?" (Matthew 27:46). Most Bible expositors call that the most difficult text in the Bible.

Our problem is that God here manifested a depth of grace and a scope of love that is beyond our comprehension. We know what the text means, but are at a loss trying to express its full application.

The text must be interpreted in the light of these Bible truths:

1. Jesus was dying in the place and on behalf of guilty sinners.
2. Those sinners would be "punished with everlasting destruction from the presence of the Lord" (II Thessalonians 1:9).
3. In bearing the penalty of sins, Jesus must endure separation from God.

That is what happened on the cross. "Christ also hath once suffered for sins, the just for the unjust, that he might bring us to God" (I Peter 3:18).

This text, so surrounded by God's mercy and grace toward sinners, is a rich source of inspiration and information. It magnifies the provision of salvation for sinners by viewing the price that had to be paid for sin. Our sins separated the only begotten Son from the favor of His heavenly Father!

THE SITUATION DESCRIBED

Jesus was forsaken by His nation. John wrote of Him, "He came unto his own (things), and his own (people) received him not" (John 1:11). Some became His disciples, of course, but they were a tiny minority in the nation. People were thrilled at His miracles and filled with His food, but they did not become His disciples. Even many of His professed disciples turned from Him when He taught them of the demands of discipleship (John 6:66). It happened as God's prophet had written centuries before: "He is despised and rejected of men; a man of sorrows, and acquainted with grief" (Isaiah 53:3).

Jesus was forsaken by His disciples. At the Last Supper in the upper room, they all committed themselves to die rather than to desert Him. They each said, "Though I should die with thee, yet will I not deny thee" (Matthew 26:35). Then came the experience of Gethsemane, the deep burden of Jesus, and their own inability to stay awake while He prayed. At last Judas came with the soldiers. Jesus was betrayed and taken away. The disciples were confused and frightened. "They all forsook him, and fled" (Mark 14:50).

Jesus was forsaken by His heavenly Father. He even addressed Him as "God" rather than "Father." What happened?

The Son shared perfect unity with the Father through the aeons of eternity. He shared perfect unity with the Father for thirty-three years on earth. He always did those things which pleased God and was never apart from God. But on the cross He took the place and bore the penalty for sinners. He was looked upon as a sin offering. He bore the wrath of God and was separated from the love of the Father!

THE SIN DELINEATED

The wages of sin is death. The death which sin brings is separation from God. In order for Jesus to pay our penalty for sin, He must be hidden from the face of God. That is what happened on the cross.

The price of sin is paid. Jesus paid that price for us. "He hath made him to be sin for us, who knew no sin; that we might be made the righteousness of God in him" (II Corinthians 5:21).

Jesus bore the sins of the whole human race and paid the penalty for them all in one single day! No wonder the judgment of God fell so severely on Him. No wonder He was forsaken by the Father. He bore the final tragedy of human sin — separation from God. He experienced man's ultimate misery — separation from God. The result was His cry of desolation, "My God, my God, why hast thou forsaken me?"

The end of sin is guaranteed. "The Son of God was manifested, that he might destroy the works of the devil" (I John 3:8). A believer is no longer a helpless victim of sin and a slave of Satan. He can identify with the victory Jesus has gained. "He must reign, till he hath put all enemies under his feet" (I Corinthians 15:25). Victory is ahead for the child of God.

THE SATISFACTION DEMANDED

The holiness of God demanded a just penalty for

sin. He is of purer eyes than to behold evil, and cannot look on iniquity (Habakkuk 1:13). He is a holy God who inhabits the praises of His people (Psalm 22:3). Justice demands that sin be dealt with in the right way. Holiness demands that sin be exterminated, totally overthrown and subdued. Let the penalty of sin fall on Jesus and He will pay its full due.

The curse on mankind demanded a just penalty for sin. That curse is set forth in Romans 5:12: "By one man sin entered into the world, and death by sin; and so death passed upon all men, for that all have sinned." "The wages of sin is death" (Romans 6:23).

Man was made in the image and likeness of God; however, that image is marred by the presence of sin in his life. God was insulted by mankind's sin and a remedy had to be effected. That is why Jesus paid the penalty on His cross.

The suffering of Jesus paid the penalty for sin. What a price He paid! The sins of humanity were placed on Jesus that He should bear them as if personally guilty. He cried, "My God, my God, why hast thou forsaken me?" He paid the full price so that any sinner who comes to Him, whatever guilt he may bring, can be accepted and cleansed by the blood of Jesus (I John 1:7).

THE SUFFERINGS ENDURED

Jesus foresaw the sufferings ahead and dreaded them. It would not have been normal for His human nature to react in any other way. That was the burden of His prayer in Gethsemane. "O my Father, if it be possible, let this cup pass from me: nevertheless not as I will, but as thou wilt" (Matthew 26:39). Again He prayed, "O my Father, if this cup may not pass away from me, except I drink it, thy will be done" (Matthew 26:42). His spirit was "exceeding sorrowful unto death" as He came to Gethsemane (Mark 14:34). He was under such emotional strain that the tiny blood vessels that surround the sweat glands erupted and He sweated blood. "Being in an agony he prayed more earnestly" (Luke 22:44). We can never know the extent of His sufferings before He ever reached the cross.

THE SALVATION EFFECTED

God made an offering for sin. Jesus Christ went to the cross and was made a curse for us (Galatians 3:13). He bore our sins in His own body as He hung on that cross (Isaiah 53:4-6; I Peter 2:24; 3:18). The purpose behind it all was to pay for our sins so we could come to God in peace.

"God so loved the world, that he gave his only begotten Son, that whosoever believeth in him should not perish, but have everlasting life. For God sent not his Son into the world to condemn the world; but that the world through him might be saved" (John 3:16, 17). The offering of Jesus was God's plan.

God provided redemption for sin. The death of Jesus on behalf of sinners is the way of redemption. Romans 5:6, 8, 10 points out mankind's weakness, wrongness, and wickedness in sin. Humans were "without strength. . . . sinners. . . . enemies. " "Christ died for the ungodly. . . . Christ died for us... We were reconciled to God by the death of his Son." Salvation is available through Jesus today.

God is the Savior of sinners. He laid the plan for salvation. He perfected the way of salvation. He calls sinners to salvation. He saves those who trust Jesus. "Salvation is of the Lord" (Jonah 2:9). The Bible says of Jesus, "He is able also to save them to the uttermost that come unto God by him, seeing he ever liveth to make intercession for them" (Hebrews 7:25).

God offers salvation from sin. It is a great offer which includes deliverance from sin. It is a great offer because it is free. It is a great offer because it is given by God Himself. It is a great offer because it provides forgiveness for the present and security for the future. It is too good an offer to pass. "How shall we escape, if we neglect so great salvation?" (Hebrews 2:3).

A father sent his little son outside the house for some chore. The darkness had come and he hesitated to go. When his father insisted, the little lad said, "It is too dark to go out there without a father!"

Jesus has gone through the darkness that we might live in the light. He has been forsaken of God that we might never be forsaken. Enter into the good of His atoning sacrifice.

I THIRST

Here is one of the most heart-rending views of Jesus to be found in the Gospels. He is shown suffering as a man (enduring the pains of consuming thirst) and as God (bearing the penalty for human sin). He who had created all the water in the universe suffered for a swallow to quench His agony.

"I thirst." In some languages the word for thirst is the same as the word for *flame*. A deep thirst will pierce the human frame like a tongue of fire. Behold the sufferings of the Lord as He bore the penalty of sin, "the just for the unjust, that he might bring us to God" (I Peter 3:18).

One of the elements of crucifixion was the consuming thirst experienced. The exposure of the body to the elements, plus the emotional and physical torture of the cross, caused its rapid dehydration. Sometimes the mouth became so parched that the sufferer's tongue would swell until it protruded from his mouth. Jesus' words, "I thirst," were real. They were not an appeal for pity but the statement of terrible truth.

We can identify only in part with the physical sufferings of Jesus and hardly at all with the spiritual burden He bore. But His sorrow was great as He bore both in effecting salvation for us.

FULFILLED PROPHECY

The sufferings of Jesus were foretold by ancient prophets. Psalm 69 has many references to the Suffering One. Verse 21 reads, "They gave me also gall for my meat; and in my thirst they gave me vinegar to drink." It happened just that way. Jesus said, "I thirst." The record states, "There was set a vessel full of vinegar: and they filled a spunge with vinegar, and put it upon hyssop, and put it to his mouth" (John 19:29). It is amazing how accurately those prophecies were fulfilled.

The Scriptures controlled the life of Jesus. He said "I thirst" because His body cried out for moisture. But there was another reason He said it: "After this, Jesus knowing that all things were now accomplished, that the scripture might be fulfilled, saith, I thirst" (John 19:28).

The thirst of His body fulfilled the Word of God. It is amazing how the ordinary affairs of life fit into the divine plan.

FULL HUMANITY

The reason Jesus thirsted was that He was human. The divine nature of God would not thirst for the water of earth. He needs nothing outside himself for completeness. But the human nature of Jesus' physical body must have water to live. His cry, "I thirst," testifies to His full humanity.

The Old Testament foretold His humanity. He was the son of the woman who would one day bruise the head of the serpent (Genesis 3:15). He was the great Prophet like Moses who would arise (Deuteronomy 18:18). He was the Son of David (II Samuel 7:12, 13) who would be born in Bethlehem (Micah 5:2). His humanity was fully attested in the Old Testament.

The New Testament reported His humanity. It tells how He did not take the nature of angels, but the nature of men (the seed of Abraham) when He came to earth (Hebrews 2:9, 14). It describes the incarnation process by which He took up human nature and came in the likeness and fashion of a man (Philippians 2:6, 7). This is one of the mysteries of divine revelation. How could He be fully God and fully man at the same time? There was a union of the two natures in divine sovereignty.

Jesus' personal experiences prove His humanity. He was born (Luke 2) and died (Luke 23). He grew weary (John 4:6), hungry (Matthew 4:2), and thirsty (John 19:28). He experienced sorrow (John 11:35) and joy (Luke 10:21). He was even tempted to sin as a man (Hebrews 4:15).

References to the humanity of Jesus must not detract from His deity. He was God and man, the God-Man, at the same time. "There is one God, and one mediator between God and men, the man Christ Jesus" (I Timothy 2:5). By being both fully human and completely divine, Jesus brings God and man together today.

FIERCE SUFFERINGS

The cross was agony for Jesus. It had been at least eighteen hours since He had received any liquid, probably at the Last Supper. In the meanwhile, He had walked a considerable distance, sweated in Gethsemane, and endured a beating by soldiers. He had been mutilated by the scourge until He had probably lost half of the blood from His body, and He probably had a fever by then. His mouth was parched, His system cried out for moisture, and the pain increased by the minute. There was no relief from that suffering so long as He was alive. It is a heart-breaking scene.

The spiritual burden was agony for Jesus. Proverbs 17:22 reads, "A merry heart doeth good like a medicine: but a broken spirit drieth the bones." Jesus suffered a broken spirit under the burden of sin. A song entitled "He Died with a Broken Heart" expresses the burden for sin which He bore. The burden of sin borne by the sinner (Psalm 32:3, 4) is but a drop compared with what Jesus bore.

Let Jeremiah say it for us in his Lamentations: "Behold, and see if there be any sorrow like unto my sorrow, which is done unto me, wherewith the Lord hath afflicted me in the day of his fierce anger. From above hath he sent fire into my bones ... he hath made me desolate and faint all the day" (Lamentations 1:12, 13).

He suffered as an unrepentant sinner will suffer some day. There is a little glimpse of that suffering given in Luke 16:24. The rich man cried from hell, "Father Abraham, have mercy on me, and send Lazarus, that he may dip the tip of his finger in water, and cool my tongue; for I am tormented in this flame" (Luke 17:24). The suffering of the rich man in hell included the agony of consuming thirst. Even the "tip" of the finger would retain enough water to give some relief. (Place the tip of your finger in water and see how much remains when you lift it out.) That indicates the extreme thirst suffered by those who are under the judgment which sin deserves. Be warned and flee to Jesus.

His sufferings ended when the price was paid. After six hours on the cross Jesus could say, "It is finished" (John 19:30). But He could not say that until "all things were now accomplished" (John 19:28). The work was carried to its end. Nothing was left undone. When Jesus commended His spirit to the Father, salvation's plan was completed to the minutest detail. That is why it is freely available to us today. He has paid it all; we have only to receive.

FINAL PROVISION

Jesus made satisfaction for sin. We shall never thirst spiritually because He thirsted physically in His atoning death. He endured thirst that every soul who believes could be satisfied with "the water of life."

Water was one of Jesus' chosen analogies by which He spoke of spiritual life. Hear Him say to the woman at the well of Samaria, "Whosoever drinketh of this water shall thirst again: but whosoever drinketh of the water that I shall give him shall never thirst; but the water that I shall give him shall be in him a well of water springing up into everlasting life" (John 4:13, 14).

Hear Him announce to a crowd attending a Jewish festival in Jerusalem, "If any man thirst, let him come unto me, and drink. He that believeth on me, as the scripture hath said, out of his belly shall flow rivers of living water. (But this spake he of the Spirit, which they that believe on him should receive)" (John 7:37-39).

How that stands in contrast to the cry, "I thirst" which He uttered on the cross. His thirst provided our drink!

His thirst is evidence of His full humanity. His thirst reveals His intense sufferings. His thirst shows the magnitude of God's wrath against sin. His thirst assures us that He shares with us in our physical sufferings. His thirst provides the water of life for us.

"The Spirit and the bride say, Come. And let him that heareth say, Come. And let him that is athirst come. And whosoever will, let him take the water of life freely," (Revelation 22:17).

IT IS FINISHED

Jesus met the divine requirements for our salvation so completely that there is nothing left to be added. "We are sanctified through the offering of the body of Jesus Christ once for all. . . . For by one offering he hath perfected for ever them that are sanctified" (Hebrews 10:10, 14).

"It is finished" (John 19:30). This sixth saying of Jesus on the cross came near the end of His six hours of agony there. The crisis had passed. The suffering was soon to end. All that was left was for Him to release His spirit and return to the Father.

"It is finished." The statement is one word in the Greek language: *Tetelestai* The root word is variously translated in our King James Version of the Bible. It is translated "made an end" (Matthew 11:1), "pay" (Matthew 17:24), "performed" (Luke 2:39), "accomplished" (Luke 18:31), and "finished" (John 19:30).

Each of those translations of the word applies to the sacrifice of Jesus. He made an end of our sin and guilt. He paid the price of our redemption. He performed the full requirement of the law. He accomplished the work given Him by the Father. He finished making full atonement. Glory to His name!

"It is finished." There is the assurance of our salvation. There is our hope of heaven. There is our peace with God. There is the heart of the Christian Gospel.

THE SON DECLARED IT

"It is finished." Jesus spoke those words after six hours on the cross. He spoke those words just before returning to the Father. He spoke those words after the crisis of physical darkness and spiritual separation. He spoke those words because they are true.

Prophecies of Jesus were fulfilled and finished. Look at the many prophecies which had been spoken of Him: His human nature as the Son of a woman, His divine nature as God in human flesh, the place of His birth, the nature of His ministry, the rejection and suffering He would endure, and His final triumph at the end. It was all done in exact detail "that the scripture might be fulfilled" (John 19:28).

Sufferings of Jesus were ended. He predicted He would "suffer many things of the elders and chief priests and scribes, and be killed, and be raised again the third day" (Matthew 16:21).

The earthly ministry of Jesus was completed. He spoke of the works which the Father had given Him to finish (John 5:36). That was done. He had taught the believers, established the church, instituted the ordinances, given the message, and made the sacrifice. Nothing more was to be done. "It is finished."

The atonement for sinners was effected. The real purpose of His coming to earth was "to seek and to save that which was lost" (Luke 19:10). His sacrifice was no second-best alternative. "By one offering he hath perfected for ever them that are sanctified" (Hebrews 10:14). What is left to be done when the Son of God completes His work? "It is finished."

THE FATHER CONFIRMED IT

God rent the veil of the temple. That meant the sacrifice of Jesus removed the separation which had existed between God and man. The rending of the veil was God's work, "from the TOP to the BOTTOM." It was a complete work, for it was "rent in twain (two separate pieces). It was a symbolic work, as Hebrews 10:19-22 makes clear. God opened the way into the Most Holy Place, the place of His personal presence and glory, to say that Jesus' sacrifice is enough! "It is finished."

God raised Christ up from death. That shows He has accepted the sacrifice of Jesus as the sufficient offering for sin. Thus Jesus is "declared to be the Son of God with power, according to the spirit of holiness, by the resurrection from the dead" (Romans 1:4). If Jesus had died as any other man dies, He would not have been raised. His resurrection is proof that "It is finished."

God exalted Christ to His own right hand. That shows the value of Jesus' earthly ministry and the Father's delight in Him. Jesus finished His work on earth as the Father had planned. "Wherefore God also hath highly exalted him, and given him a name which is above every name" (Philippians 2:9). The Father Himself is testifying, "It is finished."

God sent the Holy Spirit at Jesus' request. Our Lord promised, "I will pray the Father, and he shall give you another Comforter, that he may abide with you for ever; even the Spirit of truth... At that day ye shall know that I am in my Father, and ye in me, and I in you" (John 14:16, 17, 20). The Holy Spirit would not have been given if Jesus' sacrifice had not been sufficient. The presence of the Spirit indwelling you today is proof that "it is finished."

THE HOLY SPIRIT APPLIES IT

A person becomes aware of his sin and need of forgiveness because of the work of the Holy Spirit in him. Jesus said, "When he is come, he will reprove the world of sin, and of righteousness, and of judgment" (John 16:8). That is how a sinner is drawn to Jesus. Without that ministry of the Spirit, the sinner will not and cannot come. The Holy Spirit would not draw sinners to a Savior who could not save them, would He? Of course not! His wooing is proof of the statement, "It is finished."

He applies the blood of the atonement to the heart of the penitent believer. Jesus called that being "born again." He warned that unless one is "born of... the Spirit" he can neither see nor enter the kingdom of God (John 3:1-7). The Holy Spirit renews us and gives us life because of what Jesus accomplished in His death and resurrection. Your personal forgiveness of sins is proof that "it is finished."

He teaches Christians so they will be able to serve their Lord. Jesus taught that the Holy Spirit would have two primary ministries in the world:

1. to reprove the world of sin, of righteousness, and of judgment;
2. to guide believers into all truth. Notice the distinction between "the world" and "you" in John 16:8-15.

The Holy Spirit takes up permanent residence in the human spirit of each one who trusts Jesus. He abides there, living the life of God in him, teaching the things of God to him, and doing the work of God through him. None of that would be possible unless the work of Jesus was sufficient. Praise the Lord, "It is finished."

He empowers Christians so the life of Christ is lived through them. One of the most amazing facts for a Christian is the realization that "Christ lives in me!" But it is true. "I am crucified with Christ: nevertheless I live; yet not I, but Christ liveth in me" (Galatians 2:20).

How does Christ live in me? He lives in me by the Spirit of God who indwells me. The Christian life is not my life improved and extended. It is a new and different quality of life, the life of God lived in my human body. How is that possible? It is possible because of what Jesus did. "It is finished."

THE BELIEVER EXPERIENCES IT

We add nothing to the work that Jesus has finished. What could we add? Only our human efforts of self-righteousness. That would be condemned of God as "filthy rags" (Isaiah 64:6). We would be as hopeless as before. Salvation is totally by grace, without any mixture of our works (Romans 11:5, 6; Ephesians 2:8, 9). Jesus meant it when He said, "It is finished." We have nothing to add, and nothing needs to be added.

We receive freely because Jesus paid the full price of our atonement. The Bible emphasizes that "the GIFT of God is eternal life through Jesus Christ our Lord," (Romans 6:23). The ancient prophets knew that which is priceless can be received "without money and without price" (Isaiah 55:1). It is not that salvation is cheap, rather that Jesus has already paid the full price. There was nothing left to be paid after He said, "It is finished."

We enjoy eternally the benefits of Jesus' redemption. The Bible calls that benefit "eternal life." That term means more than a life so long that it never ends. "Eternal life" embraces all the blessedness of forgiveness, reconciliation, fellowship, power, and every other blessing of being a child of God in Jesus Christ. Jesus paid the full price and secured all those blessings to us. Then He cried, "It is finished."

Jesus said, "It is finished." There is nothing left to be done. With faith enter into the good of what He has accomplished for us. "By one offering he hath perfected for ever them that are sanctified" (Hebrews 10:14).

FATHER, INTO THY HANDS

"Father, into thy hands I commend my spirit." What a wonderful way to die! Jesus set the example for us in dying as well as in living.

Here is the seventh and last saying of Jesus during the six hours He was on the cross. It is an expression of His faith in God and loving assurance of a relationship with the Father. It assures us that when we face death "then shall the dust return to the earth as it was: and the spirit shall return unto God who gave it" (Ecclesiastes 12:7).

Jesus made seven statements to God while He hung on the cross. Three related to God, three related to man, and one was stated as if to the whole universe. The three relating to God were, "Father, forgive them; for they know not what they do;" "My God, my God, why hast thou forsaken me?" and, "Father, into thy hands I commend my spirit."

The three relating to men were, "To day shalt thou be with me in paradise;" "Woman, behold thy son. . . . Behold thy mother;" and, "I thirst."

The one which seems to embrace the whole universe was, "It is finished."

This week's study deals with the final words of Jesus on the cross. They show how He rested in His Father's care when His sufferings were ended.

PROPHECY FULFILLED

Jesus' earthly life was governed by the will of God expressed in prophetic Scriptures. "That it might be fulfilled which was spoken by the prophet" might be a theme by which to view His earthly ministry. The work of Jesus Christ was no sudden thing with God. He had planned it and prophesied it centuries before it happened. God never turned from His original plan, as indicated by the exact fulfillment of prophecies in the life of Jesus.

Psalm 31:5 reads, "Into thine hand I commit my spirit: thou hast redeemed me, O Lord God of truth." Jesus probably quoted a part of that verse when He came to die (Luke 23:46). His mind was so saturated with the Word of God that He quoted it in His temptations, when teaching

His disciples, and even at the hour of His death.

The statement of Psalm 31:5 became a part of the Hebrew evening prayer. It is reflected in different words in Psalm 4:8: "I will both lay me down in peace, and sleep: for thou, Lord, only makest me dwell in safety." That prayer was probably taught to Jesus by His mother during His childhood. He probably heard his younger (half) brothers and sisters say it. How appropriate it would be at the time of death since death was only a little sleep for His body before awaking in the Resurrection.

FELLOWSHIP RESTORED

What a change had come in the relationship of Jesus to the heavenly Father! Three hours before, He had cried out in desolation, "My God, my God, why hast thou forsaken me?" (Matthew 27:46). How different was this statement, "Father, into thy hands I commend my spirit" (Luke 23:46). How did the change come?

Jesus had drunk the cup of suffering which the Father had given Him to drink (John 18:11). He had finished the work which He had been commanded of the Father to perform (John 17:4). He had paid eternally the sin-debt. He had effected reconciliation of sinners to God.

"Father" is a title of faith and love. Jesus loved to use that title in speaking of God. He used it seventeen times in the Sermon on the Mount, forty-five times in the final discourse recorded in John 14-16, and six times in His prayer recorded in John 17. Because He loved the Father and was assured of the Father's love in response, and because He trusted the Father implicitly, He could say in peace, "Father, into thy hands I commend my spirit."

CONFIDENCE EXPRESSED

Consider the power of "hands." Jesus had been in the "hands" of sinful men and suffered greatly for it. He had recognized it was coming and said, "The Son of man must be delivered into the hands of sinful men, and be crucified, and the third day rise again" (Luke 24:7). (See Matthew 17:22, 23.) He did not draw back from such treatment, for that was God's ordained way of paying the sin-debt which man owed.

The Bible warns us, "It is a fearful thing to fall into the hands of the living God" (Hebrews 10:31). Jesus had been there also, and suffered as a sinner would suffer if he fell into those hands.

Jesus knew it was safe to commit His spirit into the hands of God when the sin-debt had been paid. He felt safe committing himself into those hands. So He prayed, "Father, into thy hands I commend my spirit." With those words, He died, by the act of His own will.

We might desire to experience such a death. "Let me die the death of the righteous, and let my last end be like his!" (Numbers 23:10).

We can die with that same sense of peace because of what Jesus has done. "Yea, though I walk through the valley of the shadow of death, I will fear no evil: for thou art with me" (Psalm 23:4). We can die in peace because of this assurance: "I know whom I have believed, and am persuaded that he is able to keep that which I have committed unto him against that day" (II Timothy 1:12).

SOVEREIGNTY DEMONSTRATED

Listen to the Lord Jesus: "I commend my spirit." That word "commend" means "to put in one's hands; to put in the care of another; to entrust." It describes an act of the will by which one turns a matter over to another's disposition. That means that Jesus did not die as a victim of murderers, or as a result of severe physical abuse; He died by the act of His will. He had said, "I lay down my life, that I might take it again. No man taketh it from me, but I lay it down of myself. I have power to lay it down, and I have power to take it again" (John 10:17, 18). That is divine sovereignty in action!

Listen to the Gospel references to how Jesus died. "Jesus . . . yielded up the ghost" (Matthew 27:50). "Jesus . . . gave up the ghost" (Mark 15:37).

"When Jesus had cried with a loud voice, he said, Father, into thy hands I commend my spirit: and having said thus, he gave up the ghost" (Luke 23:46). "He bowed his head, and gave up the ghost" (John 19:30). Every reference shows the voluntary element in the death of Jesus.

He was not a victim; He died as a victor! He did not die because others wanted it; He died of His own will. What a Savior!

SEQUEL NOTED

The death of Jesus was not the end of Him. His enemies thought to be done with Him when once He was dead. Not so!

Three days later, God raised Him up from death (Matthew 28; Mark 16; Luke 24; John 20). He could not be held by the chains of death or the power of the grave. He arose so triumphantly that in His ascension "he led captivity captive" (Ephesians 4:8). Hear the victorious tone of His words in Revelation 1:18: "I am he that liveth, and was dead; and, behold, l am alive for evermore. Amen; and have the keys of hell and of death."

Forty days later God exalted the risen Christ to heaven. "He was received up into heaven, and sat on the right hand of God" (Mark 16:19). "When he had by himself purged our sins, (He) sat down on the right hand of the Majesty on high" (Hebrews 1:3).

There He sits today, "far above all principality, and power, and might, and dominion, and every name that is named, not only in this world, but also in that which is to come" (Ephesians 1:21).

Here are two practical lessons we can learn from this study. (1) Do the will of God through all of life. "Commit thy way unto the Lord" (Psalm 37:5). "It is God which worketh in you both to will and to do of his good pleasure" (Philippians 2:13). (2) Trust the care of God at the time of death. Many of the saints of God have gone to their deaths with these words on their lips and this peace in their hearts. (Consider Stephen, John Huss, John Knox, and others.) There is no safer place to put yourself than into the hands of God. It is the place of sovereign care and perfect protection.

"Father, into thy hands I commend my spirit."

THE PREACHING
OF THE CROSS

How we Christians love to sing of the cross of Jesus: "I'll cherish the old rugged cross," "The way of the cross leads home," "In the cross of Christ I glory," "Jesus, keep me near the cross." What a list of songs we could make. The redemptive deed accomplished on the cross of Calvary is at the heart of the Christian religion.

THE IMPERATIVE OF THE CROSS

The fact of sin makes the cross imperative. Sin is not a relic of ancient superstition. It is real; it is present; and it is a high insult to a holy God.

The Bible is quite clear in reporting who of the human race has a sin problem. "There is none righteous, no, not one. . . . There is none that doeth good, no, not one. . . . What things soever the law saith, it saith to them who are under the law: that every mouth may be stopped, and all the world may become guilty before God. . . . For all have sinned, and come short of the glory of God," (Romans 3:10, 12, 19, 23). The universal sin problem in the human race makes the cross imperative for the whole human race. You need the cross of Jesus the same as I.

The justice of God makes the cross imperative. "We are sure that the judgment of God is according to truth" (Romans 2:2). That means there must be an accounting for sin. The Bible says of God, "Righteous art thou, O Lord, and upright are thy judgments" (Psalm 119:137). That means not one sin and not one sinner will escape His examination.

Sin makes humans unjust. God is totally just. There can be no fellowship between the two without one or the other changing. If God changed, it would make Him a sinner. That could never be. The human being must change. But he cannot change by himself. "Can the Ethiopian change his skin, or the leopard his spots? Then may ye also do good, that are accustomed to do evil" (Jeremiah 13:23). Something must be done outside a person to effect a change in him. The need is the cross.

The remedy of grace makes the cross imperative. God must justify sinners by a just method.

To excuse sin without judging it and exacting the penalty against it would be unjust. Therefore, an innocent substitute must bear the penalty of sinners and satisfy the just demands of the law of God. That is where the cross of Christ comes into its ministry.

Look at the difference Jesus makes. "We have redemption through his blood, the forgiveness of sins, according to the riches of his grace" (Ephesians 1:7). He bore the full penalty for our sins on His cross. He paid the debt in full. That is how salvation is offered to us in Him. "Through this man is preached unto you the forgiveness of sins: and by him all that believe are justified from all things" (Acts 13:38, 39). Jesus is God's remedy of grace.

THE PREACHING OF THE CROSS

The preaching of the cross is commanded by Jesus. We refer to His command for us to preach as the "Great Commission." It is so important that the Holy Spirit inspired it to be recorded at the end of the Gospels According to Matthew (28:18-20), Mark (16:15), Luke (24:46, 47), and John (20:21), plus the opening of the book called the Acts of the Apostles (1:8). It must be very important to God, and should be very important to us.

The early Christians felt a divine duty to preach the Gospel. When commanded to speak no more in the name of Jesus they replied, "Whether it be right in the sight of God to hearken unto you more than unto God, judge ye. For we cannot but speak the things which we have seen and heard" (Acts 4:19, 20). When called before the court for preaching the forbidden message, they said, "We ought to obey God rather than men" (Acts 5:29). Even after receiving a beating for preaching the gospel, "daily in the temple, and in every house, they ceased not to teach and preach Jesus Christ" (Acts 5:42). Because they were so committed to Christ, the Greek word for "one who gives his witness" (martus) has come over into English as the word for "one who gives his life" (martyr). Jesus commands the preaching of His cross.

The preaching of the cross is needed by all people. There are three great truths which prove that statement.

1. Sin is a problem for all. Romans 3 is Biblical proof that all have sinned. Human experience is personal proof that each person has sinned. Every person must do something with his sin. That is the major problem of his life, whether he recognizes it or not.

2. Atonement was made for all.

First John 2:2 says of Jesus, "He is the propitiation for our sins: and not for ours only, but also for the sins of the whole world." Let language have its ordinary meaning and ask, "For whom did Jesus die?" The answer of I John 2:2 will be "for the whole world of mankind, for every human being."

3. Jesus is the only way for all. Jesus said, "I am the way, the truth, and the life: no man cometh unto the Father, but by me" (John 14:6). The apostles who knew Jesus best testified, "Neither is there salvation in any other: for there is none other name under heaven given among men, whereby we must be saved" (Acts 4:12). That settles the issue. So we conclude, "God hath given to us eternal life, and this life is in his Son. He that hath the Son hath life; and he that hath not the Son of God hath not life," (I John 5:11, 12).

THE RESPONSE TO THE CROSS

There are different ways people react upon the hearing of the Gospel of Christ. Acts 17: 32-34 gives the three typical reactions.
1. "Some mocked."
2. "Others said, We will hear thee again."
3. "Certain men . . . believed."

Some still mock, some delay a decision, and some believe. Preach the Gospel!

The cross is foolishness to some. "Their ear is uncircumcised, and they cannot hearken: behold, the word of the Lord is unto them a reproach; they have no delight in it" (Jeremiah 6:10). Do you know anyone like that? There are many. It is not surprising that people who have a wisdom which is "not from above, but is earthly, sensual, devilish," should reject the wisdom of God. A person must accept God to know truth.

However wise an individual may be, he does not know truth until He knows God personally in Jesus Christ. To any such person the Gospel is foolishness.

The cross is wisdom to some. "The foolishness of God is wiser than men" (I Corinthians 1:25). To those who are called of God, Christ and His Gospel are seen as the wisdom of God.

God solved the problem of how He could justify the sinner and still be just by letting divine justice fall on His only begotten Son as the sinless substitute of sinful humanity. It was an act of divine wisdom which devised such a plan, and an act of divine grace which performed it. It worked out, "that he might be just, and the justifier of him which believeth in Jesus" (Romans 3:26). Consider the cross as if you heard its message for the first time. You will stand in amazement at the wisdom and love which perfected it.

"Who is wise, and he shall understand these things? prudent, and he shall know them? For the ways of the Lord are right, and the just shall walk in them: but the transgressors shall fall therein" (Hosea 14:9).

The cross is power to some. To whom? To "us which are saved" the preaching of the cross "is the power of God" (I Corinthians 1:18). Unto "them which are called" Christ is "the power of God, and the wisdom of God" (I Corinthians 1:24).

The apostle Paul expressed it this way, "I am not ashamed of the gospel of Christ: for it is the power of God unto salvation to every one that believeth " (Romans 1:16).

It is the power of God to convict human beings of sin. When people heard the gospel on the day of Pentecost, "they were pricked in their heart, and said . . . , What shall we do?" (Acts 2:37). That incident occurred in the very city where Jesus was crucified two months before. That is power!

One must experience coming to Him to know the power of the Gospel.

The cross is redemption to some. We who believe in Christ Jesus have found God has made Him "wisdom, and righteousness, and sanctification, and redemption" (I Corinthians 1:30). In Him "we have redemption through his blood, even the forgiveness of sins" (Colossians 1:14). The cross is our redemption because Jesus "entered in once into the holy place, having obtained eternal redemption for us" (Hebrews 9:12).

One must receive Him to enjoy the redemption He provides.

What is the cross to you? Is it foolishness, wisdom, power, or redemption? The cross is to you what Jesus is to you. There can be no faith in Jesus apart from His redemptive work.

THE FIRST CHURCH

Church is one of the most misused and abused words in the English language. It is used denominationally, as "the Baptist church, the Methodist church." It is used architecturally, as we point to a building and say, "That is my church." It is used geographically, as many speak of "the Church of England." It is used universally as some speak of "the universal, invisible church."

It is correctly used locally, as "First Baptist Church" or "Calvary Baptist Church." The New Testament uses the term *church* to refer to a local congregation of baptized believers in Jesus Christ who are covenanted together in belief of what He taught and in obedience to what He commanded.

Your church is important. She is included in the statement, "Christ also loved the church, and gave himself for it" (Ephesians 5:25). She is included in the goal, "Unto him be glory in the church by Christ Jesus throughout all ages, world without end" (Ephesians 3:21). She is "the house of God . . . the pillar and ground of the truth" (1 Timothy 3:15).

This series of studies centers on the New Testament doctrine of the church. Lesson 1 deals with the origin of the church, Lessons 2 and 3 with the ordained officers of the church, and Lesson 4 with the ordinances of the church. Lessons 5-13 examine several churches mentioned in the Bible to see our Lord's evaluation of them. We should come from these studies with our devotion increased to the head of the church (Jesus Christ) and our loyalty increased to the people and work of the church.

PREPARING FOR THE CHURCH

The church did not spring into existence by accident or as a last-minute change of God's plans. Prophecy foretold the preparation for the coming of the church.

The prophet Malachi gave God's announcement four centuries before the event, saying, "Behold, I will send you Elijah the prophet before the coming of the great and dreadful day of the Lord" (Malachi 4:5). Three centuries before that, the prophet Isaiah foretold of one who would be "the voice of him that crieth in the wilderness. Prepare ye the way of the Lord" (Isaiah 40:3). God's Spirit of prophecy rested on an aged priest named Zacharias at the birth of his long-awaited son, saying, "He shall go before him in the spirit and power of Elias ... to make ready a people prepared for the Lord" (Luke 1:17).

But what does that have to do with the New Testament church? The one who was to come as "Elijah the prophet" and "in the spirit and power of Elias" was John the Baptist! He was born with the prophetic announcement, "Thou, child, shalt be called the prophet of the Highest: for thou shall go before the face of the Lord to prepare his ways" (Luke 1:76). John the Baptist came preaching, "Repent ye: for the kingdom of heaven is at hand" (Matthew 3:2). From among those who received the baptism of repentance at the hands of John the Baptist, Jesus chose certain ones to constitute the first church.

The New Testament church had been in the plan of God from time immemorial. He planned for her in eternity. By the mouths of His ancient prophets He predicted the material of which she would be constituted. He brought her into existence in the personal ministry of Jesus. The church is important, for she is a part of God's redemptive activity in the world.

GATHERING THE CHURCH

The church is an *ekklesia* (ek-lay-SEE-ah), a "called-out assembly." So we may speak of the "gathering" of the church. Jesus personally called together those who made up the membership of the first church. He "added to the church daily such as should be saved" (Acts 2:47) as the church grew in Jerusalem. Even today He is saving people and adding them to the church. The church is still a called-out assembly gathered by the Lord.

The time of the calling of the first church is disputed. Those who believe that Jesus called His disciples and instituted the church during His personal ministry on earth differ as to the time and place where the calling was given. It is evident that there was no church in the Old Testament period (Acts 7:38 does not teach that), for the New Testament church was instituted in New Testament times. But when in New Testament times was she instituted?

Was the church instituted when disciples of John the Baptist became disciples of Jesus (John 1:35-51)? Was the church instituted when the first-called disciples left their professions to follow Jesus full time (Matthew 4:18-22)? Was the church instituted when disciples were called apart and twelve of them were ordained as apostles (Mark 3:13-19) in light of 1 Corinthians 12:28? The Bible does not say clearly, and good men have held each time as the original institution of the church.

Some would say the church was instituted on the day of Pentecost (Acts 2:1-41), but that was the day of her empowering, not the day of her beginning. There is not one verse in the Bible which refers to that first Christian Pentecost as being "the birthday of the church" as many believe.

The church was instituted by Jesus Himself during His personal ministry on earth. We can rest content in that fact.

The nature of the calling in Jesus' forming the first church is evident in the Bible. It was a personal call by which Jesus selected chosen men (John 1:35-51) who became foundational, with Christ as the chief corner stone, for the church (Eph. 2:20). It was a sacrificial call at which the chosen men left their sources of livelihood to follow Jesus (Matthew 4:20; 19:27). It was a permanent call by which people were challenged to serve the Lord "unto death"

(Revelation 2:10) and not depart because of a love for the present world (2 Timothy 4:10). It was a privileged call by which a person could become a member of the Lord's own church!

How would you like to have been there to share the call of Jesus to membership in His church? You are no less privileged today; you can still be a member of His church. You can be added to it by the will of Christ Himself as you follow the leading of the Holy Spirit. Glory!

THE NATURE OF THE CHURCH

There are so many uses of the term *church* today that we have difficulty knowing what is meant by its use. What is the nature of the church according to the New Testament?

The church is composed of persons. It was persons whom Jesus called to constitute the first church (John 1:35 ff; Mark 3:13 ff). It was persons whom the Lord "added to" the church as they were saved (Acts 2:47). The church is a body of baptized believers in Jesus Christ.

The church is composed of saved persons. Only those who gladly received the gospel were baptized and added to the body of Christians in Jerusalem (Acts 2:41). Only those who were being saved were added to the church by the Lord (Acts 2:47). When an inquirer asked to be baptized, he was called on to give a profession of faith. He responded, "I believe that Jesus Christ is the Son of God" (Acts 8:37). Only then was he baptized.

The church is composed of saved persons who have confessed their faith through baptism. Those who gladly receive the Word and are baptized are counted as members of the church (Acts 2:41). Jesus' commission was to make disciples (lead people to personal faith in Him) and baptize them (Matthew 28:19). That is how a person enters one of the Lord's churches today. Unsaved people may have their names on the membership rolls of churches, but only one saved by repentance and faith can be truly a member of the Lord's church.

The church is composed of assembled persons. Every reference to church in the New Testament has its primary reference to a local assembly of baptized believers in Jesus.

You have seen the Greek word *ekklesia* before. It is translated "church" or "assembly" throughout the English New Testament. The term occurs more than one hundred times in the Greek text of the New Testament. Three times it has a secular meaning (Acts 19:32, 39, 41).

Three times it is used in an institutional sense, as we speak of "the home," "the school," and "the state" (Matthew 16:18; 18:17). Ninety times it refers to the local congregation as is evident in the congregation being named 17 times, the word being in the plural 35 times, and the context making the local meaning clear 38 times. All other usages of the word indicate that the same meaning applies. So we say with confidence that every time the New Testament uses the term *church* in a religious sense its primary application is to a local congregation.

THE WORK OF THE CHURCH

The church has three great ministries to perform in this world. (1) She is to evangelize, to win souls among all nations (Matthew 28:19, 20) by preaching the gospel to every person (Mark 16:15). That is her most basic ministry. (2) She is to mature and equip the saints by teaching new converts to observe all that Jesus has commanded (Matthew 28:20). Jesus put office ministries in the church to train her for ministry (Ephesians 4:11-16). (3) She is to glorify God "by Christ Jesus throughout all ages, world without end" (Ephesians 3:21).

That is the mission of every church. Your church is fulfilling her mission on earth if she is winning souls, maturing and equipping saints, and glorifying God by it. Does a church have any right to exist unless she is doing that?

THE PROSPECT FOR THE CHURCH

The church will continue on earth until Jesus comes. God is to receive glory "in the church by Christ Jesus throughout all ages" (Ephesians 3:21). The church will be here through all the ages in order to glorify God. She is not about to go out of business.

The church will continue to grow and multiply. "The church" became "the churches" under God's blessings. From the first church in Jerusalem, there grew to be dozens, hundreds, and thousands of churches. Now there are Bible-believing, God-honoring congregations of baptized believers in Jesus in many, if not all, nations of the world. There are churches today with scores of members, with hundreds of members, and with thousands of members in a single congregation. Yes, the church is alive and well. Praise the Lord!

The church will be presented to her Lord "a glorious church, not having spot, or wrinkle, or any such thing . . . holy and without blemish" (Ephesians 5:27). What a day that will be! You and I can have a part in it to the glory of God."

That is the heritage, nature, ministry, and prospect of your church. Think of it! Your church is important to God and to your community. Show your love to Christ by serving Him faithfully through your church. That is how you will fulfill the divine purpose: "Unto him be glory in the church by Christ Jesus throughout all ages, world without end. Amen" (Ephesians 3:21).

THE PASTOR'S DESIRE

What do you think of your pastor? Do you esteem him as a man of God? Do you follow him as your spiritual leader? Do you give time to intercessory prayer for him?

The pastor is vital in the church as Jesus instituted it. Jesus is the head of the church. The Bible is the guidebook of the church. The pastor is the servant of Jesus and the shepherd of the church. The deacons are assistants to the pastor and the servants of the church. Your attitude toward your pastor reflects your attitude toward the God who called him and the Holy Spirit who set him over you in the Lord. You can strengthen your pastor's hands and aid the growth of your church by heeding the biblical principles set out in the following discussion of the pastor of a New Testament church.

ORIGIN OF THE OFFICE OF PASTOR

The church was designed by Jesus so that she needed the office of pastor, one of five offices which He gave: "apostles . . . prophets . . . evangelists . . . pastors and teachers"

(Ephesians 4:11). The Holy Spirit calls men to a special ministry and places each one in the place He assigns them as "overseers" of the churches (Acts 20:28). Here is an office planned by God the Son and filled by God the Spirit. What a sacred ministry it must be!

QUALIFICATIONS OF THE PASTOR

First Timothy 3:1-7 joins Titus 1:6-9 in listing the qualities required in a man who would be the pastor of one of the Lord's churches. The standard is high. The qualities demanded are very strict. The qualifications deal with the whole of one's life, not just his abilities as a preacher.

The qualifications relate to one's moral, mental, personal, ethical, domestic and spiritual life. No man meets that standard to perfection, but the pastor must exemplify it and seek always to grow toward it. A man must have those qualities before he becomes a pastor; they are to be sought in every mature and maturing man of God. The church who is seeking a pastor should read and pray over the biblical list of qualifications, asking God to direct her to such a man. If she chooses a man who does not measure up to God's standard, she has asked for trouble and cannot expect God's blessings.

TITLES OF THE PASTOR

What is the biblical title by which to refer to a pastor? Three Greek terms are used most commonly in the New Testament to refer to the man and the office.

Poimen (poy-MANE) occurs ten times in the Greek New Testament. It means "shepherd." It occurs five times in its natural meaning, four times in reference to Christ, and one time in reference to a preacher.

Presbuteros (pres-BEW-ter-ahs, translated "elder") occurs 75 times. It refers to those of advanced age (Luke 1:18, 15:25) or of advanced rank and responsibility (Matthew 16:21).

Episkopos (eh-PIS-kah-pahs, translated "overseer") occurs 11 times, and six times it refers to the Christian pastor.

Elder refers to the maturity of the men involved, while *pastor* or *bishop* ("overseer") refers to the work they do. The same men are called "elders" in one reference and "bishops" in another (Acts 20:17, 28). The two titles are interchangeable, depending on the emphasis on position or ministry.

Our English term *pastor* is most commonly used today, but it was seldom used in the New Testament to refer to the spiritual leader of the church.

NUMBER OF PASTORS

Each New Testament church had several pastors. There is no specific reference to a single church having a single pastor (as is most common today). Notice the singular and plural words in the following scriptures.

When Paul arrived in Miletus he sent to Ephesus and "called for the elders (plural) of the church (singular)" (Acts 20:17). He addressed them saying, "Take heed therefore unto yourselves (plural), and to all the flock (singular), over the which the Holy Ghost hath made you overseers (plural), to feed the church of God (singular), which he hath purchased with his own blood" (Acts 20:28). That same system of plural pastors of single churches is seen as Paul and Barnabas ordained "elders (plural) in every church (singular)" when on a missionary tour (Acts 14:23).

The church at Philippi had "bishops and deacons" (both plural) in the one congregation (Philippians 1:1). James said prayer for the sick should be made by "the elders (plural) of the church (singular)" upon the sufferer's request (James 5:14).

Why did a church have plural pastors? (1) They met commonly in homes, not in a large auditorium as is customary today. Many leaders were required to guide them in the faith. (2) Since the pastors had differing spiritual gifts (as in Romans 12:6-8 and 1 Corinthians 12:8-11), each man ministered in the area of his spiritual gift. Would it strengthen the witness today if churches had plural pastoral leadership? Yes. It would stop the problem of "burnout" which many preachers are experiencing today because of a work overload.

AUTHORITY OF THE PASTOR

The pastor has much more God-given authority in the congregation than many people are willing for him to exercise in many churches. Even a casual review of New Testament teaching indicates his authority among God's people.

He is the "overseer" (Acts 20:28) who bears a relation to the congregation that the father bears to his children (1 Timothy 3:4, 5). He is to be counted worthy of double honor if he will "rule well" (1 Timothy 5:17). He is to "take the oversight" of the flock of God as God's assigned leader (1 Peter 5:2). He has the "rule over" God's people; they are commanded to "obey them that have the rule over" them (Hebrews 13:7, 17, 24).

Three different terms are used in the Greek New Testament to indicate the pastor's position and authority. *Proistemi* (prah-IS-tay-me) means "to stand before; to superintend" and is translated "rule" or "are over" in 1 Thessalonians 5:12 and 1 Timothy 3:4; 5:16. *Kubernesis* (koo-BER-nay-sis) means "to guide; to steer" and is translated "governments" in 1 Corinthians 12:28. *Hegeomai* (hay-geh-AH-my) means "to lead; to go before; to have authority over" and is translated "rule" in Hebrews 13:7, 17, 24. The pastor is nowhere given authority as a dictator, but he is responsible for the leadership of the congregation.

What is to be the response of the church to her pastor? She is to recognize his God-given authority and honor him (1 Timothy 5:17). She is to protect him from wicked persons (1 Timothy 5:19). She is to honor and obey him in the Lord (Hebrews 13:7, 17, 24). That is the way God ordained it to be.

PURPOSE OF THE PASTOR

What is the pastor to do? Four blessed and solemn ministries are set out in the New Testament to guide the men who guide the Lord's churches.

The pastor is to direct the church. He has been made her overseer by the Holy Spirit (Acts 20:28). He has "rule" over her and is accountable to God for her (Hebrews 13:17). There can be no leadership unless there is a willingness to follow on the part of the congregation. God holds both responsible.

The pastor is to teach the church. That is why each man must be "apt to teach" (1Timothy 3:2). Each is to take the things of God and commit them to "faithful men, who shall be able to teach others also" (2 Timothy 2:2). That teaching is to continue "till we all come in the unity of the faith...unto a perfect man, unto the measure of the stature of the fulness of Christ" (Ephesians 4:13). Since new believers are continually added to the church, the pastor's ministry will continue until Jesus comes.

The pastor is to feed the church (John 21:15-17). He teaches them the Word of God to give them "knowledge and understanding" in the things of God (Jeremiah 3:15).

The pastor is to mature the church so her members will be able to serve God (Ephesians 4:11-16; II Timothy 2:2). He is not to do the work of the church; he is to train the church to do the work of the church.

PREACHING OF THE PASTOR

The pastor is primarily a teacher of God's people. Preaching and teaching are his basic ministries and must come before any other thing. Jesus said to "teach" (Matthew 28:19) and "feed" His sheep (John 21:15-17). So "we preach, warning every man, and teaching every man in all wisdom; that we may present every man perfect in Christ Jesus" (Colossians 1:28).

The early Christian preachers were said to "teach" as they went about their ministries (Acts 5:42). The purpose of all speaking in the church is to edify the church by speaking the Word of God (1 Corinthians 14:3-5, 12, 19, 31, 37). The example of Bible churches was to "continue stedfastly in the apostles' doctrine (teaching)" as in Acts 2:42. "They assembled themselves with the church, and taught much people" (Acts 11:26).

Honor your pastor. He is Jesus' servant and your shepherd. Follow his leadership. Encourage his spirit.

DEACONS WHO SERVE

The typical New Testament church is composed of "the saints in Christ Jesus...with the bishops and deacons" (Philippians 1:1). The saints are the members, the bishops are the shepherds (pastors), and the deacons are the servants. So a New Testament church is an assembly of saints, some of whom have been designated shepherds, some servants of the Lord, and others the congregation.

Consider the deacons, the servants of the church. Their title (Greek, *diakonos*, dee-AK-ah-nahs) means "one who serves." Their qualifications indicate that they were to fill a need for service in the church (1 Timothy 3:8-13). Their original selection was for the purpose of service to the members of the church (Acts 6:1-8).

To say the deacons are the servants of the church does not indicate that they are inferior. Quite the contrary; it magnifies them. Only men of spiritual stature and great commitment can fill the office of deacon as the New Testament describes it. Honor them personally; pray for them

regularly; encourage them by speaking a word of appreciation once and again.

Faithful deacons strengthen the church through example and ministry.

NATURE OF THE DIACONATE

The nature of the office and ministry of the deacon is seen in the origin and meaning of the title by which he is called. The term *deacon* is a transliteration of a Greek word *diakonos*. (*Transliteration* means that each Greek letter in the word is changed to its English equivalent. (That is what makes the two words "favor" as you look at them.) The word is "servant" or "minister" when it is translated.

Diakonos occurs scores of times in the New Testament. It is used of the men and office of deacon, but it has many other applications beyond that. It describes the domestic servant (John 2:5, 9), the civil ruler (Romans 13:4), Christ (Romans 15:8; Galatians 2:17), the followers of Christ in relation to Him (John 12:26; Ephesians 6:21; Colossians 1:7;

4:7), the followers of Christ in relation to one another (Matthew 20:26; 23:11), the servants of Christ in the work of preaching and teaching (1 Corinthians 3:5; 2 Corinthians 3:6; 6:4; 11:23), those who serve in the churches (Romans 16:1; Philippians 1:1; 1 Timothy 3:8, 12), and it even refers to false apostles who are servants of Satan (2 Corinthians 11:15). Those uses indicate that the basic meaning of the term is "one who serves another."

The office of deacon is, therefore, an office of service. Authority is given to deacons for particular ministries, but their purpose is to serve. Blessed is the church whose deacons have the serving spirit.

ORIGIN OF THE DIACONATE

Acts 6 is the only indication in the Bible as to the origin of the ministry of deacons in the church. The growth of the congregation was so rapid and it became so large that twelve preachers (the twelve apostles) could not keep up with the daily needs of the widows in the church. (A daily distribution of food was made to those who were in need, Acts 2:45; 4:34, 35; 6:1.) The number of Christians in Jerusalem reached to the thousands. Benevolent ministry was so great the apostles were being taken away from "prayer and ...

the ministry of the word" (Acts 6:4). What could be done?

The apostles called the group together and said, "It is not reason that we should leave the word of God, and serve tables. Wherefore, brethren, look ye out among you seven men of honest report, full of the Holy Ghost and wisdom, whom we may appoint over this business. But we will give ourselves continually to prayer, and to the ministry of the word" (Acts 6:2-4).

The Bible does not clearly state that is the origin of the office and ministry of deacons. But it seems to have begun in Jerusalem under the blessing of God and was adopted by churches in other places.

These things can be said about the origin of the office of deacon in Acts 6. (1) It began in response to needs among God's people. The widows needed food and the apostles needed help in distributing it. (2) It demonstrates the validity of ministry gifts. The apostles exercised the gift of teaching, evangelism, etc.; the deacons exercised the gift of serving (called "ministry" in Romans 12:7). Each worked in the area in which God had gifted him. (3) It began under apostolic authority. They exercised the spiritual gift of wisdom (I Corinthians 12:8) and told the church what to do in that situation. (4) It began by the church's obedience to her spiritual leaders. The church obeyed the apostles in setting apart seven men who met particular qualifications; the men obeyed in committing themselves to serve (full time!) in meeting the widows' needs. (5) It continued under the blessings of God. "The word of God increased; and the number of disciples multiplied in Jerusalem greatly; and a great company of the priests were obedient to the faith" (Acts 6:7).

WORK OF THE DIACONATE

Visualize an advertisement in the Classified section of your newspaper. Suppose it read, "Must have neat appearance, excellent telephone manner, experience in filing and light typing, plus ability to work neatly and accurately with frequent interruptions." You would know from those qualifications that a business was looking for a receptionist, secretary or administrative assistant.

Since the qualifications indicate the nature of the work, you can look at the qualifications of deacons and see what their duties are. Read Acts 6:3 and 1 Timothy 3:8-13. Make a list of the duties of the deacon based on his qualifications.

It is a spiritual work. The deacon must be "full of the Holy Ghost" (Acts 6:3).

It is a public work. The deacon must be careful of his attitude ("grave"), his speech ("not double-tongued"), his personal discipline ("not given to much wine"), and his ambition ("not greedy of filthy lucre"). He must be a man against whom an accusation of wrong-doing cannot be proven ("blameless").

It is a home-related work. The deacon's wife must be praiseworthy ("grave," not a slanderer, "sober, faithful in all things"). He must have one wife only and have well-trained children (1 Timothy 3:11).

It is an intellectual work. The deacon must be "full of . . . wisdom" (Acts 6:3). That does not mean formal education necessarily, but sanctified sense in dealing with people in the name of God.

It is a responsible work. The deacon must not be a "novice," one who is inexperienced and immature.

It is a rewarding work. "They that have used the office of a deacon well purchase to themselves a good degree, and great boldness in the faith which is in Christ Jesus" (1 Timothy 3:13).

THE PRESENT DIACONATE

Do churches need deacons today? Yes! As servants of the church, deacons can make a great contribution to the peace of the church and the spread of the gospel. Pressure on pastors is increasing year by year. Some have broken health. Some have left the ministry. Some are frustrated as they serve. Faithful deacons can help relieve that burden and enable the pastor to do a more effective work.

Churches need deacons today. Human need is still about us. There are people who are sick. Some are confined to their homes. Others need food and clothing. Deacons can meet that need as effectively as preachers can and relieve the pastors to go on with a ministry of the Word. Many churches have instituted a "Deacon-Led Family Care Program" for that purpose.

Not only do churches need deacons, but the deacons also need the church. They need the confidence and support of the church. They need encouragement expressed personally by members of the church. They need the prayers of the church.

Give honor to the office of deacon. Give respect to men who fill that office according to the New Testament pattern. Help the deacons in your church to recognize and fill their office. Your concern will strengthen their resolve, and God will be glorified as the church serves people in the name of Jesus.

The pastors and deacons work together as a team. They are fellow-helpers, not competitors. The fundamental purpose in creating the office of deacon was to reinforce the pastors. They form one team which works to the good of people and the glory of God.

TRUTH IN SYMBOLS

The church ordinances are important. Jesus Himself set them in the church and commanded their observance. A person cannot be fully obedient unless he receives the ordinances in the manner and for the purpose prescribed by the Lord.

Christians have not always agreed on the number or the nature of the church ordinances. Baptists hold that there are two. The Bible identifies baptism and the Lord's Supper as the two Christian ordinances instituted by the Lord Jesus Himself.

Each ordinance is a witness to a past event and a testimony to a present reality. Together they speak of Jesus' redemptive deed and of the Christian's new life in Him. Beautiful!

THE TRUTH ABOUT BAPTISM

Christian baptism is the immersion in water of a believer in Jesus Christ, in the name of the Father, the Son, and the Holy Spirit, in token of his previous entrance into communion with Christ's death and resurrection through repentance and faith.

Christian baptism was instituted by Jesus. He received baptism at the hands of John the Baptist (Matthew 3:13-17) and recognized that it was from God (Matthew 21:25). He continued the practice of the immersion of believers (John 4:1-3). He commanded that all who became His disciples, through all human history and in all parts of the world, should receive baptism in water as a witness to their faith in Him (Matthew 28:18-20).

Christian baptism is to be received by those who are converts to Christ. It is administered to those who become disciples (Matthew 28:19), who receive the Word (Acts 2:41), who have repented (Matthew 3:2-6), and who believe that Jesus Christ is the Son of God (Acts 9:36-38). The order always is "hearing," "believed," "were baptized" (as in Acts 18:8).

There is no basis in the Bible for infant baptism. Nowhere does the Lord command it. Nowhere is there a clear example of it. The occasions in which a whole household was baptized (Acts 10:44, 47, 48;

16:14, 15; 16:32-34) show that all in the household were old enough to believe in Jesus before baptism. Infant baptism is based on a superstitious reverence for the ordinance, which is totally unfounded in Holy Scripture.

Christian baptism must be a confession of faith. It is not a "sacrament" by which one receives redeeming or sanctifying grace. One must be a child of God by repentance and faith before he is a candidate for baptism in water (Acts 8:36-38). It is a testimony of what one has already received, not a method by which one seeks to receive. It is "the answer of a good conscience toward God" (1 Peter 3:21).

Christian baptism must be by immersion. The Greek term *baptizo* (bap-TIDZ-oh) is translated "baptize" in English. That term means "to plunge, dip, immerse." Immersion, not sprinkling or pouring, was unquestionably the original form of baptism. Immersion was the practice of the ancient churches. The Bible refers to being baptized "in" water, not "with" water (Mark 1:4, 8, 9).

Figurative allusions to baptism show it to be burial and resurrection, indicating that its mode was immersion (Romans 6:4). As Israel crossed the Red Sea, going down with a wall of water on either side of them and the cloud of God above them, they were "baptized unto Moses in the cloud and in the sea" (1 Corinthians 10:2). Immersion is the evident method of baptism.

Actual descriptions of baptism show immersion. When Philip baptized the Ethiopian eunuch (Acts 8:38, 39), they followed three steps. (1) Both went down into the water. (2) Philip immersed him. (3) Both came up out of the water. That is the way New Testament churches practice baptism today.

Christian baptism must be by the right authority. There is no plain statement of Scripture which says, "This has the authority to administer Christian baptism." But from the tenor of Scripture, Baptists have traditionally held that the authority of baptism is vested in the local congregation of Christians. That is based on the Great Commission our Lord gave to the church (Matthew 28:18-20).

A New Testament church has the authority not only to administer baptism, but also to judge whether a person coming to transfer membership from another church has received valid baptism. The authority is so centered in each church that there is no higher power to appeal to when one differs from a church's decision. How careful a church must be to preserve that ordinance in the purity Jesus gave it originally!

THE TRUTH ABOUT THE LORD'S SUPPER

The Lord's Supper is a ritual in which the assembled church eats bread and drinks the fruit of the vine in token of its constant dependence on the once-crucified, now-risen Savior as the source of its spiritual life.

The Lord's Supper is a biblical ordinance. It is the Christian equivalent of the Passover meal eaten by the Hebrews (Exodus 12). Jesus instituted the Lord's Supper after observing the Passover meal with His disciples in the upper room of a house in Jerusalem (Matthew 26:26-29). It came originally and directly from the hands of our Lord Himself. The early churches observed the ordinance. They met on the first day of the week for the "breaking of bread" (Acts 2:42). (See also Acts 2:46; 20:7.) Even their ordinary meals must have reminded them of the Lord's ordinance.

The Lord's Supper was authorized by Jesus Christ. It vividly portrays His death. He said of the bread, "This is my body which is given for you" (Luke 22:19). He said of the drink, "This is my blood of the new testament, which is shed for many" (Mark 14:24). The broken bread and the poured drink speak eloquently of His sacrifice on our behalf.

Jesus wants His churches to observe the ordinance. He said twice, "This do in remembrance of me" (1 Corinthians 11:24). It is intended to "shew the Lord's death till he come" (1 Corinthians 11:26). Therefore, it is to be observed until He comes again.

The Lord's Supper is a symbolic ordinance. It is not another sacrifice of our blessed Lord, as some believe. It is not a sacrament by which one secures saving grace to his soul. It is a picture of a spiritual reality we enjoy in Christ.

It speaks of the death of Christ for us. Here is how the new covenant was sealed and made available to us who believe in Jesus Christ (Mark 14:24; Hebrews 13:20): His blood was shed and His body was broken to make that blessing possible.

It speaks of our personal appropriation of the benefits of His death. His body was broken for us (1 Corinthians 11:24). We receive the benefits of His provision as we "eat" and "drink" of Him.

It speaks of the unity of Christians in Christ. Though it is primarily a communion with Jesus, there is an element of communion between the saints as they partake (1 Corinthians 10:17). "We being many are one bread, and one body: for we are all partakers of that one bread." Since each of us is related to Him, we become related to one another in Him.

It speaks of the coming joy in the kingdom of God. The Supper looks back to Jesus in humility and love. It looks forward to the victorious kingdom with delight and anticipation. Jesus said He would not drink of the fruit of the vine again until He drank it in the kingdom of God (Luke 22:18; Mark 14:25; Matthew 26:29). Partake of the Supper with an eye on the future and rejoice!

The Lord's Supper can be misunderstood. What did Jesus mean when He said, "This is my body...This is my blood"? What does that say about the bread and drink of the Lord's Supper?

Roman Catholics hold to transubstantiation, by which the bread and drink are changed into "the actual body and blood, soul and divinity" of Jesus, even though they retain the appearance of bread and wine. Lutherans hold to consubstantiation, by which the bread and drink remain material but the worshiper partakes of the veritable body and drinks the veritable blood of Christ. Presbyterians hold to spiritual presence, in which Christ is present in a special and spiritual way to bring blessings to the participant; Christ is conveyed through the elements. Baptists and others hold to a symbolic ritual. It is merely a memorial supper which commemorates the grace of God in the sacrifice of His Son and our Savior.

The Bible makes these facts quite clear: It is available only to one who is saved (1 Corinthians 11:27-29). There is no example in the Bible of a non-Christian partaking of the meal.

It is available only to the baptized (Matthew 28:19, 20; Acts 2:41, 42, 46, 47; 1 Corinthians 10:1-3). There is no example in the Bible of an unbaptized person partaking of it.

It is available only to those who walk orderly. By that is meant moral purity, in obedience to Christ, with no false doctrine, and causing no disharmony in the church (Romans 16:17).

On the basis of the above principles, many churches make the ordinance available only to her local members. Only those can she certify to be saved, baptized, and to be walking orderly.

Baptism and the Lord's Supper have been ordained by Jesus Himself in His church. Believers in Jesus should receive those ordinances. They should respect them and recommend them to others.

WHERE HE BELONGS

Behold the relationship of Christ to the church! This is a greatly encouraging picture as we apply it to His relationship with our own congregations today. The truth is, "As their sovereign Lord, Jesus stands in the midst of His churches."

Revelation 1 is the beginning of a glorious "Revelation of Jesus Christ" (1:1). That revelation was written by the inspiration of the Holy Spirit and sent to the churches. It begins with a revelation of the person of Jesus and His personal involvement with each church. It is a blessing today when it is read and applied to the Lord's churches now. Jesus walks among His churches, beholding their order, holding their pastors in His hand, commending their good, condemning their error, sending them His messages, encouraging their obedience, and promising His rewards for their faithfulness. What an encouraging word for today!

Jesus ministers to His church by the Holy Spirit: "He that hath an ear, let him hear what the Spirit saith unto the churches" (Revelation 2:7, 11, 17, 29; 3:6, 13, 22).

Jesus ministers to His church by the pastors. He holds the pastors in His hand (Revelation 1:20) and speaks His message to the church through them (Revelation 2:1, 8, 18). Behold the interest and involvement of our Lord with His churches — with your church! He is where He belongs — among His churches today.

JESUS' AGENTS

The Holy Spirit is the agent of Jesus. While we must not think of Father, Son, and Spirit as being of varying importance, the Spirit is subordinate to the Father and Son in this present dispensation. He is the agent of Jesus in our world.

Jesus promised, "I will pray the Father, and he shall give you another Comforter . . . even the Spirit of truth" (John 14:16, 17). He spoke of the Holy Spirit, "whom I will send unto you from the Father" (John 15:26). So the Spirit was sent by the Father and the Son to minister in our world.

The Holy Spirit came at the word of Jesus to be the teacher of believers in Jesus. Jesus said, "When he, the Spirit of truth, is come, he will guide you into all truth. ... He shall take of mine, and shall shew it unto you" (John 16:13, 15). The purpose of the Holy Spirit among believers is to teach them the things of Christ and sanctify them increasingly into the image of Christ.

The work of the Holy Spirit includes each true church today. He is speaking to the churches (Revelation 2:7, 11, 17). Since the church is the local, visible body through which Christ manifests Himself today, that is a primary place of the ministry of the Spirit in the lives of believers.

The pastors of the churches represent Jesus. Jesus is the head of each church, large or small (Ephesians 1:22; 5:23). As Head, He has the authority to speak to her and govern her as He wills. There is no appeal from the authority of Jesus over your church.

The pastors are the overseers (shepherds, guides) of each church. They are appointed by the Holy Spirit (Acts 20:28). Their business is to "rule" the church and the business of the church is to "remember," "obey," "submit" to, and "salute" them as the representatives of Jesus Christ (Hebrews 13:7, 17, 24).

JESUS' CONCERN

Jesus is concerned about the churches. That is indicated in Revelation 1 in His standing "in the midst of the seven candlesticks" because "the seven golden candlesticks . . . are the seven churches" (1:13, 20). He is so concerned about His churches that He walks among them constantly to behold them, speak to them, and enable them for ministry.

Jesus' concern for the church is indicated in His claiming the church. He predicted, "I will build my church" (Matthew 16:18). His term for church was *ekklesia*, "assembly." There were many assemblies in the world in Jesus' day — political, economic, religious, social — but Jesus would build His own assembly. Notice the personal pronoun, "I will build MY church." We use Bible terms when we speak of Jesus' church, His own assembly. He is concerned about the churches, for they are His own.

Jesus' concern for the church is indicated in His love for the church. Ephesians 5:25-27 reads in part, "Christ also loved the church, and gave himself for it; that he might sanctify and cleanse it...that he might present it to himself a glorious church." So great is His love for the church that it is an example for the husband to follow in loving his wife. Ephesians 5:25-33 shows that Jesus' love for the church is sacrificial, purposeful, unselfish, affectionate, and unending. He is concerned about your church the same as He is about all others.

Jesus is concerned about every church. Revelation 1:11 lists seven congregations which were in each of seven cities in the ancient province of Proconsular Asia. Some churches were small; some were large. Some were devoted; some were negligent. Some were doctrinally pure; some were in error. Some were popular; some were persecuted. But Jesus loved each and all. He walked among them and held His messengers to them in His hands. What does that say about your church? Jesus is concerned about her as well.

JESUS' INVOLVEMENT

What picture could John have painted to show the Lord's personal involvement with His churches more impressively than the picture in Revelation 1? Examine it carefully.

Jesus is personally present among His churches. Can you imagine the sovereign God of the universe having time and concern to be walking among congregations of Christians? He is and He does! Since the church is His body (the visible expression of His person and work in the world), He is wherever the church is. There is encouragement in the revelation that He is involved with us, whether we know it or not.

Jesus sends His messages to His churches. He spoke through the apostle John in the book of Revelation. He also spoke through others such as Paul, Barnabas, Silas, and Peter. Today He is speaking to you through your pastors and teachers.

Jesus holds His messengers to His churches. In His right hand is a place of special importance and power. That does not magnify the messengers; instead, it shows the Lord's concern for His churches so that He personally holds the messengers He sends to them. What a blessed truth!

JESUS' MESSAGE

Jesus comes to us today, through the record of Revelation 1, to minister to us. What does He do?

(1) He inspires us with His glory (1:13-16). (2) He consoles us with His peace (1:17). (3) He assures us of His victory (1:18). (4) He instructs us with His message (1:11, 19). (5) He encourages us with His presence (1:13, 16, 20). (5) He assures us with His concern (1:20).

WORKING BUT WANTING

"What thou seest, write in a book, and send it unto the seven churches which are in Asia" (Revelation 1:11). Jesus' command to John resulted in the seven letters which will be our subject of study the next seven weeks.

The letters to the seven churches in Asia Minor have much in common. Each letter comes to the church through her pastor ("the angel of the church"), reveals some truth about Jesus Christ, closes with an appeal to hear and heed ("he that hath an ear, let him hear what the Spirit saith unto the churches"), and reveals some truth about the second coming of Jesus.

Each letter carries the same arrangement of material. (1) The city is identified where the church is located. (2) The Christ is identified under some symbol. (3) Commendation is extended for the good in the church. (4) Complaint is registered against any evil in the church. (5) Counsel is given concerning what to do. (6) A Covenant of promise is offered for faithfulness and obedience.

The first letter was addressed to the church in Ephesus. With what excitement they must have received a letter from the Lord Jesus, written by the hand of their beloved former pastor (the apostle John), and addressed to their peculiar situation. Read their letter in Revelation 2:1-7 and imagine their feelings when they read it first.

THE CITY

Ephesus was called "The Supreme Metropolis of Asia." As the Roman capital of the province of Proconsular Asia, it was an important center for commerce, politics, and religion. The Cayster River provided one of the finest seaports in the ancient world. Three major trade routes converged at Ephesus. It was a commercial center for the whole world.

Ephesus was also a political center of great import. It had the right of self-government as a "free city" in the Roman Empire. The most important legal cases of the province were tried in its courts. The Panionian Games (which challenged the Olympic Games in importance) were played in its stadiums. The city witnessed all the pageant of Greek and Roman life at its greatest brilliance.

Ephesus was an important religious center. The temple of the goddess Diana was one of the Seven Wonders of the World at the time John wrote his letter.

The Greeks had a saying, "The sun sees nothing finer in his course than Diana's temple." There had been a temple to Diana in Ephesus from before recorded history began. In John's day it was 425 feet long, 220 feet wide and 60 feet high. It had 127 pillars donated by 127 different kings. Thirty-six pillars were overlaid with gold, set with jewels, and bore intricate carvings. It was breathtaking in splendor. But the worship in Diana's temple was weird, ecstatic, and grossly immoral.

The gospel of Jesus Christ was introduced in Ephesus in A.D. 54 by the apostle Paul on his second missionary journey. Aquila and Priscilla became leaders in the early church. Paul spent almost three years here on his third journey. A great Christian congregation arose in Ephesus. So many people became Christians that the silversmiths raised a riot when the sale of silver images of Diana dropped sharply (Acts 19).

Tradition states that the apostle John was pastor of this congregation for a long time. Paul wrote his epistle to the church about A.D. 63. Then John wrote this last letter in A.D. 95 to 100.

THE CHRIST

Jesus presented Himself to the church as "he that holdeth the seven stars in his right hand, who walketh in the midst of the seven golden candlesticks" (Revelation 2:1).

Jesus is the Lord of the church. The "stars" are the pastors (Revelation 1:20), the Lord's messengers to the church. He holds them in order to direct their ministries, controlling the leadership of the church. He shows himself as Lord of the church.

Jesus is intimately acquainted with the church. He is walking among His churches (Revelation 1:20) and knows them intimately. He beholds their order, knows their hearts, listens to their speech, weighs their motives, and examines their activities. There is no hiding from Him.

What was true of the church in Ephesus is true of your church. Listen for His message to you.

THE COMMENDATION

Revelation 2:2, 3, 6 recounts three things in the church at Ephesus which the Lord approved. Examine them to see if they are in your church also.

"I know thy works, and thy labour" (verse 2). The emphasis is on their self-denying effort. "Works" are any kind of purposeful activity. But "labour" refers to "effort unto weariness," a strenuous and exhausting effort for God. Their selfless service for Jesus brought them to the point of exhaustion.

That teaches us that the church is a place to work. It is not intended to be a comfortable place to conserve the energies of the saints. We are saved to serve.

"(Thou) hast borne, and hast patience, and for my name's sake hast laboured, and hast not fainted" (verse 3). Christians were very unpopular in Ephesus. (It was the center of emperor worship in Asia.) They were hated, suspected, and falsely accused. Some merchants refused to sell to them. They were faithful and busy for Jesus in spite of unjust sufferings. Jesus recognized and complimented that devotion.

"Thou const not bear them which are evil...Thou hatest the deeds of the Nicolaitans" (verses 2, 6). False teachers had come (as Paul had warned in Acts 20:29ff), but they were tested and rejected. Not even the Nicolaitan heresy was permitted to remain. Here was a doctrinally pure church.

THE COMPLAINT

"Nevertheless I have somewhat against thee, because thou hast left thy first love" (verse 4).

Could anything be wrong with a church like that? It carried on its services in the face of difficulties; it rejected false teachers; it hated sin; it did not grow weary in the Lord's work. Could anything be wrong there?

The relation of compliment to complaint is seven to one: seven items of approval and only one item of disapproval. But that one error was so serious as to make the whole letter appear in a different light.

"Thou hast left thy first love" is the tragic complaint. What is that first love? It is devotion to Jesus Christ. Divine love is given us by the Holy Spirit (Romans 5:5), commanded of God (1 John 4:21), proof of new life in Christ (1 John 3:14), and essential to every Christian service (1 Corinthians 13:1-3).

If any church should have been filled with love, Ephesus would have been that church. She knew by experience the redeeming love of God in Jesus Christ. Paul wrote the great love chapter of the Bible (1 Corinthians 13) from Ephesus. John, the apostle of love, was a long-time pastor there. But she lacked it.

Can a church be doctrinally pure, unquestionably loyal,

unceasingly busy, amazingly patient, and still not love Jesus as she should? The Lord answers, "Yes!" Jesus values loving devotion to God so highly that neither work, endurance, nor orthodoxy can substitute for it. How do you measure up?

THE COUNSEL

"Remember therefore from whence thou art fallen, and repent, and do the first works" (verse 5). The appeal can be summarized in three words: remember, repent, return.

"Remember" means to "continue mindful." That appeal was in keeping with the prophet's advice to God's people, "Look unto the rock whence ye are hewn, and to the hole of the pit whence ye are digged" (Isaiah 51:1). Remember the need for deliverance, the grace that brought it, and the sacrifice by which it was made possible. That will quicken your devotion to Jesus.

"Repent" means to turn from whatever stole away one's devotion to God. The point of departure is the place where a return must begin. When a person or a church loses love for Jesus, nothing but real repentance will restore it. Service apart from loving devotion and pure living is superficial and counterfeit. God will never accept it.

"Repent!"

"Return" is a call to do the "first works." Service which issues from love is the only service God will accept. The heart which turns from the world and is centered on Jesus will experience a vigor in work, a singleness of mind, a purity of motive, a secret joy in trials which comes from no other place. That makes service a new thing, like the "first works" which characterize the new convert's devotion to Jesus.

Consider the warning which accompanies the counsel to remember, repent, and return. To fail to respond means the forfeiture of the right to exist as a church. The "candlestick" was to be removed out of its place in Ephesus. (The candlestick is the church in Revelation 1:20.) There must be repentance!

No church has the right to exist if she fails to obey the Lord's commands and fulfill His commission. Be warned!

THE COVENANT

"To him that overcometh will I give to eat of the tree of life, which is in the midst of the paradise of God" (verse 7).

What a promise! To eat of the fruit of the tree of life means that one lives forever. God forbade fallen man to eat it; consequently, He sent Adam and Eve out of the Garden of Eden (Genesis 3:22-24). In the new earth, however, the tree of life will be readily available to all (Revelation 22:1, 2). Its fruit will be new and fresh every month of the year; its leaves will be for the healing of the nations. Jesus promises that those who are faithful to Him will be given free access to the tree of life in the paradise of God.

But He is saying more than that. Jesus promises to provide the needs of those who trust and serve Him now. Faithfulness may involve labor unto weariness, but the demand will not be beyond the supply. Jesus promises, "I will give spiritual food to the one who is loyal to Me."

Ask the saints of God. They will say they have food to eat that others know not of. It is the spiritual food promised by the Lord in Revelation 2:7.

Be warned that God expects more than "busyness" in His churches. The church in Ephesus probably had all the programs, ministries, and activities one could imagine (to speak in terms of today's church). They were so busy working for God that they forgot to love Him. Be aware that devotion to Christ supersedes well-intentioned activity. Hold the doctrines. Be involved in activities. Serve in the church. But always keep your fire of devotion to Jesus burning brightly.

Here is the divine imperative under which all service must be rendered. "Thou shalt love the Lord thy God with all thy heart, and with all thy soul, and with all thy mind, and with all thy strength" (Mark 12:30). There is no substitute for love.

Good works will not counteract the ill effects of misplaced love.

TRUE RICHES

Do you know anyone who is truly rich? Be careful in your answer. Not everyone who has a large bank account, has vast holdings in real estate, or owns large blocks of stocks and bonds is truly rich. Real wealth is of the heart.

Real wealth is found in surprising places. If you had lived in Asia Minor at the time John wrote the book called the Revelation of Jesus Christ (1:1), and had been asked to select a wealthy church, you would hardly have selected Smyrna. But the Lord said to that church, "I know thy...poverty, (but thou art rich)." A church which Jesus called "rich" is worthy of our study.

How did the church in Smyrna come into existence? We do not know. It is not mentioned in the book of Acts or in any epistle in the New Testament, but only in Revelation 1:11 and 2:8. Tradition says the apostle Paul visited there on his third missionary journey about A.D. 58; however, there is no proof. It is most likely that the gospel passed from Ephesus to Smyrna in the witness recorded in Acts 19:10: "All they which dwelt in Asia heard the word of the Lord Jesus, both Jews and Greeks."

Smyrna still exists as a city of western Turkey. Its modern name is Ismir. The present population exceeds 200,000. About half of the population of the city claims to be Christian. It is a leading center for learning and piety in Greek Orthodoxy.

THE CITY

"The Glory of Asia" was the title by which Smyrna was often called. Its streets were straight and wide, running from one end of the city to the other. Beautiful temples to various gods were scattered throughout the city. There was a famous stadium, an equally famous library, and the largest public theatre in Asia Minor. Smyrna was a model city, built in the fourth century before Christ, which challenged Ephesus and Pergamos for the right to be called "First in Asia."

Smyrna was a great commercial center. It had a magnificent harbor on a deep gulf. It stood at the end of a road which ran through the valley of the Hermus River. Trade flourished from that region. The land was so fertile and the climate so ideal that some vines produced two crops of grapes each year. Situated thirty-five miles north of Ephesus, Smyrna was a city of great wealth.

Smyrna was a political city. It was a "free city" which was permitted to govern itself. Roman court was held there.

Smyrna was a religious city. Temples to gods and goddesses were everywhere. Cybele, Apollo, Asclepius, Aphrodite, and even Zeus were worshiped there, plus the wine-god Dionysus.

Christians in Smyrna saw the splendors of heathen worship on every side. Their humble little meeting places looked pitiful in comparison.

Two things made their daily lives a peril. (1) Smyrna was a center of emperor worship. Citizens were required by law to burn incense to Caesar and call him "Lord." To refuse was to be branded a traitor. But the Christians recognized no one but Jesus as Lord. To be a Christian in Smyrna was to live in daily danger.

(2) Smyrna had a large Jewish population which was opposed to the Christians. They used their political influence with the Roman governor to incite persecution of Christians. They pretended concern for pagan gods to incite opposition to Christianity. Jesus called them blasphemers and said they were of "the synagogue of Satan."

But there were faithful Christians in Smyrna, even in the face of those terrible conditions.

THE CHRIST

Jesus identified Himself to the church as "the first and the last, which was dead, and is alive" (verse 8). What an encouragement to the suffering Christians in Smyrna!

As "the first and the last," Jesus assured His presence with them. He was before creation (as the first) and will be after present creation is gone (as the last). Let suffering saints persevere; they have a King and a kingdom which are enduring. Jesus will not be defeated. Weeping may endure for a night, but joy comes in the morning.

As one who "was dead, and is alive," Jesus gives hope to the martyrs and their relatives. He has been through death and conquered it. He has the keys of death and hell (Revelation 1:18). There is no need to fear; the Conquering One is with them. That must have been quite an encouragement to the heroic saints in Smyrna who faced the dangers of death daily. The eternal and unchanging Christ guarantees victory.

Such a Christ was the head of the church at Smyrna. Such a Christ is the head of your church, also. Glory!

THE COMMENDATION

The Christian congregation in Smyrna was one of the few churches to which Jesus gave unqualified praise. He recounted her sufferings, warned of further trials to come, and encouraged endurance. In His commendation, Jesus approved the church in several specific areas.

They were busy working for the Lord. "I know thy works," Jesus said (verse 9). The opposition of sinners could not stop their witness of the gospel, their acts of benevolence, and their prayers for people in need. Jesus knew every work they did.

They were faithful in tribulation. "Tribulation" signifies "pressure of persecution." It is pictured by two stones pressed together turning back and forth to grind grain. The enemies of that church were aggressive and cruel. They ground the church to pieces. Still the believers were loyal to Jesus.

Christians are not free from such pressures today. Worry, work, material needs, spiritual opposition, and kindred evils are common. Jesus makes the difference and keeps life from becoming too heavy to bear. He gives victory in the jaws of seeming defeat.

They suffered great poverty. Citizens who refused to worship the Roman emperor Domitian would suffer the confiscation of their property. Thus many believers in Smyrna lost all their material possessions. They were very, very poor.

Christ assured them, "You are rich!" They had riches of a different kind. Their reduction to the state of beggars set their spiritual wealth in sharp contrast. Loyalty to Jesus had cost them their social standing, material properties, and even the bare necessities of life. But through faith they were rich in Him.

They bore slander and insult. All sorts of evil tales were told on them. But they followed Jesus' example. He was reviled, but He did not answer back. He suffered, but He did not threaten. He committed it all to God, the righteous Judge, knowing that He would deal justly in it all (I Peter 2:23).

They suffered imprisonment. That was not uncommon. Jails in Jerusalem, Caesarea, Philippi, Rome, and most other major cities heard the prayers and praises of believers who were imprisoned because of their faith in Jesus. God had not forgotten them. They honored Him through their sufferings.

They suffered martyrdom. Here is the record of the martyrdom of Polycarp, one of the last disciples of John and pastor of the church in Smyrna in subsequent years.

On a festival day the Jews aroused the crowd of pagans to seize Polycarp. They cried out, "This is the teacher of Asia, the father of the Christians, the destroyer of the gods who teaches many neither to offer sacrifice nor to worship (the pagan gods)."

The good Christian pastor was arrested and given a choice to sacrifice to Caesar as a god or be burned at the stake. He answered, "Eighty and six years have I served Christ and He has never done me wrong. How can I blaspheme my King who saved me?"

He was condemned to death. Though it was the Sabbath day, the Jews led the pagans in gathering wood for the fire to burn Polycarp to death. "It is well," said Polycarp. "I fear not the fire that burns for a season and after a while is quenched. Why do you delay? Come, do your will." As the flames licked his body, he prayed this great prayer, "I thank Thee that Thou hast graciously thought me worthy of this day and hour, that I may receive a portion in the number of the martyrs, in the cup of Thy Christ."

THE CONSOLATION

"Fear none of those things which thou shalt suffer" (verse 10).

Suffering saints are consoled by the thought that their Lord knows their condition.

When Jesus says, "I know," He means He knows by experience. He endured tribulation, poverty, slander, arrest, trial, and death. "In that he himself hath suffered being tempted, he is able to succour them that are tempted" (Hebrews 2:18).

There is no promise that the sufferings will soon end. They are assured that they experience nothing for Him which He has not already experienced for them.

Yet, their sufferings will have a limit. They will have tribulation "ten days," a limited period (verse 10). Jesus seems to say, "You are not in a position to know how long your trials will last, but I know, and I assure you that there will be an end to them. Know assuredly that every trial is carefully weighed in the hand of an all-knowing and loving Father, who will not allow you to be tempted more than you are able to bear."

Be comforted that Jesus still identifies Himself with His people who are in trial. He knows and He cares.

THE COVENANT

The Lord offered two blessed features in His covenant with the church in Smyrna. Here is a covenant you can enter.

"Be thou faithful unto death, and I will give thee a crown of life" (verse 10). The believer is not expecting the grave. He is awaiting a crown of life.

The crown of life symbolizes three things. (1) It indicates the royal environment entered by the overcoming Christian at death. He will not be defeated by death; he will receive a crown which is life itself. (2) It symbolizes victory. The winner in the Olympic Games received a crown of laurel leaves as a sign of his victory. The overcoming Christian will receive a crown of life upon his ultimate victory. (3) It indicates that great joy will be experienced when the Christian steps through the doorway of death. A crown of flowers was worn at banquets as a sign of joy. So the overcomer will enjoy a heavenly banquet with overflowing joy.

Who receives the crowns? One who is faithful "unto" death, faithful to martyrdom. Such a person will wear the crown of life!

"He that overcometh shall not be hurt of the second death" (verse 11). The first death is the death of the body. The second death is "the lake of fire," or the eternal state of the wicked. (See its description in Revelation 20:14, 15.)

Learn these truths well. The Lord knows the sufferings of His people; He has experienced them all. He enables His children to endure them as they are brought by the enemy of God, the devil. Such trials do not mean that God has forsaken His children. He makes them temporary and gives a reward far beyond whatever His children may have suffered. "I reckon that the sufferings of this present time are not worthy to be compared with the glory which shall be revealed in us" (Romans 8:18).

NEAR SATAN'S THRONE

How would you like to be a member of a church located next door to Satan's throne? You would be in a great mission field, wouldn't you?

The church in the city of Pergamos had such a situation. That brought a twofold pressure on them. (1) They were opposed fiercely. Open persecution had broken out against them so that some of the believers had been killed. A brother named Antipas was among the Christian martyrs. (2) There was a constant pressure for religious compromise in order to live more at peace. Some members had surrendered to that pressure. "The doctrine of Balaam," along with "the doctrine of the Nicolaitans," was already in the church.

The Christian congregation in Pergamos was no different from your church or mine. Some members compromised their spiritual integrity. Others were faithful unto death. To such churches the Lord addressed a letter.

There is no record of the gospel entering Pergamos. It may have come during Paul's three-year ministry in Ephesus when the good news of Jesus sounded out through all Asia.

The church in Pergamos was small. Surrounded by anti-Christian idolatry, it faced physical and spiritual opposition. But the church as a whole was faithful even to martyrdom. In this letter from our Lord there is a call to faithfulness.

THE CITY

Pergamos was a major city in the province of Proconsular Asia. For over three hundred years it had a place of strategic political importance. The seat of the Roman government was there. All seven of the cities to which John addressed his letters were under the political jurisdiction of the government centered in Pergamos. The nerves of political and social life of Proconsular Asia branched out from Pergamos. But worst of all, it was a center of emperor worship in the province.

Pergamos could never become a city of great commercial importance. It was located fifteen miles from the coast, with no major trade routes passing through it. But what it lacked in commerce, it made up for in politics.

That city had one of the most famous libraries in the world. It contained over 200,000 volumes. Only the great library in Alexandria, Egypt, surpassed it in those days.

Two major religious systems were centered in Pergamos. (1) It was the center of the worship of Asclepios, the pagan god of healing. Sufferers from all over the world came to the temple of Asclepios to be healed. The temple had medical wards, a medical school, priests, and votaries. The emblem of the god was a serpent. The temple had tame snakes with which sufferers were permitted to spend the night in the darkness of the temple. They thought that one would be healed by touching a snake slithering past in the darkness. The touch of the snake was thought to be the touch of the god.

(2) It was a center of worship of the Roman emperor. As an act of allegiance to the state and as an act of worship of the "divine Caesar," all citizens were required on pain of death to offer incense to the emperor. While that was required through all the empire, Christian citizens in Pergamos faced jeopardy every day of the year. One took his life in his hands (humanly speaking) if he was loyal to Jesus in Pergamos.

What was "Satan's throne" which was located in Pergamos? It probably was the Concilia. That was a committee charged with preserving the state religion (worship of the emperor) and to enforce obedience to its requirements. To appear before this committee and not do worship to Caesar would be certain death. The committee was the murderer of the Christian martyrs.

THE CHRIST

Jesus identified Himself to the struggling, persecuted church in Pergamos as "he which hath the sharp sword with two edges" (verse 12).

A two-edged sword was a formidable weapon in New Testament times. People stood in awe of the man who could handle it with expertise. Jesus said He was such a person!

What is suggested by the symbol of the Lord with the two-edged sword? (1) It may mean the Lord is able to protect His people even in the persecutions where martyrs are falling. (2) It may mean the Lord will move in judgment to punish those who cause His church to suffer. The same sword can both defend and punish. It defends God's people and punishes their enemies.

What a comforting thought

for believers in trouble! When they were brought before the magistrates, they had an advocate who was greater than any magistrate on earth. On the other hand, they were obligated to be loyal to Him, for He could discipline as well as protect with His sword.

The same Lord Jesus is walking in the midst of His churches today. He is holding their pastors in His hand. He is talking to the congregations through them. He is wielding the two-edged sword even now. That is the Lord with whom we have to do. Bless His name!

THE COMMENDATION

"I know thy works, and where thou dwellest, even where Satan's seat is: and thou holdest fast my name, and hast not denied my faith, even in those days wherein Antipas was my faithful martyr, who was slain among you, where Satan dwelleth" (verse 13).

"I know thy works" suggests energy. They were engaged in unceasing effort to promote the kingdom of God. Every deed was known to Him. They kept on serving when it was not popular. They kept on serving when it was dangerous. They kept on serving when it was deadly, costing Antipas his life. Jesus saw all that and commended the church for her faithfulness.

"I know . . . thou dwellest . . . where Satan's seat is." What a place for a church to be! They had a mission field at their doorstep. And the church is said to have "dwelt" there.

This is not the common term used in the New Testament to refer to the Christian's residence in the world. He is called a pilgrim and sojourner because his residence here is temporary. But the church in Pergamos had a permanent and settled residence right next to Satan's seat.

"You are living in a city where the influence and power of Satan is strong. You have to go on living there. You cannot escape. Life has set you where Satan's seat is. There you must live, and there you must show that you are a Christian." That was Jesus' message.

The believer cannot run just because a situation is difficult or dangerous. He must bear fruit where God plants him.

What is Satan's "seat"! The Greek term translated "seat" is *thronos* (THRAH-nahs). Notice how it looks like the English word *throne*. It means much more than a seat; it refers to a seat of special authority — a throne. Pergamos was more than the place where Satan dwelt. It was the place where he exercised special authority. It was the place where the anti-God forces had their Asian headquarters! It was there that a little congregation of Christians gave forth their testimony for Christ.

"Thou holdest fast my name, and hast not denied my faith." In an alien and hostile environment, even in the shadow of the high and awful throne of Satan, a little Christian congregation raised her colors and stood firm in giving out a witness for her Lord. It was not easy. One of her members named Antipas had paid with his life-blood for his witness for Jesus. Each day there was the possibility of others being killed, yet they stood fast in the faith. The Lord Jesus saw it, honored it, and commended it. That is the kind of loyalty the Lord expects from each of His children and each of His churches.

THE COMPLAINT

The Lord complained that the church had some who held "the doctrine of Balaam." Balaam was a prophet who tried to make money by the use of his prophetic gift. When God would not let him speak against Israel, he conceived a scheme to bring God's own curse upon the nation. The women of Moab seduced the men of Israel, and God judged them for their immorality and idolatry. What a tragedy!

Some brethren in the Pergamos church were advising believers to go through the form of emperor worship to escape persecution. Jesus warns against any such compromise with evil. The end does not justify the means if the means are not right.

The Lord complained that the church was infected by "the doctrine of Nicolaitans" (verse 15). The word is composed of two words which mean "to conquer the people." It may refer to the dictatorial power of the clergy over the laity in the church.

Not everyone in the church held those two doctrines. But some did, and the rest did not purge the church. They tolerated them; so, there was a danger that the whole church would be contaminated. Each church must hold faithfully to the truth.

THE COUNSEL

"Repent!" That is the counsel the Lord extends to a church which tolerates false doctrine. It means to change, to reject evil teachings and those who propagate them.

The Lord gives the church opportunity to correct her errors. If she does not, He will come and correct her. He warned the church, "Repent; or else I will come unto thee quickly, and will fight against them with the sword of my mouth" (verse 16).

The Lord wants His churches to be pure. It is no sign of

Christian love to tolerate error. An erring member should be disciplined for his own sake and for the sake of the church. "If we would judge ourselves, we should not be judged" (1 Corinthians 11:31).

THE COVENANT

Two precious things are offered to him who overcomes. "To him that overcometh will I give to eat of the hidden manna." Reference may be to the pot of manna placed in the ark of the covenant by Moses. Tradition reports that Jeremiah took the pot of manna and hid it in an unknown cave in the mountains when the temple was destroyed. Some believe the Messiah will bring forth that pot and feed His impoverished people when He comes.

We understand the hidden manna to represent Jesus Christ, "the true bread from heaven" (John 6:32). The one who overcomes certainly shares a communion with the Lord that no other person can ever know.

"To him that overcometh ...I... will give...a white stone, and in the stone a new name written, which no man knoweth saving he that receiveth it" (verse 17). The "white stone" is probably a reference to the pebble of friendship called *tessera hospitalis*. It was engraved with some legend, name, or sign which gave to its possessor a claim of hospitality from him who gave it. Jesus said He would give the overcomer access to the resources of God through Christ. It would be a shining, glistening white stone such as humans have not seen before. It is His personal gift to overcomers today!

Be faithful. Be faithful in the worst of situations. Be faithful, and the Lord will reward you gloriously.

"He that hath an ear, let him hear what the Spirit saith unto the churches."

BEWARE OF DECEPTION

"That which ye have already hold fast till I come" (Revelation 2:25).

That appeal summarizes the letter from Jesus to the congregation of Christians in the city of Thyatira. This is the longest of the seven letters addressed to the seven churches in Asia. This longest letter was addressed to the church in the smallest of the seven cities.

We do not know when the gospel was first preached in Thyatira. We do not know details concerning the founding of the church there. It is possible that the church arose as a consequence of the conversion of Lydia while she was in Philippi on a business trip (Acts 16:14, 15). It is likely that she took faith in Jesus back home with her.

The church in Thyatira was strong and flourishing. Some scholars have concluded that the majority of the city had become nominal Christians at the time this letter was written.

The church was not as strong spiritually as she was numerically. The same heresy which was in Pergamos was in Thyatira; the influence of that heresy was much stronger there. The standards of the faith had been lowered and the world had entered the church.

The church in Thyatira was as busy as the church in Ephesus and had the love Ephesus lacked. She preserved the faith which was in danger at Pergamos. She shared with Smyrna the virtue of patient endurance of tribulation, yet she had one problem which imperiled the effectiveness of her ministry.

THE CITY

Thyatira had a strategic location, situated at the mouth of a long valley which connected the Hermus and Caicus rivers. Since all-weather roads were few in ancient times, trade routes followed the rivers. So the major trade roads of Asia Minor passed through Thyatira.

For more than four hundred years Thyatira had been a military center. It was set to repel invaders and protect the capital city of Pergamos. It was a sentinel town whose business was to fight until captured, be destroyed and rebuilt, and fight again. Her reason for existence was to protect the capital.

Special religious importance was attached to Thyatira. A temple to Artemis and a temple to Apollo were there. Worship of the Roman emperor was practiced in the city, but of major religious fame was the sibyl (female prophet or witch in ancient times) called Sambathe. People came from distant places to consult that oracle. But, surprisingly, the Christian congregation in Thyatira faced no great danger from the heathen religions.

Commerce was particularly important in Thyatira. Half of the trade of the then-civilized world passed over roads in that area. The city was famous for its wool trade and its dyeing industry. The purple dye (which Lydia was selling in Philippi) was very expensive. Labor unions were common in that city. There were unions of bakers, bronze workers, clothiers, cobblers, weavers, tanners, dyers, and potters. Each union had a religious bond; worship of a particular idol god was a part of membership in a labor union then.

THE CHRIST

"These things saith the Son of God, who hath his eyes like unto a flame of fire, and his feet are like fine brass" (verse 18).

"Son of God" occurs only here in the book of Revelation as a title for Jesus. It suggests supreme authority. The church must hear Him.

He has absolute authority and perfect knowledge. The expression, "his eyes like unto a flame of fire," suggests penetrating vision which discerns every detail in the church and each member who composes her fellowship. As the light of fire pierces darkness, so the eyes of the Son of God discern the most profound secrets. His knowledge is intimate, detailed, and perfect. His judgments concerning the church are true and righteous altogether.

Total authority and perfect wisdom are accompanied by sure judgment. "His feet are like fine brass." Principles of truth and right were applied to the character and conduct of the church then; those same principles apply now.

Here is the Christ of the church. He is infallible — the Son of God. He is omniscient — piercing vision of flame. He is authorized to judge — feet as fine brass. Such was the Lord of the church then; so He is today.

THE COMMENDATION

What a beautiful bouquet of virtues adorned the church in

Thyatira! Jesus commended her works, love, service, faith, patience, and further works. Examine that list.

The works of the church are commended. There is no detail as to the specific deeds of the church, but there were many of them. The terms *works* and *service* suggest busy activity in a good cause. The church's efforts must have been increasing, as indicated in the phrase "the last to be more than the first." The beauty of the church is seen in her becoming increasingly busy about the service of her Lord.

The love of the church is commended. Work was inspired by the right motive-love. Blessed is the congregation whose service walks hand in hand with devotion to God. That gives meaning to her work (1 Corinthians 13:1-3).

The church in Ephesus had abandoned her first love, but no such charge could be brought against the church in Thyatira. That loving devotion to God which is the spring of all true spiritual service flowed freely there.

The faith of the church is commended. They not only trusted Jesus as Savior, but they were also faithful to Him as Lord. Fickleness might mark others, but steadfastness was the quality which characterized the church in Thyatira.

The works motivated by the love of those Christians were steadfast. Constancy marked their efforts for their Lord. Their service was neither occasional nor spasmodic. Jesus looks for constancy in individuals and congregations today.

The patience of the church is commended. They had power to stay under the load, the ability to hold on, and the spirit of peace under pressure. The Lord places great importance on this virtue. It is the condition of character which results from the activity of faith and love. G. Campbell Morgan calls it "the flower of fidelity." The apostle Peter urges us to give all diligence to its nurture and maturity (2 Peter 1:5-8). Patience assures faithfulness and fruitfulness in the work of the Lord.

THE COMPLAINT

What a tragic and surprising thing it is to find in such a great church a confessed prophetess teaching and seducing the people of God! Who would have thought such a church would tolerate it? The one in Thyatira did.

Jezebel was her name (perhaps a title given her by the Lord as a reminder of the Jezebel who was the wicked wife of King Ahab). Compromise was her theme. She taught Christians "to commit fornication, and to eat things sacrificed unto idols" (verse 20). The joining of "fornication" and "idols" suggests that her sin was spiritual adultery — a spiritual compromise.

Jezebel probably encouraged the Christians to participate in the meetings of the pagan-dominated labor unions. That would involve the recognition of idol gods and perhaps even participation in immorality. (Ceremonies of worship of pagan gods often included unbridled licentiousness.) The Christians were denying their allegiance to Christ.

Who was this woman Jezebel? Some think she was the pastor's wife. Others think this was an allegorical way of presenting evil doctrine as an evil woman. Most likely she was a woman in the church who taught false doctrines under the guise of having some special revelation since she called herself a prophetess.

The church had committed a grievous error; she permitted heresy to be taught. Ephesus hated heresy. Pergamos was contaminated by tinges of heresy. But Thyatira tolerated the teaching of heresy in the very assembly of the church. Jesus warns that judgment will come upon such evil. But even the warning is a sign of grace. Between the time of warning and the time of judgment there is time for repentance. That is grace.

The judgment upon the sin would be in the very corruption which had been encouraged. The Lord warned that they would be cast "into a bed," the bed of sin becoming a bed of sickness and death. If that sounds hard and harsh, be reminded that God always judges sin. "It is a fearful thing to fall into the hands of the living God" (Hebrews 10:31).

THE COUNSEL

God does not condemn the innocent with the guilty. He whose eyes are like a flame of fire will distinguish between people, punishing the guilty and rewarding the righteous.

No extra burden is laid on the righteous in Thyatira. The Lord wants them to remain consistent in their purity. The unfaithfulness of some might bring pressure on them, but they have no duty other than to be faithful to their Lord. "That which ye have already hold fast till I come" (verse 25).

THE COVENANT

"He that overcometh... to him will I give power over the nations: and he shall rule them... And I will give him the morning star" (verses 26-28).

The Lord will vindicate His people. The Christian movement will not be swallowed up and exterminated by the waves of paganism or by hostile political powers. Total triumph awaits the people of God. The menacing power of Rome was nothing compared with the gracious power of God. Those who were so opposed by political powers will one day rule the nations as the representatives of God. Praise the Lord!

The morning star is seen just before the sunrise. It may have seemed that darkness would never end for the Christians in Thyatira. It may have seemed that the darkness of sin would forever reign. But that was not so. The day star would arise; the morning would come. Jesus promised relief from the darkness of sin and the full light of the day of righteousness. That is His sacred covenant to His people.

What have we learned from the situation in Thyatira? We have learned that the church should never seek "peaceful coexistence" with sin. To cease fighting sin is to submit to it.

It is not enough to be a large church and a busy church. A church is required to be faithful. The letter to the church in Thyatira teaches that lesson.

Any doctrine or philosophy that makes it easy to sin (whether by excusing it, minimizing its enormity, or denying its existence) is of hell. God holds guilty those who teach such a doctrine, along with the church which is not clear and outspoken against it. "He that hath an ear, let him hear what the Spirit saith unto the churches" (verse 29).

RESTING ON LAURELS

Look at this church! She has great influence in her community. She has a reputation of strength, life, and progress. Her members are enthusiastic. Her doctrines are pure. It is difficult to find anything wrong with her. She appears to be an ideal church.

Yet the Lord spoke His severest condemnation against her. That is the church which was located in the ancient city of Sardis, the fifth of the seven churches in Asia to whom the Lord wrote by the hand of the apostle John.

The great fault of the church in Sardis was her resting on her great reputation and neglecting present duty. That was so serious that Jesus did not compliment a single thing in the church, but warned her against apostasy.

Melito was one of the pastors of the church in Sardis. He wrote the first known commentary on the book of Revelation. What comments do you suppose he made concerning the Lord's letter to his own congregation?

We have no information concerning how the gospel first came to Sardis. Likely it came from the witness Paul established in Ephesus. The whole province of Proconsular Asia received the gospel from there.

The church at Sardis had a wonderful opportunity. There was no persecution by the pagans. There was no opposition from the Jews. No doctrinal heresy or schism in fellowship hindered her. She had the greatest evangelistic opportunity of any church in Asia. The problem was that she failed to take advantage of her opportunities. Undisturbed from within or without, the church fell into a spirit of complacency. The church of Sardis enjoyed peace, but it was the peace of death.

THE CITY

Sardis was located at the junction of five major roads in the Hermus River Valley. It was located thirty miles southeast of Thyatira and fifty miles east of Smyrna. It drew trade and wealth to itself and was the major city of the area.

A river bearing gold dust flowed through the city. The first coins were minted here during the reign of Croesus, the amazingly wealthy king. Sardis was the capital city of the kingdom of Lydia as far back as 560 B.C. The woolen industry of the area was centered in Sardis. Costly dyes were made there, as well as in Thyatira. It was a commercial and banking center.

But Sardis had a blemish on its beauty. It was notorious for its loose-living, pleasure-seeking, and luxury-loving people. Its name became a byword among the pagans for slack and effeminate living. It was typical of a broken-down aristocracy. Easy living had brought a voluptuous decadence to the city. And as the city had sunk, the church had gone with her.

THE CHRIST

The Lord Jesus identified Himself in a figure found in Revelation 1:4, 16. He is "he that hath the seven spirits of God, and the seven stars."

The "seven spirits of God" refers to the Holy Spirit. He is said to be "seven spirits" because seven is the number which symbolizes completeness. He is the Spirit of God. He is the fullness of God. He is complete.

The great need of the church in Sardis was to be awakened from her lethargy and spiritual decay. That could be done only by the life-giving power of the Holy Spirit. Jesus told the church that He had the answer to her need.

The "stars" are identified in Revelation 1:20 as the pastors of the churches. The Lord Jesus, the head of each church, holds the pastors in His hands (Revelation 1:16). The pastor of the church in Sardis might have been encouraging his congregation to a fuller spiritual life, but his message was going unheeded. Jesus undergirded the ministry of the messenger by saying He was holding that pastor in His hand and guiding his ministry. Let the church hear because the Lord Jesus is speaking through His messenger.

THE CHARGE

The Lord spoke no words of commendation to the church in Sardis, as He spoke to other churches. She was spiritually bankrupt. His words are startling, sudden, and terrible: "I know thy works, that thou hast a name that thou livest, and art dead" (verse 1).

The church in Sardis did not look dead. She had popular acceptance, adequate manpower, excellent talent, and financial resources. But her excellent appearance was not the true picture. Her appearance was deceptive.

The socially distinguished congregation was a spiritual graveyard. She was busy but powerless. People applauded her; Christ rebuked her. What seemed to be great religious works before other people were incomplete and halfhearted works before God. "I have not found thy works perfect before God" (verse 2).

The church had a great reputation. But no one can live on the merits of the past. The church had a name that she was alive, but her condition did not agree with her reputation. Sardis was misnamed, God said.

Activity in the service of Jesus is wonderful, but it must be motivated and governed by love for God and submission to the Holy Spirit. Otherwise, it is an empty pantomime. Read 1 Corinthians 13!

THE COUNSEL

Five staccato imperatives burst from the lips of the Lord. What should the church do to remedy her plight? He answers, "Be watchful; Strengthen the things that remain! Remember! Hold fast! Repent! (verses 2, 3)." Sardis needed that ambition, just as do many churches today.

The city was built on a hill surrounded on three sides by precipitous cliffs. It was easily defended, since an enemy army could not scale the cliffs. During the reign of Croesus, the city was besieged by Cyrus. A reward was offered to any soldier who could find a way up the cliffs to open the gates. A soldier named Hyeroeades was successful. He saw a Sardian soldier drop his helmet over the wall by accident. The soldier climbed down the cliff, retrieved his helmet, and climbed back up again. Hyeroeades remembered the route up the cliff. After dark he led a detachment of soldiers up the cliffs. The king and all his people were asleep, confident that no one could scale the cliffs. But the city gates were opened and Cyrus sacked the city.

Jesus called to Sardian Christians, "Remember your history. It is dangerous not to be watchful. The same fate can come to your church that came to your city." That is a solemn lesson which we must ponder today if our churches are to be vibrant in the work of God.

A true spiritual life cannot prosper on ritual alone. There must be spiritual reality. So Jesus admonished that church to awake and to strengthen what remained. Death was certain unless serious attention was given at once. The whole church in Sardis had only a "few names" which were not defiled. Those should be taken as examples by the rest of the church.

Spiritual power resides in the spirit of God alone. No person or thing, however impressive or appropriate, can substitute for Him without spiritual death being the result. The true gospel had come to Sardis. It was heard and believed, and great spiritual victories were won. How tragic for the church to forget her past victories and lose the war by default.

Would Sardis hear His words? Would she repent? Would she know spiritual life again? If so, wonderful! If not, she would find the coming of Jesus to be sudden and terrible judgment.

THE COVENANT

A blessed threefold promise is given to those who remain faithful to the Lord. "He that overcometh, the same shall be clothed in white raiment; and I will not blot out his name out of the book of life, but I will confess his name before my Father, and before his angels" (verse 5).

"They shall walk with me in white." White was a sign of purity, festivity, and victory in ancient times. All three probably relate to the Lord's promise to the spiritual overcomer. He will be pure, rejoicing, and victorious. What a precious promise! Oh, to walk with the lovely Lord Jesus in white robes in the day of His triumph! I will be faithful, blessed Lord!

"I will not blot out his name out of the book of life." "The book of life" is an Old Testament term variously called "God's book, the book of the living, the book of remembrance, the book of life, the Lamb's book of life."

This is not a warning against "falling from grace" so as to be eternally lost in hell after having come to salvation in Christ. Read Revelation 3:5 in relation to 1John 5:1-5. Jesus promises, "I will never by any means blot out his name." Blessed assurance!

"I will confess his name before my Father, and before his angels." He will claim us, not deny us. He will acknowledge us before His Father, glad to call us "brethren" (Hebrews 2:11).

Here are two questions dealing with your reputation and reality as a Christian. (1) What have you done for Jesus in the past? That will determine your reputation. (2) What are you doing for Jesus now? That indicates the reality of your confession of loyalty to Him. Reputation is weak unless it is backed up by reality.

GOD'S OPEN DOOR

How would you like to be a member of a church against which the Lord Jesus makes no complaint of error? Then you should have been a member of the Christian congregation in the ancient town named Philadelphia. Whereas some of the other churches were rebuked for their error, the church in Philadelphia received abundant praise from her head.

In Ephesus there was a large congregation of Christians who were busy in religious service. But they had left their first love, and that grieved the Lord.

In Sardis there was a large, influential congregation which seemed vibrant with life. But in the records of heaven she was written down as dead.

In Philadelphia there was a struggling congregation with but a "little strength." But she received her Lord's highest commendation and praise.

How differently God judges from the way humans judge. It is imperative that we learn to see from God's perspective to approve what He approves and to reject what He condemns. We can get in on God's

evaluation of a church as we study the church in Philadelphia.

THE CITY

Philadelphia was located twenty-eight miles southeast of Sardis on the slopes of Mount Tmolus. It was surrounded by a very fertile farming region. Standing on the borders of Mysia, Lydia, and Phrygia, it occupied one of the most strategic sites in the world. Philadelphia was the gateway between two continents.

Attalus founded the city of Philadelphia to bring the barbarians of Phrygia into contact with Greek culture. The city had a missionary purpose — to represent Greek life. Jesus may have made a reference to that when He said, "I have set before thee an open door" (verse 8). As the city was to spread Greek culture, the church was to spread the Christian gospel.

Philadelphia was a famous city. The grapes produced in its fertile volcanic soil produced wine that was famous throughout the world.

Volcanoes produced springs of hot water where people came to bathe for medicinal purposes.

But the city had a serious problem — earthquakes! When a tremor was felt, the people would run into the open fields to escape injury from falling masonry. It was common for them to run from the city in fear and return with hesitation. Jesus promised of the overcoming Christian in Philadelphia, "He shall go no more out" (verse 12). That indicates the safety He would bring. "I can rid you of your fears, your terrors," Jesus said. "I can rid you of your nervous uncertainty. I can give you a safety which will preserve you in life and in death."

Philadelphia was a religious city. It was the center of worship of Dionysus, the god of wine and merriment. Temples throughout the city were devoted to other gods, also.

When a citizen served the state well, a pillar was erected in one of the temples and his name was inscribed upon it. All who came to worship would see the pillar and remember the illustrious citizen. Jesus had this in mind when He promised the faithful Christian, "Him . . . will I make a pillar in the temple of my God . . . and I will write upon him the name of my God" (verse 12).

The message to the Christians in Philadelphia was in words and pictures they could understand from their daily life. To this day, Philadelphia is a Christian town.

THE CHRIST

In character, the Lord is "holy and true." "Holy" refers to His consecration to God's service as one set apart for God alone. "True" indicates His perfection in contrast to the shadow, the antitype in contrast to the type, the ideal which is the only real.

He is holy in character and true in action. He is holy in His person and true in His government. He alone is King by divine right because He only is "holy" and "true."

In authority, the Lord of the church has "the key of David." He claims to be the fulfillment of Isaiah 22:22, "The key of the house of David will I lay upon his shoulder; so he shall open, and none shall shut; and he shall shut, and none shall open." He alone is King over kings and Lord over lords. He has authority over the whole earth. He has the keys!

In administration, the Lord is actively engaged in His kingly work in relation to the church. He is opening doors and closing doors according to His sovereign will. He is involved with churches around the world. The gates of hell shall never prevail against them. The King of all authority is on their side.

THE COMMENDATION

"I know thy works." There is no hiding them from God. Knowing what the church had been doing faithfully, He set before her greater opportunities for enlarged service. The "open door" He sets is not a way to escape but an opportunity to serve. Praise the Lord for that.

"Thou hast a little strength." The church in Philadelphia was weak, but she had served her Lord with all the strength she had. Though experiencing poverty in both numbers and resources, she persevered without faltering in service. Though small, she was faithful. Using her best for God, she was given opportunity to do more for Him.

There is a lesson here for churches today. If you wish an open door for service, serve faithfully with what is at hand. God knows whom He can trust with His blessings.

"Thou . . . hast kept my word." The weakness of the Philadelphian congregation was not in the area of their loyalty to the Word of God. Opposition had increased her commitment to Holy Scripture as the ship depends on its anchor in a storm.

To "keep" the Word of God means to know it, believe it, and obey it. The Word of God is kept by defending its letter; it is kept also by obeying its teachings. No man can keep the Word of God as doctrine unless he follows it in duty.

"Thou . . . hast not denied my name." What is His name? It is "Jesus Christ." Jesus means "Savior." Christ means "Anointed." Christians in Philadelphia were faithful to the name — the anointed Savior sent from God.

The name of Jesus is not kept by quoting it, but by manifesting sincerity, fidelity, and loving devotion to Him. The Lord expects each believer to be faithful to His name. He looks for these traits in you. Does He find them there?

THE COVENANT

Examine the structure of this letter to the church in Philadelphia. One verse (7) identifies the Lord of the church. One verse (8) commends the points of virtue in the church. Five verses (9-13) speak words of promise to the church. What a thrill that must have brought that congregation! God's promises were as certain as if they had already been fulfilled. His promises were guarantees of blessings. The promises were not to the church in Philadelphia alone, but to every faithful church through the ages. Here are promises to your church.

The faithful church will be honored in the presence of her enemies. "I will make them to come and worship before thy feet, and to know that I have loved thee" (verse 9).

The church in Philadelphia faced special opposition from the Jews. In the name of God they opposed the gospel of Christ. They were called "the synagogue of Satan" because they were doing Satan's work. How they despised the Christians!

But let the believers in Christ remain faithful. One day the persecutors will see the church vindicated, manifest as those whom God loves. The Christian religion (though outlawed by the Roman Empire) will become the dominant force for righteousness. Then those who have been abused and mistreated will be acknowledged and honored.

Take that promise as your promise. God will vindicate His people. We will not be left to shame.

The faithful church will have security in times of trial. "I also will keep thee from the hour of temptation" (verse 10). He who keeps the Word of God will be kept by the God of the Word. A great wave of tribulation was about to sweep over the world. But Jesus promised His sustaining grace to faithful saints then; that grace is available now.

The believers in Philadelphia found His promise to be true. You will experience His faithfulness also. He does not promise to keep us from all trials, but He does promise to keep us in the midst of trials. God will keep His own.

But verse 11 carries a warning. Do not presume upon God's grace. He is coming soon. Hold fast His word, His patience, His promise, and fill the opportunities for service He provides.

The faithful Christian will become a pillar in the temple of God (verse 12). Earthquakes in Philadelphia demanded that houses be built of the strongest material. They had pillars which added support, built in as a part of the building. Jesus promises that the faithful Christian will have a permanent position in the great Christian temple (Galatians 2:9). His position will be conspicuous, abiding, joyous, significant, and to the glory of God. After a brief life of faithful service here, one becomes a glorious pillar in the temple of his God. That is your home and mine.

The faithful Christian will be clearly identified as belonging to God. "I will write upon him the name of my God, and the name of the city of my God... and I will write upon him my new name" (verse 12).

The name written upon one

indicated to whom he belonged. A tattoo on the body of a slave indicated ownership. So when Christians bear God's name, the name of the city of God, and the glorious name of Christ, it indicates that a unique relationship exists between them and their God. God is theirs and they are His. The name of God indicates ownership. The name of the city of God indicates the place of his habitation. The name of the triumphant Christ designates the one through whom the believer gains the victory. There is no promise in the Bible more glorious than this one. Rejoice in it!

The Lord sent a blessed message to the "little" church in Philadelphia. And yet, there is no such thing as a "little church" in the eyes of God. The congregation in Philadelphia was few in numbers and limited in strength. But God reserved His choicest promises for her. She was given an open door of service such as no other church had. That should encourage your church, whatever its size. God loves you, too.

The church in Philadelphia was small, but if she entered the open door the Lord set before her she did not remain small. The opened doors must have been opportunities for evangelism and discipleship. Do not be discouraged in trials. They often are followed by enlarged opportunities.

Finally, with added opportunity comes added responsibility. When God opens a door of service, He holds us responsible to go through it to His glory.

"He that hath an ear, let him hear what the Spirit saith unto the churches" (verse 13).

COMMUNION WITH THE LORD

The letter to the church in Laodicea is the saddest of the seven letters to churches in Asia Minor. Not one word of commendation is expressed. The whole congregation had lost her devotion to Jesus. The Lord said of her, "I know thy works, that thou art neither cold nor hot...So then because thou art lukewarm, and neither cold nor hot, I will spue thee out of my mouth" (verses 15, 16). What a tragedy!

But wait! This is also the tenderest letter to any of the seven churches. It has the longest invitation of any of the letters. Judgment is threatened, but it is tempered with the explanation: "As many as I love, I rebuke and chasten: be zealous therefore, and repent" (verse 19).

To this lukewarm church the gracious invitation is extended: "Behold, I stand at the door, and knock: if any man hear my voice, and open the door, I will come in to him, and will sup with him, and he with me" (verse 20). How like our gracious Lord!

This letter is applicable today. It gives an exact description of the respectable, sentimental, nominal, skin-deep religion that is so common. It describes how flabby and anemic such religion is before God.

There is a warning here. Be sure you evaluate your life and your church life as God does. At the very time the church in Laodicea was saying, "I am rich, and increased with goods, and have need of nothing," the Lord was saying, "Thou art wretched, and miserable, and poor, and blind, and naked" (verse 17). They felt they needed nothing; God knew they needed everything. Oh, that we might see through the eyes of God!

THE CITY

Laodicea was located forty-three miles southwest of Philadelphia and about one hundred miles due east of Ephesus. It was set in the valley of the Lycus River, along with Hierapolis and Colosse. Those three cities were about ten miles apart.

It was a strategic location, guarding a narrow valley which was the gateway to Phrygia. The trade route from the east flowed through Laodicea to the west coast of Asia Minor. One route led to Attalia and Perga (where Paul passed on his first missionary journey). A second led to Philadelphia and Sardis. The third reached into Phrygia. It was a major city.

The history of Laodicea was glamorous. It was founded about 250 B.C. by Antiochus II, who named it after his wife, Laodice. It became part of the Roman Empire in 133 B.C. The city developed under Roman influence. The Roman governor visited there often and held court there, adding to the city's political importance.

The wealth of Laodicea was fabulous. It was a major commercial center. The city even minted its own coins. Destroyed by an earthquake in A.D. 60, she rebuilt herself with her own money, refusing help from the Roman government.

The wealth of the city was related to the fertile land and good grazing grounds for its black-wool sheep. That violet, glossy black wool was made into garments which were prized around the world. Clothing factories in the city made garments that were exported throughout the civilized world.

The medical resources of Laodicea were likewise famous. The pagan god called Men, the god of healing, was worshiped there. A famous medical school was located there. A powder to treat a common eye disease was manufactured there and shipped all over the world in the form of a tablet.

All of that is reflected in the admonition of the Lord to the church: "I counsel thee to buy of me gold tried in the fire, that thou mayest be rich," a reference to her wealth; "I counsel thee to buy of me … white raiment, that thou mayest be clothed, and that the shame of thy nakedness do not appear, " a reference to her garment industry; "I counsel thee to buy of me . . . eyesalve, that thou mayest see, " a reference to her medical school and eye medicine. He called the church to a spiritual inventory which would correct the evils He saw in her.

THE CHURCH

There is no information as to how the gospel of Christ came to Laodicea. Possibly, a faithful Christian preacher named Epaphras was used of God to establish that church. The apostle Paul did not visit there, but he knew of the church and wrote a letter to her (Colossians 4:16). We cannot now identify the epistle to the Laodiceans.

Archippus was pastor of the church in Laodicea at the time John wrote this letter. Paul had admonished him, "Take heed to the ministry which thou hast received in the Lord, that thou fulfill it" (Colossians 4:17). He needed that admonition as pastor of a seriously sick church which showed the outward signs of spiritual life and health.

THE CHRIST

Jesus is "the Amen." He is one with the God of Isaiah 65:16, the God of all truth. The words He speaks are absolute truth. The letter He sends must be heeded. One neglects its revelations only at his own peril.

Jesus is "the faithful and true witness." As a true witness, He bears testimony to what is correct, genuine, and right. As a faithful witness, He declares the whole truth whether people like it or not. He tells "the truth, the whole truth, and nothing but the truth," as we say.

Here is the perfectly qualified witness. He possesses in himself all those qualities which a witness should possess: a firsthand knowledge of the events, competence to relate correctly what He has seen, and willingness to bear a factual witness. He has examined the church. He knows the facts. He speaks the truth of God.

Jesus is "the beginning of the creation of God." That does not mean He was created, but that He created all things. "By him were all things created...

and he is before all things, and by him all things consist" (Colossians 1:16, 17).

Listen earnestly to the Lord of the church. He knows. He is faithful. He has authority. He who has an ear should hear what the Lord says to His churches.

THE COMPLAINT

Lethargy and pride were the two faults Jesus found in the church at Laodicea. What serious faults they were!

Spiritual lethargy is evident in the words, "I know thy works, that thou art neither cold nor hot." That solemn accusation indicates that there can be no true religion without zeal.

It is surprising to hear Him say, "I would prefer that you were freezing cold or boiling hot." Lukewarm is better than freezing cold, isn't it? Our Lord says, "No!" There is more hope for winning a down-and-out sinner than one who is refined and disciplined. Jesus calls for a clear-cut decision. "Be with Me or against Me," He requires. The Laodiceans readily understood the Lord's comparison. The area had many beautiful springs of water. A traveler might stop at one to refresh himself, only to discover it had mineral content and a tepid temperature. If one drank much of it, he would actually vomit.

Jesus said that is the way He feels about a church without enthusiastic commitment. Even the active, energetic, wealthy, and popular church is disgusting to Him if she lacks spiritual zeal.

The cause of Christ needs "hot hearts." Christians should be wholehearted, full of zeal, fervent in spirit.

The lukewarm church is in danger. Jesus warns, "I will spue thee out of my mouth" (verse 16). It is a picture of disgust. Jesus calls us to boil or freeze, never to simmer in a tasteless tepidity.

The proud and self-complacent spirit of Laodicea had permeated the church without her knowing it. She looked at herself and grew proud. Jesus looked at her and felt sick.

Jesus was on the outside of the Laodicean church. He was not kept out by doctrinal error or ungodly practices. He was excluded by the lack of love and zeal. How tragic it is if He is excluded from your church by that same spirit today.

THE COUNSEL

"Look at yourself." That is Jesus' counsel in verse 17. What a glaring contrast there is between what a lukewarm Christian thinks he is and what he truly is! A church may be popular and prosperous with adequate buildings, trained leaders, and liberal offerings. She may feel no need at all. But Jesus may say to her, "Look at yourself; you are not what you think yourself to be." Spiritual complacency blinds. Jesus calls today, "Look at what you really are. Then look at what I can make you. Be zealous, therefore, and repent."

"Receive what you need from Me." Jesus calls us to "buy" from Him that which is priceless (Isaiah 55:1). What is the currency? What we need is purchased by repentance, confession, and faith.

That is no easy requirement. The proud Laodiceans would find it difficult to admit their poverty. But admit it they must, or their need would go unmet.

In place of material wealth, Jesus offers spiritual treasures. In place of medicine for physical eyes, Jesus offers spiritual sight. In place of their famous black wool garments, Jesus offers the white raiment of practical righteousness. All they needed (wealth, raiment, healing) was available in Him.

THE COVENANT

"If any man hear my voice, and open the door, I will come in to him, and will sup with him, and he with me. To him that overcometh will I grant to sit with me in my throne" (verses 20, 21).

What a promise of

fellowship! To eat and drink with Him is an honor beyond imagining. But for Him to come and eat and drink with us is nothing less than amazing grace.

The promise is for fellowship, and more. Authority is there, also. Christ has conquered the world and the devil. He has the keys of death and hell. He reigns with the Father (Revelation 1, 4, 5). Those who trust Him conquer in Him; thus they reign with Him.

To be complacent and halfhearted is so distasteful to Christ that He threatens vehement rejection. But to be wholehearted toward Him, opening the door to one's life and inviting Him to come in to reign, is to share His fellowship on earth and His reign in heaven.

Each person has his own choice. When a whole church in Laodicea was lukewarm, Jesus offered His invitation to persons one by one. He did not say, "If the whole church will open the door." He said, "If any man hear my voice, and open the door, I will come in to him." You can be that "man."

In Holman Hunt's famous painting *The Light of the World*, he placed Jesus before a door with no handle on the outside. Just so, the human heart must be opened from within. We will either throw open the door by an act of our will or keep it fast closed in His face. Are you willing to invite Him in to occupy your whole life?

"He that hath an ear, let him hear what the Spirit saith unto the churches."

ASSURED OF OVERCOMING

A discouraged brother lamented, "I don't know what the church is coming to." Another replied, "I do. God says she is coming to victory that brings glory to God." That reply is Bible truth!

Your church is important. She is important in view of her worthy heritage, her present ministry, and her future prospect. She is the public representative of Christ in your community. She is the body which makes Him knowable before mankind. She is so important to the work of God that you should give your best service to God through her.

The Bible principle is, "Unto him be glory in the church by Christ Jesus throughout all ages, world without end. Amen" (Ephesians 3:21).

The churches may experience temporary setbacks, but God will be glorified through them in the end. One church may fail and another succeed, but God's purpose will be realized. Overcoming is assured.

OVERCOMING THROUGH FELLOWSHIP

The great emphasis of Philippians 1:3-7 is the unity of spirit which Jesus establishes between those who trust Him. It is developed further in Ephesians 2:11-22. Racial, national, and social prejudices fall before the love of God which is placed in the hearts of believers by the Holy Spirit (Romans 5:5).

"I thank God for you," (verse 3). That is the spirit of one Christian as he thinks of fellow believers at home and abroad (Romans 1:8; 1 Corinthians 1:4; Ephesians 1:15, 16). You experience that as you hear of an evangelistic harvest being reaped in a sister church or on some mission field. You find a prayer in your heart for the converts, the congregation, and the spiritual leaders who are involved.

"I pray for you" (verse 4). Prayer offered daily and sincerely for one's fellow Christians can avail much. But for what do you pray after you have said, "God bless..."?

Ephesians 1:16-23 says we should pray that our brothers and sisters in Christ may have spiritual insight, full hope, appreciation of God's power, and a personal knowledge of God. Philippians 1:9-11 includes abounding love to God, increasing knowledge and spiritual discernment, pure lives, and fruits of righteousness. Colossians 1:9-12 adds a worthy walk and overflowing thanks to the list. Use those three passages to guide your praying for Christians.

"I share fellowship with you" (verse 5). This is a fellowship based in the gospel, which involves a mutual relationship with God in Jesus Christ (I John 1:3). Such a spirit will encourage believers in times of suffering (Acts 16:12-40), will encourage their supply of one another's needs (Philippians 4:10-19), and will overcome all differences which would otherwise separate them (Ephesians 2:11-22). Fellowship means mutual sharing, to be one in spirit. Jesus makes that possible.

"I have great expectations for you" (verse 6). There are "things that accompany salvation" (Hebrews 6:9) which we delight to see in our fellow believers. We are confident the good work God began in salvation will follow through to sanctification. We expect the best because "it is God which

worketh in you both to will and to do of his good pleasure" (Philippians 2:13).

"I love you" (verse 7). What a blessing it is for one brother to write to other brothers and sisters in Christ, "I have you in my heart." Such love is possible because the love of God is shed abroad in our hearts by the Holy Spirit who is given to us (Romans 5:5). It is not according to the natural dispositions of the flesh, for it is proof that one is truly saved (1 John 3:14). Christian love is the love of God flowing through man to man.

OVERCOMING A FIERCE OPPONENT

Revelation 12:7-10 reaches beyond our human comprehension. It describes war in the heavenly sphere. It tells of the downfall of the devil and his angels. Interpreters are not agreed on details. The following is one opinion of the meaning of the event.

When? The warfare occurred when Jesus returned to heaven to present His sacrifice before the Father in the heavenly tabernacle. Where? The warfare took place in the spiritual realms above the earth. Who? The warfare involved angelic beings, not mortal men. Why? The warfare was the final attempt of the devil to prevent the victory of Jesus Christ. What results? The atoning sacrifice of Jesus was presented and accepted before God so that the overthrow of the devil was certified and sure.

Though the defeat of all demonic forces is guaranteed, it is not yet executed. The devil is still in the world raging with all his power against God, "having great wrath, because he knoweth that he hath but a short time" (Revelation 12:12).

A fierce warfare is involved (verses 7, 8). Here on earth the warfare continues. We are admonished to put on the whole armor of God, to be strong in the Lord and the power of His might, and to stand against the devil until the warfare is ended (Ephesians 6:10-18). Though the devil rages as a fierce beast of prey seeking to devour (I Peter 5:8), we can be confident knowing that Jesus has given us power "over all the power of the enemy" (Luke 10:19). The battle is fierce, but victory is assured.

A sure victory is ahead (verse 9). Cast out of the heavenly spheres, the devil is sure to be subdued on earth also. Jesus went to the cross with the assurance, "Now is the judgment of this world: now shall the prince of this world be cast out" (John 12:31). Christians live and serve with this assurance: "The God of peace shall bruise Satan under your feet shortly" (Romans 16:20). The victory is as certain as if it were already attained.

Glory to God will follow (verse 10). Imagine sharing in this glad announcement: "The kingdoms of this world are become the kingdoms of our Lord, and of his Christ; and he shall reign for ever and ever" (Revelation 11:15). "Now is come salvation, and strength, and the kingdom of our God, and the power of his Christ" (Revelation 12:10). What glory that will bring to God!

You and I will share that glad occasion as children of God. We will be with Jesus in His kingdom. We will reign upon the earth. What a day that will be!

OVERCOMING BY JESUS

How was the victory over the devil and his angels attained? Revelation 12:11 answers, "They overcame him by the blood of the Lamb, and by the word of their testimony; and they loved not their lives unto the death." Three things were involved in the victory, according to that verse.

Calvary is the basis. They overcame the wicked one "by the blood of Jesus." We do not understand the details, but we know that when Jesus died on the cross our redemption was secured. More than that, the claim of the devil on the whole of creation (including the curse which sin brought) was broken forever.

Confession is the method. By "the word of their testimony" victory came. Not just the fact that they spoke, but the truth which they spoke was accompanied by God's power and victory was gained. "The testimony of Jesus is the spirit of prophecy" (Revelation 19:10). Commitment is the evidence. "They loved not their lives unto the death" (verse 11). That is a challenging example to all Christians. "Christ shall be magnified in my body, whether it be by life, or by death" (Philippians 1:20). Jesus said, "Whosoever will save his life shall lose it: and whosoever will lose his life for my sake shall find it" (Matthew 16:25). But He promised further, "Be thou faithful unto death, and I will give thee a crown of life" (Revelation 2:10). Behold the blessings God gives to overcomers. They can eat of the tree of life, eat of hidden manna, have power over the nations to rule them, be clothed in white raiment with their names written in the book of life, be pillars in the temple of God, and sit with the Father in His throne (Revelation 2, 3). They will overcome the devil (Revelation 17:14) and inherit all things (Revelation 21:7). What promises!

But who will overcome? "Whatsoever is born of God overcometh the world: and this is the victory that overcometh the world, even our faith. Who is he that overcometh the world, but he that believeth that Jesus is the Son of God?" (1 John 5:4, 5).